CLEFT
of the
Rock

From Sill

Jess 29ill

Book One in the Ordinary Man trilogy

CLEFT
of the
Rock

Based on a True Story

Frances Smith

Gazelle
PRESS

Mobile, AL

Gazelle Press
P.O. Box 191540
Mobile, AL 36619
800-367-8203

DEDICATION

To Dr. Charles Stanley, pastor of First Baptist Church in Atlanta, Georgia. Dr. Stanley's inspiration and teaching were the catalyst for the events described in these pages, and he continues to feed us spiritually through his sermons and books.

To Dr. Hollie Miller, senior pastor of Sevier Heights Baptist Church in Knoxville, Tennessee. Brother Hollie, as he insists on being called, is our current pastor, a mentor and a friend. He is a huge part of our continued spiritual growth and nourishment and that of our family.

We are profoundly grateful for the life-changing messages and discipleship of both.

"...I WILL PUT YOU IN THE CLEFT
OF THE ROCK AND COVER YOU
WITH MY HAND UNTIL
I HAVE PASSED BY."

EXODUS 33:22

PREFACE

The best stories are usually true, or at least based on events that actually happened. Knowing that a story is factual gives it more credence and impact.

When I first heard about Mark Smith's year of mission work in Nome, Alaska, it seemed unbelievable. A nineteen-year-old boy did all that? Come on, really? But the more I heard, coupled with a trip to Alaska in 2013 to see the actual locations of his mission work, the more I knew the story begged to be told.

Cleft of the Rock is a story of one person's year of immense spiritual growth. It shows vividly how faith can literally conquer mountains. And it depicts in graphic detail the triumph of the human spirit and the power of unshakable conviction when faith is placed in the one and only Almighty God.

Almost all of this story actually happened. Because a tiny fraction didn't, I call it fiction. Because the truth is often raw and rough, some events may be difficult to read. But it needs to be told. And it's my honor and privilege to tell it.

FRANCES SMITH
JULY 2014

PART 1:
SUMMER

1

The plane steadily descended toward Nome. The view below was completely different than several weeks before, when I'd last seen it. Then, the tundra was green. Now, it was covered in snow.

I'd given up everything to come back to Alaska. My car, my apartment, my job, my status as a college student—all gone. Everything I owned was either in my pockets or in my trunk. I felt no fear or trepidation, just excitement to find out what the future held. Not only would I have the opportunity to serve here, but this job opened up the door to my entire future. I intended to work hard and go home next June with not only the money from the job I'd been offered, but as much additional cash as I could earn.

I felt a tremendous sense of excitement to be back working at the church I had helped build from the ground up, working with kids I had grown to love at the group home. I sensed I would be making an even bigger difference now. What difference, I had no idea. But I knew there was something I was supposed to do, and I would discover what it was as I went.

My supervisor and ministry mentor was again waiting at the tiny airline terminal. My first impression of Will West, three months ago, had been that he in no way looked like a pastor. He was a little taller than me but much heavier—probably solid muscle—and he wore a plaid flannel shirt with a pipe in the pocket and sleeves rolled halfway up his forearms, well-worn jeans, and cowboy boots. He had straight dark, slicked-back hair, brown eyes, and an impressive handlebar mustache that made him look more like a prospector than a preacher.

And he sported a .44 magnum under his arm that looked like it meant business. Now, as before, I couldn't take my eyes off that gun. Will carried himself with an assurance and a confidence that said he knew exactly what he was doing and why he was here. That confidence was contagious.

I felt the same sense of peace and elation to see him. I walked straight to him and shook his hand.

"Hey, Will!"

"Hi, Mark!"

"It's so good to be back. I can't even tell you."

"It's good to have you back. Wait until you see the church. We've gotten a lot done since you left."

"I can't wait to see it. How is everybody?"

He filled me in on everyone as we stood in the baggage claim area and waited for my footlocker. He'd left his wife, Denise, at home preparing a welcome meal for me. The kids at the group home couldn't wait for me to get back. Being away had made me realize how much I loved them, and I couldn't wait to see them.

We got my footlocker and walked out of the airport toward the car. As soon as we hit the fresh air, I caught my breath.

"Holy cow," I said as we climbed into the familiar two-toned Bronco, and started toward town.

"What?"

"It's a whole lot colder now than when I left."

"Yes, summer is short and it gets cold very quick. We pull out our cold weather gear right about this time of year." He turned toward town. "Mark, I've got some bad news for you. I found out last week when you were in Anchorage, and it seemed pretty pointless to tell you then. I decided to wait until you got here and tell you face to face. I'm so sorry." Will's voice was sincerely apologetic. "The state pulled the funding for the position we offered you at the group home. There's no job. We can pay you for one month, but then the funding goes away."

I just stared at him. It didn't sink in at first, and then it hit with the force of an arctic blast. "You can't be serious! I flew seven thousand miles for this job . . . I quit my job in Tennessee . . . withdrew from college . . . gave up my housing, everything. I don't even have the money for a plane ticket back home. What am I supposed to do?"

I was overcome with a blinding anger, frustration, and sense of betrayal, and suddenly I couldn't stand to be with anyone. Before the mud-covered Bronco even came to a full stop in the Wests' driveway, I jumped out and started walking. Where I was going, I had no idea, but the thought of being here for one more second was unthinkable.

I've always had a temper, and it came boiling out. How could God do this to me? All I'd done was try to obey Him. Coming here had been the ultimate sacrifice, and all for Him. Aren't people supposed to be blessed for things like that? This didn't feel like a blessing. As I walked, my rage mounted. My fists clenched.

"What are you doing, Lord?" I shouted at the heavens as I charged along. "This was something I was doing for You! I was going to do Your work here!" Tears streamed down my face. "Did I do something wrong? Was I prideful?"

I stormed on and on, with the vague idea of not stopping until I got to the North Pole. The terrain grew more rugged as I got into the foothills north of Nome. Higher and higher I walked, almost running now, railing at God and myself the whole way. What was I supposed to do now? I had no money to get home, and even if I had money, there was nothing to go back to. I'd given it all up. All I wanted was to be obedient and serve. I walked and walked, with every intention of raising my fist and shouting my displeasure at every mountain peak along the way from Nome to the North Pole.

Wind started to blow, strong from the west, pounding rain and sleet ahead of it. I began to shiver. It was late afternoon, nearly October. The Nome area no longer had constant daylight every day. I had left Will's house with nothing but the clothes I'd worn on the plane. Jeans, sneakers, and one thin long-sleeved shirt, all soaked with sweat now. No jacket, no gloves, no hat—nothing to protect myself from the cold. I rummaged through my pockets and found only a Life Saver wrapper. An Eagle Scout should have known better. My emotions and pride had gotten ahead of my spirit and reason.

I had huffed my way for six miles to the top of Anvil Mountain, the highest place anywhere around Nome. Ahead was nothing but snow-capped mountains and beyond them, the Arctic Circle. Standing on the peak, soaked with sweat, I met the brunt of a powerful new storm sweeping in from the north. The front of my shirt froze as I faced the wind. Feeling dizzy, thirsty, and suddenly very weak, I knew hypothermia was minutes away. There was no way I could make it back down the mountain.

In desperation, I looked around. The majestic formation of Anvil Rock stood sentinel before me, a silent testament to the majesty of God. Not knowing what else to do, I crawled into the only space available to get out of the wind—a cleft right below the anvil formation. I squeezed myself as far up as I could into the rock sandwich. I tried to pray, but it was too cold and I was shaking too badly. The wind howled around me. The air grew colder and colder. The tears I'd cried earlier were now frozen on my face and lashes. Everything went black.

* * *

Eighteen months before, in the spring of 1978, my life took a dramatic u-turn that brought me to this place. At a youth retreat, I began to feel a strong urge to do mission work. And the more I thought about it, the more I wanted to go far from home. Nome, almost to the Soviet Union—and just south of the Arctic Circle—was as far as it got with the North American Mission Board.

My mother wasn't too happy about having her nineteen-year-old son that far away for a whole year, but my dad was proud. I was the only son of a Southern Baptist minister, and when I'd made the decision to spend the summer of 1979 doing mission work, it was he who'd suggested going as far away as possible.

I hadn't always been the type of kid that my parents would have anticipated spending my summer doing the "Lord's work." In first grade, I was acknowledged as a "gang" leader in my school near the projects of Athens, Tennessee. By second grade, I'd lost that respected position and was getting pushed around myself and by third grade, I was getting bullied regularly. A group of tough kids would wait for me on my way home, and would beat me up, take my money, and stomp on my books and papers. I tried other routes and timing, including cutting across a field where a big, ornery bull lived, but it did no good. If I evaded them one day, they'd get me the next—and it would be worse. When I showed up at home with torn clothes, bleeding, and bruised, my father told me I was an embarrassment to the family and I had to stand up for myself. One day, I did.

I was watching for them. Dad had said to hit the leader once in the mouth and I'd be surprised at the result. When they came up to me I reared back and, with all my strength, plowed my fist straight into the head bully's mouth, knocked out a tooth, and knocked him sprawling. I'm not sure who was more surprised, him or me, but I used my advantage well. Before he could get up, I was on him and venting all my rage and frustration. All the other bullies fled. When that fight was over, I'd made a new friend in that bully. He and his pals never bothered me again, and I never again turned away from a fight. Truth be told, I started a good many in my newfound confidence.

I was a typical young boy in many ways, probably amplified because I was a preacher's kid. My dad always stayed after Sunday services until the last person was gone. For his family, that could be tedious. We kids had to find things to do. One Sunday, after I'd scrounged through all the Sunday school rooms and pilfered all the mints, he was still busy. I had the bright idea—and the bad judgment—to call the fire department and tell them the church was on fire. I was sitting in the very back of the sanctuary when the engines screamed into the church yard. My father looked up as the firemen came running through the vestibule looking for the fire.

"There's no fire," my father said.

"Someone called and said the church was on fire," the fire chief said.

My father's eyes immediately went to my face where I sat quietly on the back pew. He instantly knew who the culprit was, and I paid dearly for that little escapade.

My life changed forever when I was ten because of Bobby Spangler, a mentally challenged man who lived near us. We gave him a ride to church every week. He walked awkwardly, talked funny, and smelled like he needed a bath most of the time. He had one good set of clothes, and he always wore them to church. His shoes were scuffed because he couldn't walk very well. His hands shook. My sister, Mellie, seven years younger than me, got to sit in front with our parents. Either I sat next to my older sister, Lisa, which was bad enough, or I was in the middle next to her and Bobby, which was horrible. We often said nasty things about Bobby, sometimes even loud enough so he could hear us. But he got in the car week after week with an envelope filled with our favorite candies—Life Savers, mints, Tootsie Rolls. He got these at the Zesto at the bottom of the hill once a week, which was the only time he left the house alone.

Our father always corrected us when he heard us badmouth Bobby. One Sunday night he didn't say anything, and it began to gnaw at me. After we got home from church he still said nothing. It bothered me, and it kept bothering me. I realized that I had been tormenting an innocent person who was only kind to me. I realized for the first time that I was a terrible person. Finally, tears in my eyes, I found my dad and told him I was a sinner.

"Yes, I know," he said.

"No, really Dad, I am a sinner. I mean, if I die I'm going to hell."

"I know, Mark."

"Dad, I need to get saved."

He told me to think about it for a few days. My ten-year-old conviction grew stronger every day, moment by moment, as the days went by. I kept bugging him about it. Finally, on Thursday of that week, I told him I had to get saved *now*, and I'd do it with or without him. We had a long talk, and my father made sure I knew what being a Christian was all about. I was accepting Jesus' gift of salvation and turning my entire life over to Him as Savior and Lord. Did I completely understand that? I did. So we knelt together and prayed, and I confessed that I was a sinner. I believed that Jesus died as punishment for my sins, and I asked Him to be Lord in my life. Dad asked if I was ready to make it public, and I said I definitely was.

Lisa, eleven months older than me, made her decision shortly after, and our father baptized us at the same time.

My decision and dedication did change the way I treated Bobby, but it didn't change some of my other mischievous behavior. At the age of twelve, my friends and I pulled some mean pranks. We hid behind a bush and lobbed eggs at cars as they passed. We could usually filch two eggs from home without our mothers noticing. A lucky toss would splat on a car's windshield, and brake lights showed that our eggs had found their target. Reverse lights would be our signal that there was probably a man in the car. Then it was time to run. Once, a big dude started chasing us. We were escaping through back yards, an area that I was more familiar with than my friend was. I knew where the clotheslines were, and I knew when to duck. My friend did not. He caught one under the chin at full speed, and I heard a surprised yelp. I looked back to see him doing a beautiful triple gainer, and the driver catching up as he landed with a bone-rattling thud. Of course I kept running. Our motto was "every man for himself when the law arrives."

I was a resourceful kid, and I knew how to watch and learn. There was a construction site near our house, and I noticed that the heavy equipment operators didn't always use keys to start the bulldozers. I watched carefully how they did it, and one night I sneaked to the site, started a bulldozer with a screwdriver, and drove it around. It was great fun, and I got away with it several times before a policeman noticed and paid me a visit. He said he was going to take me in.

"Do you have to?" I asked. "My dad will kill me."

"What you're doing is wrong and dangerous. How did you get this thing started, anyway?"

"I watched the men during the daytime and figured out how they did it."

"If you'll show me how, I won't take you in."

So I showed him where to stick the screwdriver in and what wire to connect, and he let me go. My mother doesn't know about that to this day.

The one bright spot was my involvement in the Boy Scouts, where a nationally-recognized scoutmaster took me under his wing. When I was thirteen, I finished my Eagle rank—the highest in Scouts.

We moved to Maryville, Tennessee, in time for me to finish the ninth grade. My parents separated earlier in the year. My father, disillusioned and unsupported by his congregation, left his eleven-year pastorate in Athens and found work in a lumber business in Knoxville. My parents eventually got back together, but we were now living in an unfamiliar town. When I fell in with a shady group like I was used to in Athens, my father put his foot down.

"Find new friends," he said, "because you are not going to hang around with those boys."

I was so angry at him for making us leave Athens. I had left my lifelong friends and now he was telling me who I could and could not hang around with? As it turned out, his holding the line led to one of the best things in my life. I met Doug Taylor early in tenth grade when we both tried out for the Maryville High School tennis team. Becoming friends with him and several others set the stage for my high school years. Several guys and girls, all good friends, ran around together in a pack. We bowled, picnicked in the mountains, went to movies, and had a great time as a coed group.

All of a sudden academics began to make sense, and I graduated with honors as a three-year letterman on the tennis team and the wrestling team. Doug and I also sang with two others in a quartet, and I did photography for the high school yearbook. My action shots from sporting events sometimes wound up in the local newspaper.

Being good kids didn't mean Doug and I were angels. We had our own pranks, including the time we climbed a water tower with a supply of bottle rockets and shot them into a pasture down below. It was great fun when we realized we could shift our trajectory and make the cows run. Before long, we were shooting the rockets at one of end of the pasture and then the other, hooting hysterically at the stampede. Evidently someone called the cops, because they were waiting for us when we climbed down and eased over the barbed wire to where we had left our bicycles. Thankfully, we had used up all the fireworks and had none in hand at that moment.

One of the cops said, "You know, I bet if someone were doing something to spook those cows, they'd realize that was a mean thing to do and wouldn't do it anymore."

Doug and I agreed with the officer that that was absolutely the case, and again I escaped a brush with the law.

When high school was over, Doug went directly to Georgia Tech in Atlanta, Georgia, beginning classes in June 1977. He began attending First Baptist Church, about two blocks from campus, and the teaching of Dr. Charles Stanley changed his life. I spent some weekends at Georgia Tech with Doug after I began attending the University of Tennessee, and got a peek into life on a different campus.

Doug, studious person that he was, never got enough sleep. Freshmen in the engineering program at Georgia Tech go through a rigorous winnowing out process, and only the best survive. Doug was determined to be one of the few. One Friday night he was especially tired. I was sleeping in his roommate's bed, and I woke up to an odd sound.

Thunk-thunk. Thunk-thunk. Thunk-thunk.

Blearily I opened my eyes to see Doug at the half-open door of the room. He was sleepwalking, mumbling something about the library, trying to get out of the room. But his foot kept the door from opening very far, and his head ricocheted between the door and the jamb every couple of seconds. He was unable to figure out the problem, and kept hitting his head. A light in the hallway illuminated every thunk.

Thunk-thunk. Thunk-thunk. Thunk-thunk.

The next morning he couldn't figure out why his head was sore, and I knew he'd never believe me if I told him.

The best part of my weekends with Doug was the church services and the teaching of Dr. Stanley. Although I'd grown up in the same household with a minister, I hadn't really paid enough attention to his teaching. Does any kid ever really listen to his father? I certainly didn't. What I was hearing from Dr. Stanley went straight to my heart. It was like new stuff. Heady stuff. Stuff that made me want to actually get out my Bible and read it for myself.

Dr. Stanley talked about the Word being living and active. He said if you were a child of God, His Spirit would work within you so that Scriptures would make sense in ways they never had before. He said that Jesus Himself would be your intimate Friend, and your prayer life would come alive.

To my amazement, he was right. Doug and I fed off each other, sharing experiences and helping each other grow.

Then Doug invited me to a retreat at St. Simons Island, Georgia. I said yes because there was a tennis tournament there that weekend. But while I was there, something inside me changed for good. I knew I was already saved, but I'd never felt the conviction that I felt now. I had to do something about it. I wanted to serve. I wanted to use my gifts for God. Now. Wherever and however He wanted.

Dr. Stanley said that sometimes God calls us to fast and meditate to determine His will. I wanted desperately to know what God wanted of me, so I tried it. I told no one, as Dr. Stanley instructed that God does not want us to make a public show when we fast for Him.

After a day with no food or water, constantly blocking out the needs of my body and seeking His guidance and His will, I became more in tune with Him. The second day I clearly felt the Holy Spirit's prompting inside me. And I knew what I had to do.

*　　*　　*

I went back to the University of Tennessee, where I was finishing my freshman year, a changed person. I liked UT, and I was a good student. I was majoring in biology with the idea that I would become a dentist, for no real reason other than that I was good in math and science and dentists get to leave work early on Wednesdays. I wanted to use that time to go fishing. And they seemed to make a lot of money. Now my plan seemed pretty empty and self-serving.

My first stop when I got back to school was the Baptist Student Union. The director—who also happened to have ties with the North American Mission Board—was in his office. I knocked on his door and poked my head around the corner.

"Dr. Hall, got a minute?" I asked.

"Yes, of course! Come in. But you know you have to call me Bob."

I went in and sat on one of the comfortable chairs scattered around the office. His desk and the floor around it was a chaos of papers, files and books, but I knew he could find anything he wanted, anytime he wanted. He called it an organized mess. He was all about making college kids feel at home, and he made his office welcoming for us. The BSU was supposed to be a haven, a place kids could come to. As I prepared to put my future in the hands of this man, I had never been so appreciative of his unswerving support of all of us.

As I sat, trying to decide where to begin, he made it easy for me.

"You look like you've come to some sort of decision, Mark," he said in his high-energy, upbeat style.

"I have. I want to do mission work."

"You want to do it, or you feel called to do it?"

"Both."

"Why don't you start at the beginning and tell me all of it?"

Some of it he already knew, like my beginnings as a pastor's son and the fact that I'd never been discipled by anyone. He knew about my trips to First Baptist in Atlanta, and that I was finding fulfillment there. But this—this would be beyond anything I'd told him before.

"I just got back from a retreat at St. Simons Island."

"Yes, how did that go? Did you win the tournament?"

I'd all but forgotten about the reason I'd gone to St. Simons to begin with. The tournament seemed so small now, the satisfaction I'd gotten from winning both singles and doubles so insignificant.

"Yes, but that's not what I wanted to talk to you about."

"Okay."

"I recommitted my life to Jesus during the retreat. I know I was saved before, but now I really feel God's presence in me, more than I ever have."

"That's wonderful, Mark! I'm so happy to hear it. Congratulations."

"And I want to do something about it."

"What did you have in mind?"

"I want to go on a mission trip, as far away from home as I can."

"Really?"

"Really. Where's the farthest place the Mission Board goes?"

We stood up and looked at the map of North America on his wall. "That would most likely be Nome, Alaska."

All I knew about Nome was that it was about as far west as you could go before North America ended and Asia began, and that it was really cold and either very dark or very light all the time. The land of the midnight sun. But if it was what God wanted me to do, then so be it.

"Then I want to serve in Nome."

He sat back in his chair and studied me. The clock ticked. The squirrels in the tree outside his window chirred and skittered. Other students, ones who weren't making life-changing decisions, walked past on the sidewalk outside.

"Mark, are you sure? This is a really big decision. It's not like going on a mission trip close by. And it will cost."

"I'm absolutely sure. How do we get started?"

"Well, it starts with an application to the Mission Board. But all the trips for this summer are planned and staffed. We'd be looking at next summer. The Mission Board will help some, but you'd have to raise some money."

"How much?"

He thought for a moment. "Probably about five thousand dollars."

That was a lot of money, but I knew this was what God wanted, so it would work out. I took an application back to my dorm and filled it out, with Nome, Alaska, as my number one choice. I had to put two other choices down, but Bob assured me that no one ever requests Nome. Bob's friend, Bill Lee, was the director at the Mission Board and handled the assignments personally. Bob's letter of recommendation, which all but sealed the deal, was included with my application.

My father was happy, my mother less so, when I told them I'd actually submitted the paperwork. Alaska isn't a place you can easily come back from if you get homesick.

Around Christmas of 1978, the letter came from the Mission Board, confirming that I had indeed been selected and had received my number one choice. Come June, I would be on the mission team that was being sent to Nome to help build—literally build—a new church from the ground up. I was about to get some real-life application for the construction work I'd learned as daddy's shadow all my life.

The next months were a blur of planning, fund-raising, training, and preparation. I linked up with Corey Bennett, a counselor from

Campus Crusade for Christ at the University of Tennessee, and my faith and conviction grew stronger. I worked my bookkeeping job at a local lumber company and saved every cent, but it wouldn't be enough. My father suggested that I appeal to our old church in Athens. They considered me theirs, so perhaps they would help. I suppose it didn't hurt that Prof Powers, my old scoutmaster, was chairman of the Board of Deacons and vouched for me. The good people at that church committed money and prayer, and all my needs were taken care of.

The Mission Board was sending only two people to Alaska. Besides me, there was a Dallas Bible College student named Barry Watkins. It would be him, the pastor, and me—and we only had three months of summer. It would be a miracle if we managed to build a church that would still be standing after the first sub-zero winter.

On paper, it looked like I was the most prepared and best equipped. I was just shy of six feet tall, a rather wiry one hundred forty pounds. I'd always been an athlete, doing pretty well at every sport I'd ever tried. My mother liked to tell her friends that I had trophies, medals, and ribbons in nine different sports, plus chess. That was true, but I felt that my real contribution would be in my ability to work with available resources to figure things out and get jobs done. I'd started a lawn business from nothing at the age of sixteen, and ended up responsible for twenty-two lawns and multiple outdoor construction projects. I prided myself on being independent and able to take care of myself.

But the fact was, I'd never been out of the South, unless you counted the occasional family trips to visit my mom's family in Oklahoma. It was the very definition of stepping out on faith, but I felt it was absolutely clear that this was what the Lord wanted of me. So I planned, and I prepared, and in June 1979 I was on a plane headed west.

2

I flew out of Atlanta and arrived in Chicago to make a connection, only to look up at the screens and see "CANCELLED" beside every outgoing flight. The Federal Aviation Administration had grounded the entire fleet of DC-10s—all of them, every airline. It was only the second time in aviation history that an entire fleet had been grounded. A flaw with the cargo door had caused two crashes several years before. Evidently the DC-10 was on borrowed time, because another crash, this one because of improper maintenance to an engine, had killed hundreds and caused the FAA to ground all DC-10s.

I was handed a voucher for a hotel room and money for transportation, and was told to come back the next day to make alternate transportation plans.

"But I'm due in Alaska today. People are expecting me to start a job."

"Everybody's due somewhere. We're doing the best we can. Just sit tight."

I had never called a cab, never checked into a hotel by myself, and certainly never seen a city like Chicago. I was just one of thousands, trying to find a way, any way, to get where I was going. Never mind that I was only nineteen and had never before been away from home. Everyone had a story. I knew I had to have help. And it had to be someone special.

I watched the people at the packed, harried Alaska Airlines counter and noticed one lady who seemed to take special care with people. Her eyes were soft, her voice was kind, and she seemed to genuinely want to help. She was a small lady—I guessed in her fifties—with spectacle glasses on her nose and straight black hair fastened to the back of her head with a pencil. Her name tag said Julia. She reminded me of my mom. I walked up and stood in her line. When I finally got to her, she looked at me expectantly. I used the one Upik word that the Nome pastor, Will West, had taught me in preparation for my mission trip.

"Ainngai," I said with just the right guttural click. I hoped I'd said hello.

The lady looked startled and grinned. "How can I help you?"

"I'm a little out of my element here. I've never been out of Tennessee by myself before, and I don't quite know what to do."

She sized me up quickly. "No problem. I have a son about your age, and he'd be lost too. I'd be happy to help you however you need."

I gave her a relieved smile. "Okay. What do I do first?"

"First, call a cab and go to your hotel. The name of the hotel is in your envelope, along with money to pay. The cab driver will know where it is."

"I've never called a cab. Where do I call from, and how do I know the number?"

She looked at me with sympathy. "Don't worry about a thing. I'll help you."

So she showed me how to hail a taxi, how to pay for it, how to check into a hotel and pay, and how to get back to the airport the next day.

"Come straight here and see me when you get back tomorrow. We'll get this out and get you where you need to go."

Finally in my hotel room with some food, I stared at the phone and debated. To call home or not? My parents weren't expecting to hear from me, and they couldn't do anything but worry if they knew my situation. Why call? So I didn't. I got out my Bible and studied for a bit, especially the passages promising that the Lord will take care of His obedient children. I found one in Jeremiah that comforted me as I settled into this strange room, in this strange city:

"'For I know the plans that I have for you,' declares the Lord, 'plans for welfare and not for calamity to give you a future and a hope.

Then you will call upon Me and come and pray to Me, and I will listen to you. You will seek Me and find Me when you search for Me with all your heart.'"

And another, from Psalms:

"Your Word is a lamp to my feet and a light to my path. . . . The unfolding of Your words gives me light; it gives understanding to the simple."

I got the message—take it one step at a time and trust God. And finally, I remembered and meditated on one of Dr. Stanley's guiding principles—obey God, and leave the consequences to Him.

"Father," I prayed, "I'll take this one step at a time, and trust You to show me the way. I trust that You do know the plans You have for me, and that You will see me safely to Alaska so I can work for You. Just please guide me, and go with me, and protect me during my trip. Be with my family and with other people in the same situation I'm in tonight. In Christ's name I pray, amen."

Then I fell into bed exhausted.

*　　*　　*

I cannot stand to sit still. I have to be moving, even if it's slowly. Sitting in an airport for hours would be intolerable. So when I arrived at Julia's desk the next morning, and she presented me with several possibilities, all of which involved lots of sitting and waiting, I looked at her rather desperately. "Aren't there any other options?"

She and the other agents were still just as harried as the day before, still trying to find ways to help thousands of stranded passengers. Julia wearily looked at her computer screen again, made several adjustments, then looked up.

"If we can get you to Seattle, you could take the milk run."

"What's the milk run?"

The milk run was exactly what it sounded like. A very small plane went from town to town, carrying mostly supplies of milk. Alaska is so vast and so remote that airplanes are often the only way for perishables to get in. So, every few days, a plane arrives with a supply that has to last until the next flight.

"The planes are six-seaters," she explained. "There's no room for baggage, and if you get airsick, this isn't for you. The schedule is brutal, flight after flight, no breaks except to sleep a couple hours at night. I wouldn't normally consider it an option, but these are not normal times."

"When would I get to Nome?"

Julia looked back at her screen. "Wednesday night."

This was Sunday, the day I was supposed to be in Nome. Wednesday didn't sound so bad. "I'll take it."

I was told that my baggage would be sent on ahead via cargo plane and would be in Nome when I got there. Then I set out, with the next leg on my journey being a train ride to Seattle. From there I flew on a small plane to Ketchikan, Sitka, Juneau, Skagway, Cordova, Seward, Homer, Kenai, and then headed northeast for about a dozen more stops. Girdwood, Palmer, Wasilla, Talkeetna, Trapper Creek, Healy, Denali Park, Nenana, Galena, Selawik.

The towns ran together, but I got a first-hand look at the vastness and the untamed quality of this land. The immenseness. The majesty. We landed on skis in the fjords of the Inside Passage and saw eagles soar and whales sound in waters thousands of feet deep between shores cut by glaciers. We flew among the towering peaks of the Alaska Range and saw moose, elk, grizzlies, and mountain goats. There were peaks so high that the snow never leaves, that the people in neighboring towns almost never see because they're always cloaked in clouds. Glaciers nestle between the mountains. The rivers are glacial runoff, spectacular in their swiftness and teal color.

It was a glorious display of the awesome power of God, and one that I was profoundly and tearfully glad I'd witnessed. A non-stop flight on a DC-10 would never have given me the appreciation and perspective that I got on the milk run.

As we flew northwest, the landscape changed gradually and dramatically. The splendor of the mountains gave way to flatter, more undulating land. Greenery disappeared completely as the arctic tundra began to take over. I was to learn later, and close up, that there is lots of color on the tundra, but you have to be very close to see it.

Along the way, my prayer was answered in remarkable ways. God very obviously guided me and protected me. At every stop, an Alaska Airlines person was there to personally see to my money, lodging vouchers, and arrangements for my next leg. I began to expect to see these angels in Alaska Air uniforms.

We touched down in Kotzebue, where I had my picture taken to prove I'd been north of the Arctic Circle, then headed south on the short final leg to Nome.

Ultimately, a trip that should have taken one day turned into four. I finally arrived in Nome at about nine o'clock Wednesday evening, three days late, filthy, dirty, and exhausted. Of course, no one was waiting for me. I found a pay phone, fished out a dime, and called the pastor's number listed on my assignment letter. He answered on the first ring.

"Brother Will?" I said. "This is Mark Smith. The Mission Board sent me to work on your church. I'm at the airport."

"Mark! We'd just about given up on you! We'll be there as quick as we can."

An hour later the pastor pulled up in a beat-up, dirty two-toned Bronco with his wife, Denise, beside him. Denise looked like the nurturing type. She had short, fluffy dark brown hair and warm blue eyes, and she wore an apron over a size-twelve house dress, which told me she'd been cooking when they got my call. A light pink sweater and Keds-like white sneakers completed her outfit.

She didn't look much older than me, maybe somewhere in her late twenties, but she instantly clicked into mother mode.

"Are you okay?" She pulled me into a hug. "We were worried about you, especially when we heard your trunk arrived without you. You must be hungry and tired. There's food at the house. We want to hear your story as soon as you rest up."

They gathered my trunk from the baggage area and bundled me into the Bronco.

Will and Denise gave me a tour of Nome on the way to their home, where both of us mission workers were to stay. They told me about the town, and I told them about my unusual trip.

We came into town from the airport on Seppala Street and turned right on Bering Street. Then we turned left on Front Street and passed the Nugget Inn, the Iditarod Arch, the visitors' center, the museum, the library, and numerous saloons. To the right stretched the steely Bering Sea, which ended at the Soviet Union, less than a hundred miles away. Standing sentinel to the left was the tallest peak in sight, topped by an impressive, oddly-shaped rock. I asked about it.

"That's Anvil Rock," said Will. "That was the first place gold was discovered here in Nome. It started the whole gold rush back in the early part of the century."

"What do people do for a living here now?"

"They still mine, mainly. Some people make a pretty decent living at it, too."

"I guess I thought the gold rush was over a long time ago."

"The rush was, but there's still gold here, and people are still finding it. A lot of the people you'll see in town are miners."

"How about the others?"

"They're people like us, or they're natives. Mostly natives. White people who are here are either . . ." he held up three fingers and ticked off his points, ". . . crazy, like the gold miners; called, like us; or they have nowhere else to go."

As we bumped along the dirt roads—I was to learn later that there were only six miles of paved roads in Nome—we passed penned yards where doghouses stood in rows, their chained inhabitants alertly stationed on their flat roofs. Our passing caused howling to begin in waves, with one group of dogs passing the word on to the next. Soon, it seemed the entire countryside was howling.

"Some of those dogs will be in the Iditarod in a few months." Will's voice was clear but soft, and I had to listen closely to hear him. I'd learned from my reading that the Iditarod was a thousand-mile dog sled race that ended in Nome.

"Those are my dogs." Will pointed to an area that wasn't fenced and had just one dog house. Twelve dogs of various sizes and descriptions were chained together at short intervals. Each dog had its own food bowl and water container. They all jumped and wriggled at the sight of Will. I was to learn later that Will obtained his dogs from different sources, without any real strategy at all, and kept them for fun and convenience. When it's forty below and there's no easy way to get around, it's handy to have dogs and a sled.

As we continued our tour, my first impression was that Nome wasn't very pretty. The houses were more like shacks, with most of them looking like they were falling in. Mud covered everything. The businesses looked run-down. The people looked rough and unkempt.

Denise must have noticed my expression. "Not very pretty, is it?"

"That's what I was just thinking."

She told me why. Several decades ago, a big storm had washed away most of the buildings. The government came in and built temporary housing, and that temporary housing was still being used by a lot of people. And, taxes were determined based on the outward appearance of a house, so people didn't mind if their homes looked shabby from the outside. It saved them a lot of money.

We drove a little more, then pulled up to a run-down corner with several shacks that looked like they might fall down at any moment.

"This is it." Will got out of the Bronco.

"This is what?"

"Where the church is going to be."

I looked at the site with renewed interest and walked onto the lot. This was where I'd be spending most of my waking hours this summer. It didn't look promising.

Grass was tall around the shacks, which were several sizes ranging from outhouse to small home. They were all deserted, with doors hanging open and holes in the walls and roofs. Rotten wood hung in juts from the frames. Mosquitoes the size of large houseflies droned hungrily. I'd heard tales of these insects, with proboscises two inches long that could punch right through clothing. Some people called them the Alaska state bird. They didn't look quite that bad, but bad enough to torment a person working outside for hours at a time.

"Brother Will, what do we have to do here?"

The pastor lit his pipe. "First we have to tear down the buildings that are already here. You can see they're about to fall down anyway, so that shouldn't be too hard. Then we have to level the land, and then put up the church."

"And there's you, Barry and me?"

"Yep. We have more than twenty hours of daylight every day,

and even the dark isn't really dark. The Lord's been blessing us in a mighty way already. I have no doubt that we'll get it done this summer, no problem."

If we did get it done—and it actually stood—it would be an example of the Lord performing something impossible. Three people, none of whom were professional builders, to do this huge task and do it well? In three months?

"There's a crew coming from California around the end of the summer to look it over and correct any mistakes," Will went on.

Denise must have noticed my dazed look and took charge. "Come on honey, you're exhausted. Time enough for this later. Will, let's get him home."

A few minutes later we were pulling up to the Wests' house—the pastorium—and there was no more time for thinking or looking.

3

The pastorium was a small, one-story house a few blocks from the church site. As Nome houses went, it looked clean and comfortable. The yard had statues and some shrubs that looked like they were trying hard to live. Denise had hung drab but cheerful-looking curtains at the windows. Will picked up my trunk and Denise led me to the front door. We went in first through one door and then another.

"Why two front doors?" I asked.

"The first one is the arctic entryway," Will explained. "When it's forty below zero, you can't just open the front door directly. The cold air would be too much. You come into the entryway, close the door, take off and store your boots and cold weather gear, then go into the house. In the cold months, we have to preserve warmth any way we can."

We went into the kitchen and down a hall to the left. We passed one bedroom that seemed to have a girl's stamp on it, then another that looked like the master, and a small bathroom. At the end of the hall we entered a third bedroom and Will put my trunk down.

"Welcome home," said Denise. The room was tiny but clean. Twin beds took up almost all the floor space. In the corner was a small upright dresser with four drawers, one of which was hanging open and showed socks and underwear. One of the beds held a plump pillow and a disheveled sleeping bag, and a foot locker sat at the end of it.

"Barry sleeps on that one," Will explained. "He got here yesterday. We've just been waiting for you. He's at the group home right now, helping get the kids tucked in."

"My sister, Allie, is in the room down the hall." Denise said. "She's sixteen, and she came for the summer to help me with the house and some of the church work. It's going to be a busy summer, so I'm glad she's here.

She headed back toward the kitchen. "I know you're starving. I have some nice hot soup and homemade bread in the kitchen."

She was right, I was starving. It was a toss-up which I needed worse, food or sleep, but food won this battle. Minutes later I was sitting at the faded kitchen table, eating some really wonderful ham and bean soup, sopping it up with warm homemade sourdough bread.

"This is terrific, Mrs. West."

"Denise."

"Denise. You're a really good cook."

Her face lit up and she gave an infectious laugh. "I like to take care of people. And I like to eat, as you can tell."

The four long days on trains and planes began to hit me, and I suddenly had a hard time keeping my eyes open. Denise's eagle eyes picked up the signs of fatigue. "You need a good night's sleep."

It was hard to argue with that, so I stumbled back down the hall, shed my travel-stained clothes, and fell onto the sleeping bag that Denise had evidently spread out for me while I ate.

It was nearly eleven o'clock at night, but the sky was still as bright as afternoons at home. Even though I had always slept in pitch darkness, I burrowed into the sleeping bag and instantly dropped like a stone.

*   *   *

I awakened to bright sunlight, the sound of rhythmic, guttural snoring, and an amazing need to use the bathroom. A glance at my watch told me it was after eight o'clock. I fell back on my pillow and looked around at the room I hadn't been awake enough to see last night.

One window was situated in the wall above the two beds, which were snugged against opposite walls with a narrow walkway between. At the foot of the beds were two doors, one that led to the hallway and another that had to lead to a small closet. The dresser sat in a small alcove to the right of the closet door.

The room was decorated with various Iditarod pictures, large and small. The race had begun only six years before but was already the most important in the sport of mushing and was called "The Last Great Race." Getting up and looking closer, I saw that Will and Denise were in some of the pictures. They posed under the Iditarod arch with dog teams and their drivers, a couple of whom held trophies.

The snoring coming from the other bed got louder and was punctuated with a snort. I looked over at my roommate, but he was hunkered down in his sleeping bag and all I could see was his hair.

Suddenly the need for the toilet overcame everything else. I left the bedroom and went a few steps down the hall to the bathroom. After what seemed like ten minutes, I breathed a huge sigh of relief and went to the sink to wash my hands. In the mirror before me was a face I'd seen and known my entire life, but it now somehow looked different. I was nineteen years old, but had experienced an adventure many people only dream about. I had wanted to make a difference, to serve the Lord. The next three months would give me that chance.

Rejuvenated, I followed my nose down the hall to the kitchen, where Will and a young girl sat at the table and Denise was taking something that smelled incredible out of the oven.

I sniffed as I walked in. "Are those . . . homemade cinnamon rolls?"

"Good morning, Mark!" Denise set the pan on the stovetop. "I hope you slept well. Yes, they are. I thought you might like a little comfort food after your long trip. This is Allie."

"Hi," I said to Allie, then headed toward the stove. "I slept great. The sun didn't even bother me."

"Did you meet Barry?"

"I just saw the top of his head poking out of the sleeping bag."

"He'll be up soon. Better go ahead and get you some rolls, because that boy can eat."

Will turned the pages of the *Nome Nugget*, which I already knew was the town newspaper. "The forecast looks like we might get a little sun today. I hope we can start clearing that lot."

"I'm ready," I mumbled around a mouthful of moist, succulent cinnamon roll.

"Good, because we need to take advantage of every dry hour we have."

Dry *hour*? It hit me why everything in Nome was so muddy and dirty. "It rains a lot here?"

"It usually rains at least some every day. That's going to make what we have to do a lot harder, but Lord willing, we'll get it done."

Denise evidently knew what she was talking about, because at that moment in came a young man who I knew was just three years older than me, but looked at least twenty-five. He was wearing a Texas Christian University t-shirt, gym shorts, and thick socks. He was about my height but much more solidly built. He had a full beard and thick, wavy, brownish-red hair. He looked half asleep and at first didn't even see me.

"What smells so good?" he asked in a sleepy, gravelly voice. Just in those few words, I could hear Texas.

"Cinnamon rolls." Denise handed him a plate. "Help yourself."

He sat, took a huge bite, and finally focused on me.

"You're Mark?" My name suddenly had two syllables when he said it.

I nodded.

"You're from Tennessee."

"And you're from Texas."

"We been wondering where you were. Glad you made it."

"I'm really glad I'm here. It's been a long four days."

We sat, ate Denise's cooking, and got to know each other a little. Barry was a senior communications arts major at Dallas Bible College.

"That's just a fancy way of saying I'm a drama major," he said. "I design and build sets for plays, mostly."

Barry had a girlfriend back home, along with his parents, two brothers, and a sister. He lived in Fort Worth but went to school in Dallas. He wanted to attend Southwestern Seminary and study religious education. He seemed like he couldn't wait to get to work, which was a relief. If even one of this three-person team was lazy, we were in for a long summer.

We finished our breakfast, piled in the Bronco, and headed out.

The sky was spitting rain mist now. Gray clouds scudded overhead. I expected that we would go straight to the construction site, but we went the opposite way, back toward the airport. About halfway there, we veered off down a small road to the right.

"Going to the group home first?" Barry asked.

"Yep, got some things I need to see to."

"Group home?" I asked.

"Yes, it's a state-funded home for abused or neglected children," Will explained. "They have either alcoholic parents or no parents at all."

We jounced along the washboard road for a few more minutes, then pulled into the yard of a large two-story house that looked as run-down and drab as all the others.

"Mark, I thought you'd like to meet some of the kids at the group home," Will said. "We all help out here, and I'd like you to work with them at the Lighthouse too."

"Lighthouse?"

"It's an after school ministry we do for the group home kids and any other kid who wants to come. We usually have a pretty good crowd, all ages."

"What do we do?"

"Play games, tell stories, help them with homework, just generally give them a good, wholesome place to go. Their home life is anything but."

As the Bronco splashed to a stop, several children ran out to meet it. It was obvious they knew when that vehicle pulled up, it was a good thing. Their eyes were eager, and smiles covered their faces. At the door of the house stood a motherly-looking woman who smiled indulgently at the children's enthusiasm.

"Hi Mona," Will called.

"Morning!" she called back. "Doesn't look like you'll be doing much at the lot today."

"Prob'ly not. Not till it dries up a little. I hope we can get some work in though."

"Who's this? This the one you've been waiting for?"

"Yep, this is Mark. He got in last night. Mark, this Mona Sanders.

She and her husband are the houseparents here."

She turned her attention to me. "That took a while. Bet you've got a story to tell."

Mona was a tall, lean woman of about forty, with shoulder-length reddish-blonde hair, fair skin, and a light dusting of freckles across her nose and cheeks. She had eyes the color of blueberries that stared deep into mine. Looking at her, I would bet that these kids didn't get away with much. She wore a warm-up suit and worn Isotoner slippers and carried a whisk broom in her hand.

"I'm just happy to finally be here. It's nice to meet you, Mrs. Sanders."

"And your mama raised you right." She gave me an approving smile. "Call me Mona. We're pretty informal here."

All the kids were still bouncing around Will and Barry and were now looking at me curiously. We moved like a herd into the house.

"What's up, Darren?" Barry asked a tall, thin boy who looked like the oldest of the group—probably about twelve.

"Not much, Texas."

I counted eleven children ranging from a tiny girl with thick black pigtails, who looked to be about five, all the way to Darren. All but one had dark hair and slightly tilted eyes, which I learned later was the look of a native. The one who looked a little different was a boy of about ten with red hair, one green eye, and an eye patch.

"Pastor, can we work today?" the redheaded boy asked eagerly.

"Can't get a lot done until we have a dry day, Paul. I want you to meet Mark. He just got here from Tennessee. It took him four days. He came to work on the building and help out here with you guys."

"Where's Tennessee?" Paul wanted to know.

"A long way from here. Clear on the other side of the country."

"You mean it's in the Lower Forty-Eight?"

This was the first time I'd heard that term, but I guessed I'd be hearing it a lot more. "Yes it is. I came a long way to be here and help out this summer. You going to be helping us, too?"

"The pastor said I could help tear down the buildings." Paul cut his eyes at Will. "Right, Pastor?"

"We're going to need lots of help, cleaning out those old shacks and getting them out of the way. You're on the demolition A-team for sure."

Will spent a few minutes talking with Mona, and then we were back in the Bronco and headed to the church site.

"What happened to Paul's eye?" I asked Will.

"We're not sure. Best we can tell, it was gouged out in a mining accident when he was just a toddler. His parents died in that accident, and he's been at the group home ever since. He's ten now."

"The eye patch doesn't seem to bother him."

"He's never known anything else. He sure doesn't let it slow him down. Wait till you see him at the building site. He'll actually be a big help."

We rattled toward the church site, and I learned about the home and some of the other kids. Darren, the oldest, was the acknowledged leader of the group. He'd been at the home since he was about four, abandoned by his alcoholic mother. She was still in town but showed no inclination to see her son, which was just fine with him. The tiny girl I'd noticed was named Priscilla, but everyone called her Prissy. I could tell from the warmth in Will's voice when he talked about her that she was a favorite. She, too, was the child of alcoholic natives, but they didn't live in the area.

"They practice subsistence," Will said. "It's a lot cheaper to live that way, and it's the native way."

"Subsistence?"

Will explained that people who practiced subsistence lived completely off the land. They grew, trapped, or caught their food. Catching a large animal like a whale or a walrus was cause for celebration, as every part of the animal was used. The meat was eaten, the skin was stretched and used for shelter or clothing, tusks were used for weapons or to carve to be sold. No part of any animal went to waste. They also had large crab pots that they used to catch huge Alaskan king crabs, and restaurants bought everything they could catch.

"The natives have a great deal," Will went on. "They can kill anything they want to without any kind of permit at all. They can shoot anything—walrus, seals, polar bears, moose, whales, whatever—anytime they want. I have a permit that lets me get one moose per year, and it was really hard to get that."

Subsistence people were getting fewer and fewer, as almost everyone purchased something at one time or another. Prissy's folks seemed to be the exception. According to Will, they hadn't been into town from their hut on the tundra since they abandoned their daughter at the home when she was an infant.

"Alcohol makes these people do some strange things," Will continued. "When you get to know these kids, it will break your heart. Look at little Prissy. You'll never meet a more precious child, but we're still working with her to get her to talk. I've heard her say maybe one sentence the whole time I've known her. How could anyone abandon her? Alcohol, that's how."

Natives had never seen or tasted alcohol until the Russians and Americans introduced it to them in the 1800s. It proved to be, in many ways, the downfall of a proud people.

All resident Alaskans received a stipend of two thousand dollars a year just for being residents. Will explained that when that time of year came around, non-natives stayed indoors because they knew that the money would be used for liquor and everyone on the street would be drunk. Brawls were abundant. Murders and suicides soared. Spouses and children were beaten.

"Alcoholism is the main thing I'm trying to fight here," Will said. "It's the biggest problem and the biggest evil. If you stayed here long enough, it would amaze you and depress you to see the extent of the abuse wives and children suffer because of alcohol. It's what the group home and the Lighthouse are all about. If we can even partially solve this problem, Nome will be a better place."

Will went on to explain all the different causes and ministries he was involved in. Besides pastoring and building the church, he counseled alcoholics, manned an emergency line for alcoholics, read devotions at the Christian radio stations in town, ministered to inmates at the Nome jail, worked with the kids at the Lighthouse and the group home, and taught Old Testament courses at Nome's tiny college, the University of Alaska Fairbanks, Northwest campus. He and Denise had recently fostered two small children until their grandparents took them in right before Barry and I arrived. When the Iditarod rolled around in March, and Nome's population temporarily exploded, he and other church members would roam the streets and pass out hundreds of hot drinks, cups of soup, and invitations to come to church.

And, he had a team of sled dogs that he fed and exercised daily, which was a large time commitment in itself.

"I'd like you to get a taste of all the different areas of our ministry here," he said to me.

"I'd love that."

For now, the sky was a solid, steely gray and rain came down in a steady, drenching downpour. So we headed back to the house, where Denise had mooseburgers ready for us. I was a lifelong picky eater, but I knew I'd have to get over some of that. I bit tentatively into the mooseburger and discovered it to be delicious, much better than hamburgers. I ate every bite, then when my eyelids began to droop I realized I hadn't quite recovered from my long trip.

"Now's a really good time to catch up on your rest, Mark," Will sopped ketchup with the last bite of burger. "Once we get started working, there won't be much time for rest."

I thanked Denise for lunch, went down the hall to the bedroom, crashed on the bed and knew nothing more until almost suppertime.

4

Rain saturated Nome for the next two weeks, so I spent the time resting, reading my Bible and getting to know the Wests, Barry, and Nome. Every now and then we had a stretch of several dry hours, and then we would go to the construction site and clean out some of the old buildings. We were ready to start taking them down as soon as we got any real break in the weather.

I discovered that Nome was about as far away from my life in Tennessee as it could possibly be. Maryville, which is in East Tennessee, is nestled at the base of the Great Smoky Mountains. We have tumultuous, unpredictable weather that comes off the mountains, but it was nothing compared to what I saw in Nome. Our proximity to the Bering Sea, both south and west, made us very vulnerable to storms coming from any direction. When icy winds swept off Siberia in the Soviet Union, there was nothing to stop them until they got to us. Similarly, when winds came across the tundra from the north and east, they slammed full force into Nome.

Since I had been here, it had snowed twice. And it was mid-June.

The weather dictated a different pace of life. People rested when they could and worked when they could. Most of Nome life happened on Front Street, which was paved downtown but was otherwise mostly dirt and mud. Residences were on streets one or more blocks back from Front.

It was colder than Tennessee, but not as cold as I expected. The temperature sometimes got up into the sixties, but more often stayed in the thirties and forties. People who lived here seemed to think this was warm, and I saw them outside in short sleeves, while I wore three or four layers of clothing. Some people even swam in the Bering Sea, but I'd been cautioned that a non-native couldn't last more than five minutes in that water. There was often a stealthy mist that drenched me as completely as a driving rain. I didn't even notice I was soaking wet until it was too late.

There was no morning, no evening. The sun was out for more than twenty hours a day, and even when it went down at about two in the morning, it still didn't really get dark.

People talked different here, or maybe it was me. Maybe it was both. There were three native languages—Upik, Siberian Upik, and Inupiaq. To each other they spoke in their native tongues, which sounded like guttural grunts with some clicks thrown in. When they spoke English, it was with heavy accents. The kids at the Lighthouse used their native language with each other, but did make an effort to speak English to us adults. The younger natives were bi-lingual or even tri-lingual.

Even the non-natives sounded different. Accents were from everywhere, and mine was more Southern than most. East Tennesseans have more of an exaggerated drawl than other areas of the country, and sometimes I had trouble making myself understood. Even Barry's Texas drawl wasn't quite as pronounced as mine. Some people looked amused when they heard me speak for the first time. I handled it with good humor.

I learned that Alaska time is different from regular time. At first I got upset when people told us they would come help us at eight o'clock, and then didn't arrive until nine. Here, eight o'clock didn't mean eight o'clock. It meant eight-ish. As long as people arrived somewhere within an hour or so of when they said they would, they thought they were on time. Will just looked at me with amusement and told me, "Mark, you're on Alaska time now. You have to change your whole outlook on punctuality."

The landscape was completely foreign. In and around Nome were rolling hills and tundra, but absolutely no trees. There were chest-high willow bushes, but that was as far as the vegetation went. And little or no grass. The tundra was interesting and beautiful, but very mushy and wet. I heard that it freezes and stays green; when it thaws, the berries from the year before are still good because they were frozen. I spent some time out on the tundra, taking photos of nature, sunrises and sunsets. I was especially fascinated with the endless variety of flowers and colorful mosses. I discovered that I could pick up rocks, and find no bugs underneath them. Nome has no snakes, which I personally found to be an excellent change from home.

I discovered that hygiene expectations here were far different than what I was used to. At home, I wouldn't have dreamed of going a day without a shower. Here, in the cooler weather with far lower humidity, wearing several layers of clothing, it just wasn't necessary or expected to wash hair, trim nails, wear deodorant, or even shower daily. No one noticed or cared. So I fell into the habit of bathing about every fifth day, and I fit in just fine.

The population was not quite three thousand, mostly native. Summer brought in some tourists, and we held a worship service at six thirty on Sunday mornings for them. Until the church was completed, we held church in the federal building downtown, which had three rooms. We held three Sunday school classes, one in each room. Barry and I led the junior high and high school group. Sunday and Wednesday evenings we held meetings at the Wests' home.

Wages in Nome were high. Will estimated we'd be working more than sixty hours a week when we got going. If we had been getting paid hourly, that would translate into more than eleven hundred dollars a week at local wages. Some whites took advantage of that by coming here, working hard, living frugally, making a lot of money and not reinvesting any of it back into the local economy. Instead, they went back to their homes in the Lower Forty-Eight, or even some exotic destination like Tahiti, and lived it up. When their money was gone, they came back and did it all over again. Natives were understandably resentful.

I saw what Will was talking about when he described the alcohol problem. Natives literally could not handle strong drink. Something in their metabolism amplified the effects of alcohol by a factor of ten. Drunks were everywhere. They staggered in the streets, puked in the roads, and urinated on the buildings. One day driving along with

Barry, I saw a heap of what looked like a coat, hat and trousers in the road. I asked Barry to stop, and it turned out to be a man passed out in the street.

Family life was broken down. Lots of people lived together in small houses. The two small children that the Wests had been fostering before Barry and I arrived were small boys who had been beaten by their mother. They had been taken away from her and ultimately given to their grandparents.

We used our time well as we waited for the weather to break, getting materials lined up for our future needs. We had materials coming in by barge sometime in July, but we had to have enough on hand to make use of the good weather between now and then. That quickly turned into a ministry in and of itself, as people saw our need and responded to it. Will was known and respected for his work with alcoholics, and people rallied to support him. Commitments for building supplies poured in. A man named George Allen, who owned Nome's biggest bar, the Board of Trade, pledged to place and bulldoze gravel on the property when it was clear. A local businessman gave us a ridiculously low bid to drill and install forty thousand dollars' worth of pilings. He told us to tell no one of the bid. At an emergency line for alcoholics, a walk-in center had to fold for lack of funds. The center gave Will a phone diverter system and fifteen hundred dollars that was in the bank.

I began to see what Will meant that first day when he said the Lord had been working in a mighty way.

5

During my second week in Nome, a package arrived for me. I ripped it open and found a cassette recorder and player with several blank tapes and a package of D batteries. The note read:

> Dear Mark:
> I hope this letter finds you healthy and happy, and your work going well. We want to hear from you, but we don't want to burden you by asking you to write us when we know you're very busy there. So here is a recorder you can use to tell us what's going on anytime, even while you're doing other things. When you fill up a tape, just drop it in the mail. In the box you'll find postage-paid envelopes.
> To start you off, we've done a tape for you. I hope you enjoy it.
> We all miss you very much but are so proud of you. We see all your friends home for the summer walking down the road or riding their bikes, or other things that are so shallow and insignificant. But our Mark is thousands of miles away doing the Lord's work.
> We are thinking of you and praying for you. We look forward to getting your first tape.
> Much love,
> Mother

I felt a vague horror. Seriously? My mom wanted me to talk into a machine? I couldn't imagine. I had some time on my hands right now, but soon we'd be working sixteen hours a day. We were all watching the sky every day for chances to work.

I plugged in the machine, slid in the tape marked "June 20 for Mark," and hit play. The first voice was my mom's.

"Hi, Mark. We thought you'd like a little taste of home. Everybody is here—me, your dad, Lisa, Jerry and Mellie."

A rousing chorus of voices called "Hi Mark!" in the background. Suddenly I felt a little homesick to hear my family's voices. Although I hadn't seen much of them in the two years I'd been away at school, their voices tugged at my heart now. I had always been close to my two sisters in different ways. They were both beautiful, with thick dark hair and hazel eyes like our mother.

Lisa was eleven months older than me and had always treated me like you'd expect an older sister would treat her younger brother. She tortured me. When I was two years old, she fed me a bottle of baby aspirin, but got her just desserts when our mother found the empty bottle in her hand and rushed to the hospital. She thought Lisa was the one who'd eaten the aspirin, so Lisa was the one who got her stomach pumped. Twice. They found nothing in her, so they looked to me. Lisa had actually eaten one pill, and I had ingested the other two dozen, all of which came gushing out.

She made me play humiliating games, girl games like "Mystery Date" that no self-respecting boy should ever have to play. I'd bet I was the only boy in town who knew how to use an Easy Bake oven.

But there'd always been the knowledge that Lisa was my sister and she loved me, and I loved her. Now she was preparing with starry eyes for her wedding to a ruggedly tall and handsome local boy, Jerry Lambert. Jerry and I also had a bit of a history, having done some fishing together since he and Lisa had begun dating. The most memorable experience was the time we got bored with fish that wouldn't bite, when we could clearly see huge carp, three feet long, paddling lazily around in the shallows. I stood a net on the bottom of the lake, and Jerry startled an especially big carp into swimming right into it. We didn't reckon on the sheer strength of a fifteen-pound carp, and when it took off it dragged me along with it. Jerry grabbed my feet, and the fish dragged both of us and the boat. There we went around the cove, the carp in the net dragging me, with Jerry in the boat holding onto my feet for dear life. The fish finally tired, and we took him home triumphantly.

You just don't eat carp, which I knew very well, but hadn't really thought about. My father took one look and declared that thing wasn't going in our trashcan, so we had to find a way to dispose of the huge carcass. We came up with the bright idea of hanging him on the fence at the high school tennis courts, and to this day my coach, Dr. Ferguson—who still teaches English and coaches tennis at Maryville High—doesn't know who hung that huge fish there. The stench lingered for days.

Mellie, my other sister, was seven years younger than me and had always been a little separated from the Lisa-Mark unit. The only blemish on her beauty was an unfortunate set of buck teeth that mortified her and that she was getting fixed. Lisa and I loved her like a pampered pet. Curiously, now that I was away from home, I found I missed Mellie the most.

The tape went on for about fifteen minutes, with each member of my family giving me a little personal message. I enjoyed hearing about what was going on back home, but the thing that made my eyes sting was the in-between moments when I could hear their background interaction, the television, and doors opening and shutting as people came and went. This was life at home, and I suddenly missed it. After being exposed to family life here in Nome, with alcoholism taking its toll in such a huge way, I valued my family more than I ever had. And I vowed in my nineteen-year-old wisdom never to take them for granted again, and to give them the best I had.

"Lord," I prayed, "thank You for opening my eyes to the treasure I've always had and never fully appreciated. Help me to do my best by my family from now on. In Christ's name, amen."

From down the hall I heard Will calling my name. I took a deep, shaky breath and went to see what he wanted.

6

"Did you want me, Will?" I came into the kitchen where he was putting on shoes over the thick white socks he always wore, indoors or out.

"Yes, Mark. There's a way you can help me out if you're interested."

"Sure. What can I do?"

Will explained that feeding and exercising his dogs was taking time he really didn't have. Would I be willing to take that off his hands while I was here?

"I'd be happy to." I had no idea what I was agreeing to.

We hopped in the Bronco and drove about one mile to the yard on the outskirts of town where his dogs were chained. We drove up to the area and I noticed, as I had before, that the dogs were not fenced or protected in any way. I asked Will if he was worried that someone might steal them. He laughed out loud.

"If anyone other than me comes anywhere close to those dogs, it wouldn't be pretty."

"Why? They look really friendly to me."

"That's because I'm here. I'm the only one they'll allow anywhere near them. They'll eat anyone else alive."

This posed an obvious obstacle to the task he'd asked me to do for him.

"Then how am I going to feed and exercise them for you?"

"Very carefully."

For several days, I went to the dog yard with Will every day, always bearing food. Slowly, the dogs got used to me. Feeding them,

I discovered, was not as easy as dumping dog chow into their bowls. They were accustomed to a special mixture, which was necessary in the extreme cold of winter but also carried through to the summer months. The dogs ate household leftovers, mixed with grease to prevent it from freezing, mixed with salmon. I learned that it takes seven hundred pounds of salmon to feed the dogs for a year.

I also noticed, as I had before, that Will had eleven dogs but only one doghouse. He explained that the house was for pregnant dogs and their pups. When he became aware that one of his girls was pregnant, she got to stay in the house until she delivered and her pups were weaned.

Exercising them was another challenge. I rode with Will on the back of the dog sled so the dogs could get used to the sound of my voice. To my surprise, I learned that real mushers never utter the word "Mush!" "Hike" means go, "Gee" means right, "Haw" means left, and "Whoa" means stop. The sled has a brake that can be thrown on the ground to help stop.

Dogs are bred to have real personalities and strengths. The lead dog, Snickers, was as smart as any human. She was responsible for listening to commands and keeping the whole team in line. The wheel dogs, Sitka and Silver, were the ones nearest the sled. They were responsible for making the big load move, so they were by necessity the strongest.

Since there was no snow in June and July, we exercised the dogs on the beach of the Bering Sea. We got to the beach by putting the sled on a four-wheeled roll cart. Once on the beach, we'd stand on the sled's runners and yell "Hike!" to start the team moving. Under the direction of either Will's voice or mine, the dogs would pull us down the beach, turn around, and pull us back. They loved to run. You could see it in their bright eyes and lolling tongues.

The dogs began to recognize me and respond to me nearly as well as they did Will. And it became a part of my daily routine.

7

We also used these rainy days to work with the kids at the group home and the Lighthouse. I worked with Patricia Boston, a volunteer who ran the Lighthouse.

As I got to know the kids better, I could clearly see the reasons for Will's passion for his alcoholic ministry. These children were innocent, victims of their parents' weakness. And, their association with us was the first time they'd ever heard the Gospel. Their thirsty minds were eager for anything positive.

Young Darren had a tender heart under all the toughness. At twelve, he was the oldest kid and the undisputed leader. It reminded me of my scouting days, and how my scoutmaster handled a group of young boys with a broad age range. He enlisted the older boys as leaders. If I were to make any progress, or gain any sort of respect, it had to start with Darren.

We took him and Paul with us to the church site one day when we had a window of dry skies. We were cleaning out and pulling down the old buildings so we'd be ready to clear the lot when the rains left. One thing I liked about this part of Alaska is that there are no snakes and really no insects other than mosquitoes, so you don't have to worry about what's in there when you clear out junk. We were able to get into the old shacks and throw stuff willy nilly into dumpsters.

As we were working that day, a drunk woman staggered up. I had seen her from a distance before. Will had told me that this was Darren's mother, and that Darren wanted nothing to do with her. As she approached, I watched him out of the corner of my eye. He kept working and acted as if he didn't notice her.

"Hi Phyllis," Will greeted her. "How are you today?"

"Can't complain, can't complain. Say, pastor, I'm a little short on cash today and need to get some food. Wonder if you'd lend me a dollar or two until my check comes through?"

We all knew that she didn't work, and any money she had came from begging. And we also knew that if she got money, it would go toward her next drink, not toward food.

"I don't have anything on me, sorry," Will said. "But Denise has some good soup in the freezer and would be happy to give you some if you go over to the house and tell her I sent you. You know where it is, right?"

"Sure, pastor, I know how to get there. I'm obliged to you." And she shuffled off, but not in the direction of the pastorium.

We all worked in silence for several minutes, and I could see the upset in Darren's eyes, his posture, and the savage way he ripped boards off the house and threw them into the dumpster. He didn't look right or left, just took his frustration and upset out on the job. Paul eyed him timidly. I sized up the situation and went over to Darren.

"Would you mind giving me a hand with something?"

"Got to finish this first," he mumbled without looking at me.

I laid my hand on his shoulder. His wiry body was taut with tension. "No, really, Darren, you can finish this in a few minutes. I've got something over here I can't do by myself."

Reluctantly he came with me, and we walked over to the biggest house together. The job I had in mind was to tear some big boards off the sides of the house, which I honestly did need help with. The boards were long, rotten, and could be dangerous if handled by one person. I showed him what to do, and we worked in silence for a couple of minutes.

"You know, Darren, I've noticed that you're really the leader around the group home. All the other kids seem to look to you before they do anything."

"Really?" He kept working at a fever pitch.

"That kind of leadership is a gift. Did you know that?"

He looked at me sideways. "A gift?"

"Yes, it is. A gift from God. He gives everyone gifts. This is one of the gifts He gave you. Would you hand me that hammer?"

He handed me the hammer, then tore boards loose with a little less vehemence as he digested this. "I don't usually get any gifts."

"Well, you've got this one." I took the claw of the hammer and ripped an especially stubborn nail out of a rotten plank. "You should look at the kids' faces when you say or do anything, anything at all. God wants you to use your gift wisely, and I could use some help, too."

"You?" Darren stopped working to stare at me. "You need help?"

"Everyone needs help." I ripped another nail free. "A big part of my job is to work with these kids. They look to you for everything. If you and I are a team, they're going to listen to me. If we're not, they won't. So yes, I need your help. You're like an unofficial staff member."

Darren resumed ripping boards off the sagging building. He struggled with a stubborn one and used a crowbar to work it loose. "What do you want me to do?"

I helped him pull the big board free, and we heaved it to the dumpster. "Really just recognize how important your role here is. Show that you support me, Barry, and the pastor. If you do, the other kids will too." I paused. "And when something happens to upset you, remember that the other kids are watching and taking their cues from you."

He took a deep breath. "You think Paul noticed I was upset."

"Darren, everyone could tell you were upset."

"It's embarrassing. I wish she'd just stay away. I don't need her, and I don't want anything to do with her."

"I understand that, and that's okay for now. Someday you're going to have to deal with it inside yourself, but don't worry about it right now. Just come to me if you need to talk or let off some steam. For now, just put on a better face in front of the kids. Think you can do that?"

"Yeah, I can do that."

"Good. Now let's get this sucker on the ground."

*　　*　　*

Paul was my shadow, and he blossomed at the attention I showed him. He was all tensile strength and willingness to learn. His one eye sparkled with determination. His parents had been from Oregon. There was no other family, so Paul became a ward of the state, and a resident of the group home, at the age of two.

He was a hard worker, a kid determined to make something of himself. Foster families were scarce in the turnstile culture of Nome, but he felt being adopted was the key to his future. On the rare occasions when a foster family came to take one or two kids home with them, Paul was always spiffed up, eager, and ready to go. He hadn't yet been chosen; none of us could figure out why. He definitely stood out from the crowd, with his red hair, pale skin and freckles. But for some reason, most foster families wanted native children.

He worked like a mule—almost literally—at the construction site. No task was too tall or too nasty for him. He learned everything he could, figuring that whatever he could learn might benefit him later. I could identify with that, as I'd always been a go-getter myself. No one had ever had to motivate me or tell me to do anything. I'd gotten through two years at the University of Tennessee with zero loans and very little help from my parents. Scholarships, odd jobs, and work on campus had paid my expenses so far. I wanted to earn my own way and owe no one. I saw the same determination in Paul. He stuck by my side like a burr, and I found myself having to take my own advice, for he would model himself after me. What I did, he did.

Tiny, five-year-old Prissy was a little doll. With her thick black braids and big dark eyes, she was everyone's favorite. She was so quiet that she presented a challenge. She'd been in several foster homes, but no one could ever relate to her, and she ended up coming back to the group home. There she had a comfort level, some history, and people who knew and loved her.

Her parents were not far away in their hut on the tundra, but she hadn't seen them since they abandoned her. The group home was the only home she'd ever known, and Dan and Mona Sanders her only parents.

She was amazingly adept at making herself understood without speaking. Whenever I was around, she attached herself to my back like a little monkey. She was so light that I scarcely noticed her there. When we sat for meals, I just spun her around to sit on my lap.

She was one of my kids at the Lighthouse. All kids were invited there after school, but mostly only the younger ones went. I worked there on Tuesday, Wednesday, and Thursday afternoons and found it to be a bit like Bible school back home. The group I worked with was the King Crabs, which was kindergarten through third grade. We sang, worked with Play Doh, studied Psalms, and did skits and crafts. I was not a crafty person, but these kids were very forgiving. I found that native kids were very smart and seemed to pick up on things faster than other kids I'd been around. They also excelled at anything with their hands.

These kids soaked up the news of Jesus' love like little sponges. They hadn't seen much love in their lives, and this was completely new territory for them. Bible stories, the ones I had known my entire life, were also new. I delighted in watching their faces as they comprehended for the first time that the God of the universe knew about *them* and loved *them*. I read them the Scriptures that showed that God counts each and every speck of sand and hair on our heads, and that He created each of us to be special. Many of them had grown up with either no spiritual background or believing in the spirit world like their ancestors had for thousands of years. As smart as they were, they learned quickly.

Prissy and I were inseparable whenever I was around, either at the group home or the Lighthouse. Like many places, the Lighthouse had no running water. The only toilet was what they called the honey pot, which was located in the arctic entryway. People did their business there in front of anyone who might be passing by. When Prissy had to use the honey pot, she was so tiny that she would have fallen in. I was the one she wanted to hold her over the honey pot while she did what she had to do.

I learned that I was lucky to be here in the summer, because in the winter the honey pot would get full and would have to be emptied and buried in the snow outside. The smell was bad enough now, but at least we could dispose of it properly. I heard stories about the spring thaw, which usually happened in May. All winter long, people buried their wastes in the snow, and it was a dreadful, nasty, unhealthy situation when it thawed and ran into the streets. But no better way had yet been devised. This, thankfully, was something I wouldn't have to deal with.

8

I also got a taste of salmon fishing while we waited for dry weather. Every July, the salmon come up the Nome River to spawn. Huge fish boil and teem in the river as they fight their way upstream. Like everywhere in Alaska, catching and smoking salmon is an essential part of life, because this is a big part of the people's diet during the long winter months. So, people either have to catch them or buy them.

Salmon fishing is difficult because they don't eat after they start their migration. From the time they leave salt water until they spawn, they eat nothing. They are sometimes attracted to the bright flash of the hooks, but you can also snag them by dragging your hook across them. That is now illegal, but it wasn't at the time.

The prime time for salmon fishing is when the salmon make their run. They school up at the mouth of a river and dash upstream together, thousands upon thousands of them. They seem to know they have a better chance in a big group, but that's also when fishermen come out in masses. When salmon start schooling up, word travels fast and the fishermen come running.

One day at church, Barry and I heard the fish were schooling up and went to try our luck, using a couple of rods we borrowed from Will. In the short time I'd known Barry, I'd learned that he was not only a Texan. He was a *Texan*, so much that I called him "Texas," and he called me "Tennessee." Everything in or from Texas was better than anything from anywhere else. I couldn't even convince him that Alaska is considerably larger than Texas. He simply looked at a map, and it looked to him like Texas was bigger.

On this Sunday afternoon, we ambled along Front Street in a slight drizzle, following the road past the end of town until it turned into dirt. Our shoes had long since become filthy from all the dust and mud, and we'd given up trying to keep them clean or even dry. The Nome River is a couple of miles out of town. Locals' cars passed us in a steady stream, mostly salmon fishermen but some locals with full crab pots, on their way to sell their crabs to The Roadhouse, Nome's most popular restaurant. Some people make their living this way, in addition to catching enough food for their own families. Whenever you got a meal—any meal—at a Nome restaurant, you got a crab leg with it. Full crab dinners were expensive, so restaurants could afford to be generous with the fishermen.

I'd been fishing all my life with my father and grandfather, and I felt like I had a pretty good chance at nabbing some salmon. But I'd never seen anything like the scene that greeted us at the Nome River. Normally, it's a pretty lazy stretch of water. It's maybe two hundred feet wide at that point, with sand bars and shallow water. A bridge crosses it at the point where we arrived.

Cars were lined up along the road. People arrived on foot in a steady stream, with all types of fishing poles over their shoulders, ranging from the most elaborate, expensive setup to homemade rigs consisting of wooden poles with string and jury-rigged hooks. In the water, on the sandbars, and along the banks, people had staged themselves in strategic spots, eyes fixed downstream. Natives were positioned mid-stream in umiaks, which are light boats made of walrus or seal skin stretched over ribs of bone or driftwood. They held nets at the ready.

I assumed all the good spots were taken and that this would be a learning experience. Barry and I made our way down to a spot on the river bank with a clear shot to the water. We got in place just in time, as we heard a whoop from the people on the bridge and looked up to see people pointing downstream.

And here they came. What minutes before had been a relatively calm stretch of water was suddenly a boiling, teeming mass of fish a good two feet long. I'd had no idea salmon were this big. When Jerry and I caught the carp, we caught him with a net and that was hard enough. The biggest fish I'd ever caught with a rod was a sev-en-pound bass. I couldn't imagine what it would feel like to have one of these big boys on the end of my line.

Barry had never fished, so I tried to teach him while I did something I'd never done before. We emulated the people around us, casting, feeding out line and pulling it back in much more quickly than I was used to. The point was not so much to get the fish to bite, but to firmly snag them with the treble hooks on our lures.

On the third cast, I felt my lure sink into a big salmon, and my line took a tremendous jerk that I felt all the way down to my sternum. The fight was on. I kept my line taut, so he couldn't dislodge the hook, and let him run. As I fought him, I noticed the etiquette of the other fishermen. The ones downstream pulled in their lines, moved around me, and resumed fishing upstream so I could use the river's current to bring the fish in. I made my way down the riverbank, steadily pulling my fish toward shore. He was strong, and it took him a while to tire. My arms ached after just a couple of minutes, from the weight and the sheer pressure as the fish fought. I reminded myself not to be surprised; these fish can leap up six-foot waterfalls on their way to their spawning territory. Of course they were strong.

Barry also had a fish on his line. He was jumping and hollering and doing all the wrong things, but somehow managing to keep from losing his fish.

By now a crowd of children had gathered around, watching and cheering me on. Breathing hard, arms feeling they were being pulled from their sockets, I slowly pulled in my catch and got a good look at him as he drew near the shore. He was huge, about two feet long and weighing at least twenty pounds. I pulled him close to the shore, grabbed him firmly by his gill, and dragged him out of the water. Sure enough, the treble hooks had caught him just behind his head in two places, snagging him firmly as I pulled him through the water. I carefully worked the hooks loose, then tucked my catch away in a big bag we'd brought along.

I looked up at Barry just in time to see his rod tip drop and his line go slack. I started to yell at him to get his line taut, but it was too late. All of a sudden his line went limp as the fish took advantage of the slack line and shook himself free.

Barry looked at me, red-faced with sweat dripping off his face along with the rain. "Dagnabbit!"

"Better luck next time." I was still breathing hard.

"You got one?"

"Yep. Take a look." I opened the bag and showed him. My fish nestled there, still heaving and glaring at us.

"Good grief, Tennessee, that's a big one."

"I think so. Denise should be happy with this."

"I can taste the salmon steaks already."

We admired him for another moment, then I became aware of one child who had stayed behind. All the others had left when I put the fish into the bag, but one small boy remained. He looked to be about seven years old, and he held a fishing pole made of a big stick, a string, and a bent straight pin. He looked thin and hungry, with dark hair and strange sea-green eyes.

"That was great, mister," he said to me.

"Thanks. What's your name?"

"Atka. What's yours?"

"Mark. Do you like to fish?"

"I try, but I never caught one like that."

'I just got lucky. This was my first time fishing for salmon. It was really different."

"Your first time? Really?

"Yep."

"Can I see him again?"

I opened the bag again and showed him to the boy. We knelt together, the little native boy and me, and I realized with a jolt, as from a voice inside, that this was a God-given opportunity.

"Atka, where do you live?"

"Right down there." He pointed back toward town.

We talked for another minute or so, and I discovered that he went to the Nome elementary school and lived at home with his mother and two younger brothers. His father lived on the streets of Nome, having been thrown out of his home because he was always drunk.

"Have you ever heard of the Lighthouse, Atka?"

"No. What's that?"

"It's where kids get together after school and do some fun stuff. All kids are invited. I'd like it if you'd come and check it out."

"Will you be there?"

"I'm there on Tuesdays, Wednesdays, and Thursdays, at least until the weather breaks and we can start building our church."

"I'll see if I can come. My mom needs me after school to help with my brothers."

"I'll ask her for you if you want."

He looked at me oddly. "Why? Why do you want me there?"

"I just think you'd have fun, and I like you."

This seemed to be a strange concept to him, but he accepted it. "I'd like it if you'd talk to my mom."

Atka hung around with us for the rest of the day. He shared our lunch, and I let him use my rod to see what he could do. Within a couple of minutes, his line gave a huge jerk.

"Mark!"

"I see. Just stay calm and let him play, but keep the tip up and the line tight."

"You do it. I don't want to lose him."

"You can do it. I'm here if you need me."

He concentrated, tongue caught between his teeth, feet braced wide apart as he fought the fish. His green eyes were steely determined, his hands tight on the rod. I realized suddenly that this was more than just a fish for him. This was food for his family, food they didn't have the money to buy. I told myself if Atka couldn't bring this fish in, I'd give him mine.

Before long the fish, fighting for his life, outdueled the small boy. When Atka's arms started trembling, I gave him a break and fought the fish while Atka caught his breath, and then gave the rod back to him. I wanted him to bring it in on his own.

Slowly but surely, the fish gave in. His struggles grew steadily weaker until it became obvious that Atka would win. Seeing this, the boy seemed to get a second wind and easily brought the salmon to shore.

I thought my catch was big, but Atka's beat it. It was about the same length, but much fatter—at least twenty-five pounds. Barry and the other men standing around us whistled and cheered as Atka pulled it in. They came up to admire the fish and clapped the boy on the back.

"That was amazing!"

"Great job!"

"I can't believe you brought that thing in!"

Atka beamed and showed off his fish, and I knew this was the proudest moment of his young life. He handed me the rod, looked up with big wet eyes, and said, "Thanks."

I couldn't speak for the lump rising up in my throat, so I just nodded and took the rod. If it had been mine to give, I would have given it to him.

We started the long walk back to town, lugging our catches, and he asked if I had meant it when I said I would ask his mom about the Lighthouse.

"Sure, if you want me to."

"I'd like that. It sounds like fun, and my mom probably will say no if I ask her. She might say yes to you."

We walked in silence, and before long turned off the main road. He led us to a small house near an abandoned gold dredge and took us straight up to the front door.

"Mom? Mom!"

"I'm coming, I'm coming," we heard from a back room. A thin woman, who couldn't have been more than thirty years old but looked much older, came into the main room with one child hanging from her skirt and another suckling at her breast. She had thin, lank blond hair and eyes the color of her son's. She stopped short when she saw Atka wasn't alone.

"I made some new friends at the river," he said. "This is Mark and Barry. They're helping build a new church in town. And look what they helped me catch."

"We didn't help you," I corrected. "You caught it all by yourself. It's nice to meet you, ma'am."

"You can call me Missy. I appreciate you bringing Atka home. And oh, look at the size of that fish!" She looked at us with startled eyes. "That will be dinner for a week."

"Your son did a great job pulling it in." I became conscious of green eyes boring into me from the side. "Actually, there's something I want to ask you."

"Go ahead." Her eyes looked wary.

"Our church has a program called the Lighthouse after school. All the kids are invited. We read Bible stories, sing songs, do crafts, and play games. We'd love to have Atka if you can spare him."

"It's right after school?"

"Yes, ma'am."

"Well, I don't know. He helps me a lot around here."

"Maybe he could start with one day a week and see how it goes."

She thought about it. "I guess that would be okay. Atka, you want to do this?"

"Yes, Mom. I'd like to give it a try, if it's okay with you."

"One day a week," she relented.

"We have services on Sunday mornings in the federal building and on Sunday and Wednesday nights at our pastor's home," I added. "We'd love it if all of you could come."

"We'll see," she said, but I could tell it was time to go.

Barry and I left the house and continued the walk back to town. He hadn't said much about Atka until now.

"That was a nice thing you did for that kid."

"The Holy Spirit led me to do it."

"He did?"

"Clear as day, like a voice inside me."

He absorbed that for a moment. "That's really cool. I had something like that when I decided to come here, but it doesn't happen to me very often."

"It's happening more and more to me. I've learned to trust it and just do what it says. You know, Texas, it seems to always work out just right."

When we got home, we handed over my fish to Denise and told her and Will about our experience at the river. And when I went to bed that night after a wonderful salmon dinner, I prayed a prayer of thanks.

"Dear God, thank you for your Holy Spirit, and for the way He shows me what to do. I would have missed out on something really special today if not for Him. And be with Atka and his family, and help me to do the best I can for him and all the other kids." And I fell into an exhausted, happy sleep.

9

When I opened my eyes the next day, I blinked. Something was different. It took me a minute, then I realized what it was. Sun—actual sun—was streaming through a crack in the curtains, directly across my face. I hadn't seen the sun in so long that I lay motionless, just enjoying the sensation. Then it hit me—we could get started on the church today. We'd been waiting for so long that I felt giddy. A glance at the clock showed me it was seven o'clock in the morning.

"Texas!" I shouted.

Barry leaped out of the bed like someone had attacked him with a cattle prod. "What?!"

"Look out the window!"

He peered with bleary eyes, and then it evidently hit him too.

"Woo hoo! Let's get on it!"

We bolted down the hall to the kitchen, skidding to a stop in our sock feet. Denise stood at the stove, already ahead of us with breakfast well under way. She had planned well for three hungry men with a big day's work ahead of them. Ready and on the counter top were eggs, pancakes, potatoes, biscuits, and meat that I knew was moose sausage. Will was already fixing his plate. He looked up with a huge grin.

"You boys ready for some real work?"

"Are we ever," I answered for both of us, plowing into Denise's cooking. Barry already had a mouthful of sausage.

"You're going to get it, for sure." Will paused to swallow a huge bite. "By lunchtime, we're going to have all those houses and shacks cleared away and the site ready for construction."

I stared at him. We'd managed to clean out all the structures and they were ready for demolition, but there were still six of them and three of us. He read my look.

"Do you doubt it? Hasn't God been with us so far?"

I couldn't argue that point. Over the past two weeks, I'd witnessed some near miracles as the town had come together to get everything in place for this day. We had everything we needed to get started. All the construction materials were staged and ready, and people had promised to help in any way they could. Today, it seemed, Will was going to cash in on those promises.

"Not only that," he went on with a twinkle, "but by the end of this week, we're going to have the floor finished on the bottom level."

The Nome Baptist Family Center was going to be a two-story structure with a center section, measuring twenty-four by forty-eight feet, and two big wings. There would be a loft, a pastorium, two apartments, a chapel and a fellowship hall. Finish an entire floor? This week? With just three of us?

Then I caught myself. How could I doubt? The Lord had already shown His support and blessing. If Will said we'd do it, then do it we would.

Fifteen minutes later, we pulled up to the work site to find all the houses already on the ground. Bulldozers were pushing the debris into dump trucks, which were lined up and leaving as soon as they were filled. The man who'd given us the unbelievable bid to drive the pilings was already at work on one end of the lot. Trucks loaded with gravel were lined up on the street.

George Allen was in the middle of it all. He had come through, and in a big way. He'd promised to provide, deliver, and level the gravel, but had gone a massive step farther to complete the demolition. He caught sight of Will in the Bronco and tipped his hat.

Will sat and stared, his eyes growing moist. Finally he cleared his throat. "Well. Any more questions? Looks like we're ahead of schedule. Let's get moving."

*   *   *

We spent the morning going behind the workers who were driving the pilings. They augured deep holes in the ground, through the permafrost, into the bedrock. Then they slid thick poles into the holes. Barry and I filled in with dirt and concrete so the poles were secure. Then the gravel trucks came behind us. They poured their loads, and bulldozers spread the gravel. We helped spread it among the pilings.

In the afternoon we came back with a string level and a chain saw and cut off the poles so they were all exactly even. These would form the foundation for a church we hoped would stand and be vibrant for a very long time, so this step had to be just right. It was nearly midnight when we got home.

For the next five days, we worked like we'd never worked before. I learned to read architectural drawings, lay and secure laminated beams and cross pieces, and fix the floor on top. There had been challenges when pieces didn't fit just right, but we learned to work around them and get a quality job done.

The weather held off all week, which was a miracle in itself. Three of us worked all the time, and a fourth man named James Vaughn joined us when he could. He was Will's right-hand man when he could take time away from his FAA job at the airport. He had my healthy respect because he was the oldest member of our little construction team at forty-seven, but was in the best shape by far, running anywhere from six to fifteen miles a day. He brought his wife, Lily, and his daughter, Connie, and they all helped whenever and however they could.

The mosquitoes lived up to their reputation, giving me about eighteen bites the first day. With their long proboscises, they could bite through shirts, coats, even hats. I learned a native trick of taking vitamin B-6, which takes away the human smell so the vicious insects can't tell you're a human. That, along with a mesh hat my father had given me, saved me after the first day.

Saturday night at ten-thirty, after a sixty-four-hour work week, we reached Will's goal of finishing the floor on the bottom level. We'd worked from about seven-thirty in the morning until about eleven at night, every day. One day alone, the three of us lifted ten tons of beams. Friday we went home and took a three-hour nap in the afternoon so we could work until ten the last night.

Now we could stand back and look at the miracle. The Lord had dropped everything into our hands, including extra help when we absolutely had to have it. With only three months of building time, it should take a big crew of experienced men to finish this job. But with a core group of three, we were getting it done. And Will had already asked me to stay for an additional week, beyond the departure date of August 10 that I'd been planning for.

* * *

As I lay exhausted on my bed on Sunday night, gearing up for another long week, I stared at another, much more daunting challenge than anything I'd faced so far. I couldn't put it off any longer. It was time to turn on the infernal tape machine my mother had sent me, and tell my family what was happening in my life.

Feeling like an idiot, knowing everyone in this small house could probably hear me, I turned the machine on, slid in a cassette, and punched record.

"Hi everybody. This is Mark in Nome. Hope everyone's doing well there. I'm going to hate talking into this thing, but here goes."

For the next ten minutes, I told them about Nome in general and how life was here. I covered the town, the scenery, the weather, the town people, and the alcoholism issues we were fighting, the Wests, our ministries, and my daily activities.

"I've been getting my exercise on the construction site. We started laying the beams down on Monday and by Saturday night at ten-thirty we had the whole floor on. That was Will's goal, and we thought he was crazy, but we got it done. For this next week, our goal is to be finished with the walls on the first floor and have the trusses up for the second floor, and all the windows and doors on the first floor. It seems impossible, but I wouldn't be surprised if we make it.

"There are a lot of people who help us. Even building the church has become a ministry."

I told them about the Board of Trade and the forty-three loads of rock George Allen delivered and graded. I described the man who had provided the forty thousand dollars' worth of pilings and drilling labor for nearly no cost.

I hit pause and considered. I remembered my reaction to the tape my family had sent me, and knew they'd be blessed to hear about it. I hit resume.

"I am homesick." I realized it was true. "I miss everyone. I enjoyed the tape you sent me. The thing I enjoyed the most was the interruptions and you talking to each other. That meant more to me than anything you said. It's the kind of homesickness that I'm not hurting to be home, but I miss the love that's there.

"Dad, you and Mom both talked about the Bill Gothard seminar you went to. Dad said he wished he'd gone to the seminar before he had children. I see a big need in our family for love. We need to love each other more. I'm a part of that too.

"Lisa and Jerry, I pray that you'll get involved in a church real actively. I'm not speaking from experience, but I know you can find ways to serve the Lord, maybe even together.

"Mellie, I miss you too. Bad. I didn't know that I would miss you so much until I got up here. I think I may miss you more than anybody.

"I think I've taken a lot for granted. I'm excited to come back. I think I've got some new ideas to be more helpful around our home.

"Dad, you suggested I send some film off to see how my pictures are going to turn out, and I did that. They look good, and I'm about ready to send off some more.

"I hope you didn't wreck my car, Lisa."

I went on to tell them that I was having second thoughts about being a dentist.

"I've been thinking a lot about that. I want to look at the religious studies department at UT and at Carson Newman. I want to get some information about the courses."

I spent another ten minutes rattling on about this and that, knowing my mother would want to hear every little thing. Finally, getting hoarse, I told them I was going to bed and hit stop. I decided that for the next week, I would record a little every night, giving my family a glimpse into the daily life of a summer missionary.

10

When I appeared in the kitchen for breakfast early the next morning, Will had a new opportunity for me that made me very glad I'd spent the time with the tape recorder last night.

"Morning, Mark." He had an unusual look in his eye.

"Morning, Will." Something was up. I didn't take my eyes off him.

"I have an opportunity for you, if you're interested."

"Sure. What is it?"

Will explained that the town pastors took turns doing on-air morning devotions for the local Christian radio station. This week, it was his turn.

"I'm supposed to be there at seven, but I need to be at the work site at seven to meet a delivery. Think you can handle the devotion?"

This was way out of my comfort zone, but so was everything else I'd done here. "Just tell me what to do."

"I've got it all picked out and ready. Or, you can do something on your own if you want."

He gave me a devotional book and some selected Scripture, and dropped me off at the radio station at six forty-five, on his way to the work site.

It all sounded easy, but my heart was pounding. Teaching Sunday school and telling kids Bible stories was one thing, but this was different. Who knew how many people would be listening to my voice this morning? It was very scary. I said a prayer for strength, then walked into the station.

"Hi, I'm Mark Smith," I told the girl at the receptionist desk. Her name plate said Sheila. It looked like there was just this room and one other. "I'm substituting for Will West for the morning devotion."

Sheila led me through an adjacent door, which led to a small room with lots of buttons and dials, and a big ominous-looking microphone. A hymn was playing. No one was there.

"There's the clock." She pointed to a clock on the wall directly in front of us. "You have to start at seven o'clock on the dot. Here's the button that takes the mute off the microphone. You push that button, and just start talking. Your devotion has to last for at least ten minutes, so pace yourself. Joshua will get here about the time you finish, so you can't finish early. You can run a little long, but not short."

I said I understood, and sat down at the console. It was six-fifty, so I had ten minutes to think and pray. When I'd walked into the station, I'd fully intended to use the devotion Will had prepared. But it occurred to me that this was a new opportunity, and I'd best ask the Lord what He wanted me to do with it. I closed my eyes.

"Lord, I want to be faithful with every opportunity You give me. If it's Your will that I use Will's devotion, that's what I'll do. But if there's something else You want me to say to these people, please open my mind and eyes and ears to that. In Jesus' name I pray, amen."

Usually answers to my prayers are not instantaneous, but this was evidently a special situation. I immediately got an image in my head of the apostle Paul on one of his missionary journeys, shipwrecked, with a snake hanging off his hand and a group of men looking on in horror. I knew the story, but I immediately turned in my Bible to the book of Acts, chapters twenty-seven and twenty-eight, and refreshed my memory.

Paul was being held prisoner in Caesarea, having been accused of many violations of the Jewish law. He was a Roman citizen and had the right to appeal to Caesar, and he was on his way to Rome via ship to meet with Caesar to defend himself. After completing several legs of the journey with increasing difficulty due to weather, the ship and crew were about to depart Crete. Paul warned them that the voyage was too dangerous and they should winter in Crete, but he was ignored.

Before long, the ship was caught in a violent wind and was carried along out of control. The storm went on for days, and the crew began jettisoning the cargo and tackle to eliminate weight. Paul stood up in their midst and told them an angel had come to him the night before and assured him there would be no loss of life, but the ship would indeed be lost. He told the crew that they must run aground. They followed Paul's instructions and ran aground on the island of Malta, and all 276 people on board survived. They spent three months there, and Paul was able to minister to the natives before continuing his journey on a ship that had wintered at Malta.

I took a moment to absorb Paul's experience, and couldn't help but marvel at the difference between his time and today. Here in Nome, I had the same opportunity he'd had—to tell the news of the Gospel—but the big difference was that I wasn't going to be arrested or imprisoned for it. What incredible courage and conviction those original apostles had! They had the unbelievable privilege of listening and learning from Jesus Himself, and then they were empowered and commissioned to take that news throughout the world. I couldn't even imagine such an awesome responsibility, to all of mankind. From those original twelve men, nearly two thousand years ago, had come the good news that I was here in Nome to share. All I could do was open up and let Christ speak through me.

The clock ticked on, and the instant it struck seven o'clock I hit the button that unmuted the microphone.

"Good morning, Nome. This is Mark Smith, and I'm a summer missionary at the Nome Baptist Family Center. We've been really busy the past few weeks building a church that I hope you'll all visit when it's finished.

"This morning I want to share with you a story of another missionary. His name was Paul, but it hadn't always been. He was first called Saul, and he was anything but a follower of Christ. In fact, when Jesus had been crucified and his followers were sharing the news of the Gospel, Saul was a ringleader in tracking down Christians and putting them in prison. He stood there when Stephen, the first martyr, was stoned to death because of his faith in Christ. Saul pursued Christians into their homes and arrested them, knowing they would be imprisoned, tortured, and executed.

"What happened next is an excellent example of how God can use anyone. You probably know the story of Saul's conversion. He was on his way to Damascus when a bright light blinded him, and a voice came to him saying, 'Saul, Saul, why are you persecuting Me?'

"Just imagine. You're on your way to Council to get some silver salmon for the long winter. You're thinking about all the things you have to do when you get there, and all of a sudden you're struck blind by a bright light. And a voice speaks to you and says this. What are you going to think?

"Saul was a Jew, so he believed in God. He knew immediately that this was a God thing and the Lord was talking to him. So he said, 'Who are you, Lord?'

"The answer he got was this: 'I am Jesus whom you are persecuting. Get up and enter the city, and it will be told you what you must do.'

"Saul must have felt horrible. He knew that he had been personally responsible for the deaths of dozens of people who now turned out to be right. But on the other hand, Jesus wanted to use him. He was an instant convert.

"Over the next months and years, he became one of the most active missionaries ever. He was persecuted for Christ's sake. In time, he wrote over half of the books of the New Testament. And one of his experiences speaks to me especially.

"On one of his voyages, he was shipwrecked on the island of Malta with 275 others. The natives were kind to the castaways, and built a fire to help warm them. Paul—as he was known by then—gathered sticks and laid them on the fire. Just then a snake came out, attracted to the heat, and bit Paul on the hand. It was poisonous, and the natives knew it. According to the Scriptures, it just hung there. Listen as I read from the Word of God, the book of Acts, chapter twenty-eight, verses four and five:

"'When the natives saw the creature hanging from his hand, they began saying to one another, 'undoubtedly this man is a murderer, and though he has been saved from the sea, justice has not allowed him to live.' However he shook the creature off into the fire and suffered no harm.'

"So here's Paul, meeting these people for the first time, and he gets bitten by a venomous snake. He just flings it off like it's nothing, and they first think he's about to fall over dead. But he doesn't. So then they start to think he's a god.

"Paul used that experience for God, staying there for three months and teaching the people. He healed people in the name of Jesus. When he finally left and continued his journey, it was with the full support and affection of the people of Malta.

"That story speaks to me because I'm a missionary now. I'm trying to use every situation and every opportunity, to share and teach about Jesus. I try to live His example. It's not always easy, and I do make mistakes we call sin. But I look back at the original apostles, and everything they had to deal with, and I am excited at the opportunity we have to worship and believe as we choose. I'm happy to be here in Nome to help teach and build a church in His name.

"We invite you all to come see us at our new church. And now I'll turn the program over to your morning dee jay."

I muted the microphone. Another hymn began to play. A man, whom I assumed was the morning dee jay, had been standing in the door. When I muted the microphone he came in and shook my hand.

"Nice going, man. I'm Joshua Webster, the station manager."

"I'm Mark Smith."

"Nice to meet you. Thanks for filling in for Will. Good stuff you shared this morning. Where'd you get it?"

"Where'd I get it?"

"Yeah, what book did you use? Do you have notes you can share?"

"No book. Brother Will gave me some material to use, but he said I could do something on my own if I wanted. I prayed about it, and this story from Acts just came to me. I just felt that this was what God wanted me to say."

"It just came to you?"

"Yes."

He looked at me for a moment. "That's incredible. I've never heard such a good devotion here, in all the years I've been doing this. And it just came to you?"

"It came from God. Give Him the credit."

"Well, Mark, it was an excellent job. You have an open invitation to do a devotion here whenever you want."

Floating on a cloud of good feeling, I left the station and walked the few blocks to the church site. As usual, there was a buzz of activity. The goal this week was to get the first floor walls up, and Barry was hard at work putting one together on the ground, to be lifted into place when it was finished.

Will spotted me and came up.

"Hey, Mark, how'd it go?"

"Really well, I think."

"I was listening. I think it went better than 'pretty well.' You did an amazing job. I'm proud of you."

"Well, thanks! I appreciate that. I actually enjoyed it. I'll be happy to fill in for you whenever you need me to."

Will studied me for a moment longer with that same odd look in his eye I'd seen this morning. "Joshua just called me."

"He did?"

"Seems like you made quite a hit."

"I did?"

"You did. Joshua wanted to tell me how impressed he was that you came up with something like that off the top of your head."

"Will, you know me better than that. This was way outside my comfort zone. I was terrified and prayed for strength and courage, and then I asked God how He wanted me to use the opportunity. I just said what He put in my heart to say. He deserves the credit, not me."

"Well, Joshua tried to hire you away from me for the summer. Said he had money for a summer intern and he never hired one, and he wants you."

I was stunned. "Really?"

"Really. What do you think about that?"

"I think I'm flattered and stunned, but I didn't come here to talk on the radio. I came here to be a missionary and build a church."

"That's my boy." He hooked a thick arm around my neck and pulled me toward the work site. "Let's get back to work."

11

Through the month of July, I settled into a routine. We were up by six and at the job site at seven. We usually ate breakfast at home, and the other two meals at the site.

The church rose at an astonishing pace. And somehow, the weather held for the most part. When it didn't, I helped out with kids at the group home or at the Lighthouse. At lunch time I went to feed the dogs, and every other day I took another hour to exercise them. And always, no matter what else the day held, I reserved an hour of quiet time to spend with the Bible and in prayer.

We had challenges along the way at the church, like the day we had to hoist into place a big beam that would extend the length of the building, in the rafter area, twenty feet above the ground. That beam alone weighed nearly a ton, and there was no way the three of us could lift it into place. In a sort of mini-miracle that we'd come to expect, two burly men came along just at the right time. With them, and two well-placed ropes, we were able to get the job done.

Then there was the time when things looked really bleak, because the church construction project was out of money. The Southern Baptist Convention had given all it could, and so had the Mission Board. Will was on the verge of canceling the California crew that was due to come in August to inspect and put the final touches on the frame construction. In a last gasp effort, Will called the Mission Board for help. I overheard his end of the conversation from the next room.

"Hi, Mr. McNair? This is Will West in Nome. I wanted to update you on our progress here. Yes, yes, we're doing great. The building structure is more than half done. The boys you sent are absolutely fantastic. Yes, I'd love to keep them from now on.

"We do have a problem, though. Our funding is about to run out, and we definitely don't have enough money to finish the job."

Will listened for a moment.

"I understand, I know money is tight everywhere." Another pause. "Do you have any suggestions for me, anything at all?"

Will listened for a long time, and I could hear the scratching of his pen as he made notes. Finally, he said, "Thanks so much for this suggestion. I'll definitely give him a call. Thanks again."

Within a few days we had a visitor at the construction site. His name was Matthew Hawkins, an oil-rich Texan who spent one day with us. He strode around the site with an air of confidence and leadership, talking to all of us, and making notes into a tape recorder. Then he went away, and we heard nothing more until the barge came in.

Nome, as with most other Alaskan coastal cities, gets the vast majority of its supplies via barge. The roads are either bad or nonexistent, so people have to get supplies either by air or by water. Air is very expensive, so it's used as little as possible. A year ago, Will and Denise had figured out what would be needed for this church, down to specific nails and lumber pieces, and had ordered everything they could afford.

Barge day, I learned, was an exciting day in Nome. One moment we were hard at work on the building, and the next we heard excited shouts from the direction of the waterfront. Word spread fast, and people started running in that direction. Barry and I looked at Will quizzically. He removed his hat and wiped his face.

"Only thing that causes that much excitement is the barge. I'm pretty excited about that myself, this time."

Looking at the meager amount of supplies we had left, I could understand why. We had been hoping and praying for the barge's arrival so we could continue work. It wouldn't be enough, but it would allow us to continue. We all leaped off the building and made tracks for the Bronco, joining the crowd of people who were running for the waterfront.

The scene was a madhouse. As items were unloaded from the barge, people were there to claim them. One young man grabbed a four-wheeler, revved it up, and began doing wheelies up and down the road. Huge stacks of canned goods disappeared into people's trucks. A motorboat was lowered into the water, met by its proud new owner in a umiak.

We could see our pile on the vessel's stern, and it obviously would take a lot more than the Bronco to get it to the construction site. Just as the unloading crew got to our pile, we heard Will's name called from behind us. We turned to see George Allen in a huge flatbed truck, making his way in our direction. Once again, he was our angel of deliverance. He'd promised to provide and spread the gravel on our lot, but over the weeks he'd done so much more because of his affection and respect for Will.

We started unloading our shipment, but the ship's captain stopped us. "Are you Will West, the pastor?"

"I am."

"You're supposed to read this letter before you take your stuff." The captain handed him a thin envelope.

Will, bemused, took the envelope and tore it open. He read it silently, his smile growing as he read. He said loudly, so all could hear, "We serve a mighty God, and don't you ever forget it." He handed me the letter. It said:

Dear Rev. West:

Thank you for spending time with me during my visit to Nome. I was most impressed by your work there, and your commitment to your ministry and the people of Nome.

I believe God has blessed me financially for a reason, and I feel compelled to help in a tangible way. On this barge you will find all the materials you need to complete construction. Also, in this envelope is a check for $25,000, to be used as you see fit in other areas of your ministry.

I would very much like to return next summer and see your progress, and attend church in your new building.

Again, thank you for the time you spent with me. It helped me see the need there, and I feel privileged to help you in your work. If you require further assistance, please don't hesitate to call.

Sincerely,

Matthew Hawkins

On the barge were all the materials that Will and Denise had ordered a year ago, along with much more that had been added and paid for by Matthew. Where we had been scraping by, now we had plenty. Where we were using cheap materials, now we had something better.

We all looked at each other, open-mouthed. Will led us in a prayer of thanksgiving, and Barry and I helped load the precious supplies onto George's flatbed. We triumphantly rode it to the church site.

One of the items in that load was the baptismal tank, affectionately known by Baptists as the "dunking pool." It would be used to baptize people when the church was complete. We had built the worship center on the first floor around it, using the measurements Will provided. Now we hoped those measurements, both his and ours, were exactly right. If not, we would have to tear the whole thing out and start again. And, we were depending on the Lord for help to get it into place; the job was much too big and complicated for the three of us. The timing was exactly right, as we had just finished the walls of the first floor but hadn't yet added the ceiling.

As George helped us unload, he spied the tank.

"What in the world is that?" he asked.

"It's part of our basic belief," Will explained. "The Bible tells us that when a person accepts Jesus into his life and heart, he must be baptized before witnesses. Some churches sprinkle water on people's heads rather than immerse them, but the Scriptures clearly say that Christians are to be baptized the way Jesus was, and the way he baptized people Himself—and that's immersion. A person is a new being when he accepts Christ. Being immersed in baptism is symbolic of dying to your old ways and being reborn."

"Where does it go?"

"In the worship center." Will led George to the spot and showed him. He peered at the space doubtfully and scratched his head.

"How in tarnation are you going to get it in there?"

"We'll need some help," Will said. "A couple people and a crane."

The next day a crane showed up. First we had to get the tank out of the crate, which was dicey in itself because was made of fiberglass and could not tolerate pressure of any kind. We had to fix straps around it to get it out of the crate and fasten it to the crane. As the crane began to lower it into place, we all held our breath. And as the tank dangled from the crane, we learned someone had made a mathematical error. The tank was about three inches too wide for the space we had built for it.

So there we were, standing below the tank, which was being suspended by a crane, trying to guide it into place. And the place was too small. We looked at each other and did the only thing we could.

While the crane and our helpers stood there and waited, tank still dangling in the air, we applied a sledgehammer to the front wall of the space we had built, and began frantically enlarging it. It wouldn't be exactly flush with the rest of the wall, but it was the best we could do. Within about thirty minutes, the job was complete and the tank was lowered into its new nest.

We worked on through the month of July. Barry loved to sing while he worked, so I reluctantly learned the lyrics to all the current country tunes. Often he had nails in his mouth as he sang, so the words were garbled, but that didn't stop him. Sometimes the songs made sense, and sometimes they didn't. As he hammered nails and tapped his toes, he bellowed "All the Gold in California" by the Gatlin Brothers.

Will and I often found ourselves humming along. I hoped no one at home ever found out I'd learned these songs. Country had never been my thing, but now I could tell you the words to "She Believes in Me," "The Devil Went Down to Georgia," and "Every Which Way but Loose," among others. It was embarrassing.

Some afternoons after school, Patricia Boston brought the kids over from the Lighthouse to check out our progress. On those days, we had more help than we wanted. Prissy was always there, and she climbed on my back the instant she saw me. Often Atka was there as well. He had quickly made friends with Darren and Paul, and the three of them came running with whoops of excitement when they got in sight of the church property. Barry and I found jobs for them and spent the time overseeing their work and talking with them.

I really missed these kids. After spending hours of every day with them during those rainy days of June, it was hard not seeing them now. Atka, especially, was my special child, after our time together at the river and at his home. It was well worth the time spent, even if we had to redo some of their work after they left.

12

In early August—on my twentieth birthday—Will drove the last nail into the roof structure in the east wing. The three of us sat on our haunches and looked at the finished building and each other. It was a moment of silence, of wonderment. Will found his voice first.

"Guys, I think it's a good time to pray." He reached for our hands. We both bowed our heads.

"Lord," Will prayed, "we want to thank You for Your help and Your favor that we've seen as we've built this church. We know You are the reason we were able to get it done, and to You be all the glory. You sent good weather. You sent these fine young men to help. You sent other help when we needed it. You helped us in ways we probably don't even know. And we promise to use this to glorify You. Thank You for Your Son and Your grace, which we don't deserve—no one does—but we are so grateful for it. Now please show us Your will as we finish this job for You. In Christ's name we pray, amen."

We released hands and looked at each other with wet eyes. Barry, never good in emotional situations, lowered himself to the ground and went to start gathering up our tools.

I couldn't get over it. We'd built—actually built—a church for the Lord. In this building, hopefully, His will would be done and souls would be won. Scripture would be taught and people would grow in the Word. Missions would be launched. Families would be fed. Children and adults would be baptized. And through it all, the Lord would be glorified.

"Will," I began, only to discover a very unmanly lump in my

throat. I cleared it and tried again. "Will, what's next? What do we do now?"

"Our job is done for now. For the next few days we clean up loose ends and inspect our work, and next week the California crew will be here to make sure we did everything right. Then later in August, we'll start doing plumbing and electrical work and then we'll put up walls. Hopefully we'll be under cover by the time winter gets here, and using the church for services by the time the Iditarod rolls around in March."

That sounded depressing. I was scheduled to go home on August 17, and I had already extended my stay by a week at Will's request. After putting so much work into this building, I wanted to see it through. Of course I knew that was impossible. Classes would be starting. I was scheduled to go back to my bookkeeping job. My family and friends were expecting me home. I shook off the feeling and concentrated on helping clear up our tools.

Will saw my expression and said in a serious voice, "Mark, there's something I've been wanting to talk to you about."

"What is it, Will?"

"I'd like you to consider staying on here."

"You mean after the extra week you already asked me for?"

"Yes, after that."

"I might could work out a little more time. How long?"

"Until next summer."

"Next summer?" Surely I didn't hear that right.

"Yes." He lowered himself to the floor of the second level and held up a hand to help me down. "You're so good with the kids at the group home, and they love you so much. The Sanders need a break now and then. We'd pay you twenty thousand dollars to be a relief houseparent on the weekends and two afternoons a week. It's not a full time job, but it leaves you plenty of time to find other ways to make some money and fill in the gaps. And you could be in on finishing the church."

Twenty thousand dollars, just for spending time with kids I'd grown to love. It sounded too good to be real. I didn't know what to say, so I said what was in my heart.

"Will, I don't know what to say."

"You don't have to say anything right now. It's a big decision."

"When do you need to know?"

"It's a government-funded position, so the job would start October 1, which is the beginning of the fiscal year. Go home in two weeks as planned and think about it. Talk with your family. Pray about it. When you can give me an answer, call me. I'll be waiting."

13

I didn't have much time to think about Will's offer over the weekend, as we cleared stuff up from the construction on Saturday and conducted classes and services on Sunday. The crew arrived from California on Monday, August 6. About a dozen of them came, most with their wives. They looked over every inch of our work, looking for anything unacceptable or unsafe for a building that had to endure what this one would have to endure. They looked at our plans, and they looked at what we'd done, and they went to work.

They stayed one week. They had brought tools to fix anything they might come across. They worked as a seamless unit, reworking where they could, tearing out and rebuilding areas where necessary. Will, Barry and I, along with the crew's wives, served as runners. We got them the materials and tools they needed, and helped however we could. And in one week, we learned more about good construction than we had all summer.

With the team was a young man named Jack Barker. He was a trapper by trade and a construction man by necessity, doing this work as a summer mission project. He looked about my age, with hair short on the sides and longish on top. It was blond at the tips from the California sun. He had black eyebrows, and a scruff of a beard that reappeared every day. Although young, he knew what he was doing and applied himself to his work with an admirable focus. He could swing a huge hammer and drive a nail home with one blow.

James Vaughn was there for much of the rework. Lily came part of the time, and Connie came every day after school. Jack Barker took one look at dark-haired, petite Connie Vaughn and fell head over heels in love. Soon he was spending all his off time with her, and by the end of the week both had stars in their eyes, and he was making plans to move to Nome and find work and a place to live here.

I was wrestling with what God wanted from me down the road, and I wanted to spend time with my family and talk to them about it. Should I come back to Nome until next summer or go back to school as planned? Should I continue with my plans to be a dentist or go into the ministry? Then I came across a verse in Isaiah that stood out like a beacon:

"Then I heard the voice of the Lord, saying, 'Whom shall I send, and who will go for Us?' Then I said, 'Here am I. Send me!'"

I knew then that I had part of my answer. My future belonged in service to the Lord. I didn't know when or what form it would take, but I simply trusted that He would continue to guide me and show me the way, one day at a time.

When my plane took off from Nome on Friday, August 17, I didn't know if I would be back or not. I locked my eyes on the skeleton of the new church for as long as I could see it, remembering an amazing summer that would always be part of my personal history—whether or not I returned to Nome.

PART 2:
FALL

14

From the time I landed in Atlanta and saw my parents waiting for me, it was great to be home. My father gave me a firm handshake and a big smile, and my mother enfolded me in a rose-smelling embrace with tears in her eyes.

"I'm so glad you're home," she kept saying. "I'm so glad you're home."

I felt completely different, but my parents seemed the same. My father, Richard, was a little shorter than me, a barrel-chested man with white hair at the age of fifty. He had the booming voice and big presence of a pulpit pastor. My mother, Sharon, barely five feet tall, had curly dark hair and the green eyes she'd given her daughters. Her height had always given her issues with weight. When you're five feet tall, you don't have much margin for error. But she'd always kept herself trim and neat.

My mother, never at a loss for words, kept up a constant conversation during the three-hour drive home. A debate champion in college, she's skilled at extracting a lot of information in what seems like a casual conversation. We arrived home to find Doug, Jerry, Lisa, and Mellie waiting on the front porch. My sisters flung themselves at me as I came up the steps, almost knocking me backwards. It was definitely, to this day, the happiest they have ever been to see me.

My mother had planned a big homecoming/birthday meal, since my birthday had been less than two weeks before. She had prepared my favorites: enchilada hamburgers and homemade ice cream. I ate like a sumo wrestler, catching up on life at home. Between bites, my mother grilled me for details about my summer. I told them about everyone on the mission team, the kids, the work, the town, and Alaska in general. I described the countryside, so beautiful but so different from our East Tennessee mountains.

"I hope you realize that this experience is going to impact the rest of your life," my mother said.

"I do realize that. It was surreal sometimes, the things I saw and did. It was so different from anything I've ever seen or done before." I paused. "And it may not be over. Will wants me to come back until next summer. He offered me a paying job at the group home."

My family stopped eating and stared at me with their mouths open. My mother was getting tears in her eyes again.

"How much does the job pay?" My father wanted to know.

"Twenty thousand dollars a year, and it's not even a full-time job. I'd be a relief houseparent on the weekends and two afternoons a week."

"You mentioned salaries in Alaska are really high," he said. "I see what you mean."

"I haven't made up my mind yet. I need to think and pray, and spend some time talking to you guys. I just have to let him know in the next couple of weeks."

15

For the next week I just relaxed, visited with my friends, and let my mother take care of me. To my surprise, I couldn't relate to most of my friends anymore. The only exceptions were Doug and a girl named Sandy Petre. Sandy and I had never dated because the timing had just never been right, but we were good friends. I could tell Doug and Sandy about what I had been through and the decision that faced me now, and they would listen. They seemed to understand and accept me as I was now—which was different than before I left for Alaska. The other people that I had called friends now seemed so shallow. Their lives were all about their cars, their friends, their problems, their futures, their clothes. They didn't seem to get that life wasn't about them at all, but something far bigger.

I came to realize, more and more, that my heart was still in Nome with Atka, Darren, Paul, Prissy, and all the other kids. I wondered how the church was coming along and how Will and Denise were managing alone.

I spent some dedicated time in prayer and in the Word, asking, looking, and listening for more specific guidance. I have never been one to look for signs, because the Scriptures and my own inner voice usually provide crystal clear guidance. I didn't pray for a sign now, but when one came, it was unmistakable. It was more like a kick in the pants.

I was at home one afternoon when the telephone rang. I heard Will West's voice on the other end.

"Hey, Mark!" His normally quiet voice was hearty and enthusiastic. "How's it going in the Lower Forty-Eight?"

"Warm. It was above ninety today. That's been pretty hard to get used to."

"Have you given any thought to what we talked about?"

"I've thought and prayed about very little else, Will. I'm a little closer to making a decision, but I'm not there yet. I want to be sure I stay in God's will, whatever decision I make."

"This may help. I've been working with the Mission Board, and they're prepared to make you a semester missionary, with room and board covered. That's in addition to the salary I mentioned."

That did change things. Twenty thousand dollars—free and clear—with the chance to earn more. Money had been my one stumbling block to the seminary. I wasn't afraid of hard work, and I was confident I could find other ways to earn money and bump up my savings. With the scholarships I had in place for my final two years at the University of Tennessee, the money I would earn in Alaska would pay my entire tuition at any Baptist seminary. I knew the Lord would work it out, and now He had. There was very little else to think about. This was a sign in big, bold, flashing letters that I was to go back to Alaska.

"That money is an answer to prayer. You've got yourself a missionary."

Will's loud exclamation made me hold the phone away from my ear, and I grinned. It was a relief to have the decision made. A load had been lifted off my shoulders, and I absolutely knew I'd made the right decision.

"So, when do you want me back?"

"Plan to leave in mid-September. The Mission Board wants you to stop off in Anchorage and spend some time with a couple there who works with young missionaries. Then you can be back here the last week of September and start your new job on October 1."

The next couple of weeks were madly busy. I withdrew from school, sold my orange-and-white Firebird for money to buy my one-way plane ticket, gave up my guaranteed dorm space, and quit my bookkeeping job. I figured I had a pretty good idea of what clothes I would need for the next nine months. After all, I'd just spent three months listening to natives talk about the Nome winter. I had jackets, hats, gloves, boots, and warm socks I'd used for hiking. It got pretty cold in Tennessee in the winter, so I thought that if I layered all the warm clothing I had, I should be just fine. For good measure, my dad bought me a good down vest, and I figured I was set. I spent several days collecting these things and packing them into a metal footlocker.

I spent some devoted time with Doug and Sandy. It was during one of these times that I got a rare glimpse into how dark forces operate. Sandy and I were walking in one of Maryville's beautiful creekside parks that stretch throughout the downtown area. We stopped and sat on a wooden bench under a big tree. I was explaining to her why I'd made the decision I had.

"It wasn't just the money. I started realizing that I didn't finish what I went there to do. The church isn't done. My heart is still with those kids. I need to finish what I started, and the money was the icing on the cake."

"I can hear it in your voice. Your eyes just light up when you talk about the kids."

"They're so smart, and so open to new ideas. When they hear the Bible stories we've known our whole lives, their hearts just open up. It's the best feeling in the world to be able to share that with them."

As we talked, a feeling of blackness began to come over me. It crept up slowly, steadily, noiselessly, getting darker and thicker by the moment. I saw it in Sandy's eyes, too.

"Do you feel that?" I asked her. The birds stopped singing and the park went dead silent.

"Yes, it's like . . . something evil. And it's getting closer."

I looked around and could find absolutely nothing ominous in this beautiful September evening. The air was warm but not hot. The sun was setting. Dusk had always been my favorite time of the day. The leaves were still green but starting to change colors at the very top of the trees. Kids were running and playing. People walked their dogs right in front of where we sat. No one else looked like they felt anything amiss.

But it was there, all right. Sandy and I looked at each other with increasing alarm. Then it was like something grabbed me by the back of the neck and jerked me off that bench. I grabbed Sandy's hand and pulled her with me. And at that moment, a huge limb broke high up in the two-hundred-year-old oak tree and crashed onto the sturdy bench where we had sat a few seconds earlier, breaking it into splinters.

We got a safe distance away, then turned. We stared at the bench, then at each other. Sandy was white-faced. "Whoa."

"Double whoa."

"How did you know to get up?"

"I didn't. It was like something grabbed me and dragged me."

"I'm glad you hung on to me."

We stared back at the bench.

"I think your guardian angel just saved us," Sandy said.

16

I had to make one last trip to the University of Tennessee to close out some details, and I stopped by the BSU. I wanted to talk to Bob Hall to update him on what was going on, and get his take on what had happened in the park. He was in his office.

"Hey, Bob."

He looked up and grinned. "Well, Mark! Good to see you!"

I went forward and shook his hand. "It's good to see you, Bob."

Bob Hall was the consummate encourager. He looked for the best in people, and I never heard him say anything negative. When a student went to see him, he never talked about his own problems or issues. He concentrated solely on the student. I had tried to get him to talk about himself and tell me how he was doing, and he would say a little but always turned the conversation back to me.

He also knew a great deal more than I did about Scripture and theology, and had served as a mentor to me in the two years I'd been at UT. I needed his guidance now.

"Did you hear that I pulled out of school?" I asked him.

"Yes, I did. Tell me about that."

So I told him about my summer, in much more detail than I'd told anyone else. It took a very long time. He never interrupted me, except to ask a few short questions. His attention never wavered. He never looked bored. When I got to the part about becoming a semester missionary, and the job I'd been offered, his eyes got very big.

"Mark, that's incredible."

"I thought so too. That's what made my decision for me. I decided while I was there that I want to go to seminary, but I didn't know how I was going to afford it. God provided."

"Indeed He did. But I can sense there's more. You've been leading up to something."

I told him about the incident in the park. He stopped me several times for clarification and more information.

"You and Sandy both felt something?"

"Yes."

"But no one else seemed to."

"Not that I could tell."

"And you literally felt something pulling you off that bench."

"Literally."

"Mark, Sandy was right."

"About what?"

"Your guardian angel. I have good news and bad news for you."

"Okay."

"The good news is, you definitely seem to be walking in God's will."

"That *is* good news. How do you know?"

"Because the devil doesn't like it. What happened in the park is an obvious attempt. That's also the bad news. You can expect stuff like this to continue."

Of course I believed in Satan and his minions, but I'd never had anything like this happen to me before that I remembered. So, I was a little skeptical that the forces of evil, in this day and time, would take such an active role on earth. I expressed my thoughts to Bob.

"Have you ever had anything remotely like this happen to you before? Anything threatening or unexplainable? Think carefully."

I started to say no, but stopped and thought about it. When I was ten, I fell on my head from the top of a forty-foot tree and was completely unhurt. I'd always chalked that up to good luck and my own hard head.

Then there was the time when I was fifteen, when I was riding my bike down Montvale Road in Maryville. It was, even then, a busy road, but I only had to be on it for about one hundred feet. A car swerved in front of me and I went through its windshield, breaking several bones. The police on the scene shook their heads and said I should have been killed.

Just months after that, a doped-up, money-seeking drug addict found his way into an unlocked window in our kitchen and fumbled into my bedroom at the front of the house. I woke to find a shadow in my doorway and rolled to the edge of my bed—just in time to avoid a baseball bat slamming into the headboard. I evaded the intruder and ran upstairs for my dad, but by the time he came down with his gun, the man was gone. My mom's purse was missing, but a church offering envelope with a substantial amount of money was untouched. The man was caught nearby, and my mom's purse was recovered minus the money. I identified the man from his profile, which I'd seen in the moonlight.

I would have discarded these instances as luck and coincidence, but then another scrolled across my brain. When I was sixteen, I was in the hospital after major surgery. My whole life, I'd had a sunken chest, but it had gradually worsened so that my heart and lungs were compressed and my sternum was actually touching my spine. The doctors opened up my chest, broke all my ribs, pulled my sternum up to give my heart and lungs room, and patched me back up.

As I lay in intensive care, in the most weakened, vulnerable state of my young life, a nurse somehow misread a drug order. She came into my room and started to administer a strong chemotherapy drug intended for a cancer patient. It would have killed me. My alert mother, stationed at my bedside, asked the nurse conversationally what the drug was and was able to stop the injection seconds before it would have been inserted into my IV.

The doctors and my family shuddered in disbelief that such a mistake could be made, and my mother insisted that, despite the extra cost, a guard nurse be posted at my bedside to double check any medicines. The horrified hospital immediately agreed.

Remembering all this, I said to Bob, "Now that you mention it, there have been a few things," and shared the stories with him.

He shook his head. "I was serious about your guardian angel. There are Scriptures to support this. Check out Psalm 34:7 as an example.

"I believe the devil was behind all of this. Have you read Job?"

"Yes, of course."

"It is probably the oldest writing in the Bible and says clearly in the first chapter, verse seven, that Satan does roam the earth." Bob turned to that verse in the Bible, where Satan showed up in heaven for a meeting of God's angels. He read aloud to me.

"'Now there was a day when the sons of God came to present themselves before the Lord, and Satan also came among them. The Lord said to Satan, 'From where do you come?' Then Satan answered the Lord and said, 'From roaming about the earth and walking around on it.'"

He looked up at me. "That's just one verse. It says the same thing in the New Testament in 1 Peter, chapter five, that he 'prowls about like a roaring lion seeking someone to devour.' Why would you think Satan does things any differently now than he did then?"

"I've just never had it happen to me before."

"Maybe you've never walked in God's will before. Or maybe you're about to do something so big and special for the Lord that Satan will do anything he can to stop you."

"That's a great thought, but it's also a little scary."

"That's good, Mark. If you weren't scared, you wouldn't be careful."

"I'll be careful, all right. But how do I guard against something like this?"

"The Bible tells you how. Turn to Ephesians 6:10-18." Again, he read aloud:

"Finally, be strong in the Lord and in the strength of His might. Put on the full armor of God, so that you will be able to stand firm against the schemes of the devil. For our struggle is not against flesh and blood, but against the rulers, against the powers, against the world forces of this darkness, against the spiritual forms of wickedness in the heavenly places. Therefore, take up the full armor of God, so that you will be able to resist in the evil day, and having done everything, to stand firm. Stand firm therefore, having girded your loins with truth, and having put on the breastplate of righteousness, and having shod your feet with the preparation of the Gospel of peace; in addition to all, taking up the shield of faith with which you will be able to extinguish all the flaming arrows of the evil one. And take the helmet of salvation, and the sword of the Spirit, which is the Word of God."

I felt a sense of elation. Here was solid guidance for standing firm and protecting myself. "How exactly do I do this?"

"It tells you exactly what your defense is, Mark. Look at the last verse."

"'The sword of the Spirit, which is the Word of God.'"

"Exactly. Study the Word. Use concordances to help you find other similar verses. God's Word and His Spirit will help you understand what you need to. All of us need help. Prepare beforehand. Memorize verses. Find passages that state what God's will for everyone is and be absolutely sure you do what it says. Then search for His will as it pertains to you. If you do all the other things, you'll find it. Guaranteed. And if you're in God's will, and doing something He wants you to do, He will protect you."

"The Boy Scout motto is 'Be Prepared,' but this is amazing. I've never heard it put quite that way before."

"I hope I've helped you."

"You really have, Bob. Thank you."

"I wish you success and good health over the next year, Mark. When you come back next year, there'll be a place for you here at the BSU."

"I appreciate that." I gave Bob a hug, not a handshake, and left him.

*   *   *

I was in the homestretch now of my time at home. My flight back to Alaska was booked for Monday, September 17. I was to stay in Anchorage for a week and travel on to Nome on Monday, September 24.

My mother had taken it amazingly well so far. She was weepy, but didn't say much. I thought my father had probably advised her to keep her feelings to herself, and for this I was grateful. It had to be difficult for her to see me go back to Alaska for the better part of a year. For the first time in my life, I wouldn't be home for the holidays.

The night before I was to leave, she came into my room. I was sitting on my bed, packing the last few items. A damp-looking tissue was wadded up in her hand, and her eyes were red. She came straight to me and folded me in her arms. I returned her hug, my face buried in her bosom. It had been a long time since she'd hugged me like this, like a small child. I found that I didn't mind at all.

"I worry, Mark."

"I know, Mom."

"It's so far, and you're still so young."

"I know."

"You're sure you're being called to do this?"

"I'm absolutely sure." I hadn't told her about the incident in the park or my conversation with Bob Hall; I knew that would put her over the top.

"Then I'll just pray every night for your safety and blessing." She blew her nose. "I'm putting you in His hands."

I felt tears prick at the back of my eyes. Here was unconditional love, complete understanding, and unswerving support. No one would ever love me quite like this. Someday my wife and children, hopefully, would have a deep love for me, but not quite like my mother. I really would miss her. I hugged her back and cried along with her. "Thanks, Mom." I managed a watery smile. "Try not to worry so much. If I'm in the Lord's hands, what more could you ask?"

"We are all in His hands, whether we realize it or not." She left the room and softly closed the door behind her.

17

My parents dropped me off at the airport two hours early, which was plenty of time in those days before 9/11. I checked my trunk, then wandered empty-handed through security and toward the gate. Now that all the goodbyes were behind me, all I felt was excitement and anticipation to be going back to Alaska. There was so much unfinished work, so many people I missed more than I would have thought possible. I could hardly wait to get back.

I was also excited to be spending a few days in Anchorage with Charles and Patsy Chandler, who had themselves been missionaries in Alaska. They'd met on a mission, and loved it so much they made their home there and now enjoyed mentoring young missionaries on their way to and from assignments. Anchorage was a city I'd never seen at all, except a brief landing there on my way home several weeks earlier.

The flight was uneventful. I felt like a seasoned traveler now, after the tumult of my first trip. A regular flight was almost boring. We flew non-stop to Anchorage and arrived a little early. I could see the blue ocean on one side and majestic, snow-capped mountains on the other.

The Chandlers were there to meet me, with a sign reading "North American Mission Board." Charles Chandler was a tall, thin man with vivid blue eyes, a gray crew cut, and a welcoming smile. His wife was a perfect complement to him, with her short, soft figure, bouncy bronze waves, and deer-brown eyes. They helped me gather my trunk from baggage claim and loaded me and my baggage into a muscular-looking black pickup truck.

Over the next few days, the Chandlers treated me like a son.

Watching them together was like a manual on how a marriage is supposed to be. My parents sometimes showed casual affection toward each other, but nothing like this. The Chandlers were loving and affectionate and obviously adored each other, even after thirty years of marriage. They had children, but they were all grown and gone. They went through my trunk and looked with pity at my cold-weather clothing, which kept me plenty warm in the Tennessee winters. Our coldest temperature, though, was usually in the teens.

"We're going to the Army surplus store," Charles announced, and we went that very day. They outfitted me with a warm coat, fur-lined boots, a thick wool sweater, and several pairs of warm wool socks. Feet, I learned, were the most important thing to keep warm. It gets down to forty below in Nome. That temperature, combined with the constant brisk wind that can gust up to forty miles an hour, makes the temperature feel like eighty below. I couldn't even imagine cold like that.

I also learned that when the temperature drops to twenty below zero, it's essential to keep all skin covered.

"If you expose it," said Charles, "even for a few minutes, you will lose it."

They quizzed me about the kinds of activities I'd be doing. When I mentioned mushing dogs, they counseled me about snow blindness. With sun shining on the snow blanketing the tundra, the brightness would be literally blinding. To protect my eyes, I should use glasses that let only slits of light through.

Most of my other activities would be indoor, because by now the church would be under roof. I would sometimes be taking the group home kids on short trips or the Lighthouse kids outside to play, but outdoor activities would be relatively rare. I thanked them for their advice and gratefully packed the warm clothing into my trunk.

On my final day in Anchorage, Charles took me on a sightseeing trip to Gunsight Mountain, north of the city. I'd done a lot of hiking during my scouting days, but I quickly learned that hiking here was far different from the well-marked trails of the Great Smoky Mountains. I got my first clue when Charles stopped the truck at the base of a tall mountain and we got out. I was used to starting hikes at a trailhead, where signs clearly showed how long the trail was and where it went. It was difficult to veer off our Tennessee trails because they were well-used and well-maintained.

There was no such thing here. We used game trails. We started across country, hip deep in tall grass. When we topped the first rise, a ridge of mountains was visible to our right. The trees here were mostly aspens, and they were beginning to turn in a sea of undulating yellow. As we continued to walk, I could hear the sound of rushing water. We came alongside a river that was the spectacular green-gray color of glacial runoff, and hiked beside it for a while before veering off again. Up we climbed, up until we were looking down into the valley where we'd parked the truck. We stopped for a snack and water break.

"Isn't this spectacular?" Charles leaned back and stretched.

"It's incredible." The view was like nothing I'd seen in the Smokies. I loved my mountains, but they didn't compare to this. Alaskan mountain ranges are much younger than the Smokies, so as a result they are much taller and more rugged. The Smokies are worn down by age and erosion.

And the wildlife here was incredible. On my Tennessee trails, we sometimes saw a black bear. More often, we saw deer, raccoons, squirrels, and perhaps a skunk. In some places we might see elk.

Here, antelope grazed in the far distance. Charles told me that antelope can see for about two miles, so it would be impossible to get close to them. A mama moose and her calf crossed our path, and we saw evidence that huge grizzlies were in the area. Charles kept his gun handy, just in case. On the hillsides were immense Dall sheep, with their sweeping, curving horns. Charles told me how he'd bagged one of those sheep the previous year.

"You have to understand the animal and their habits. They rarely look above their perch for potential danger. I came at them from above to get a shot." He paused, and we basked in the complete silence. "I think Patsy is planning to serve sheep for dinner tonight. You'll like it."

Charles was a wealth of useful information. He used this whole trip as a teaching opportunity, showing me berries and other things I could eat if I ever found myself stranded outside for any amount of time. He took special care as he demonstrated several ways to keep warm, to make sure I understood how to protect myself in the extreme cold. As we walked, ate berries and talked, he tested my emotional well-being and physical and spiritual health.

I found a ready ear for my story of the park and the limb. Charles completely agreed with Bob Hall's assessment and the advice Bob had given me.

"Mark, you need to spend time in the Word, and find Scripture that speaks to you specifically. One thing's for sure—Satan isn't finished trying to derail what you're here to do."

"What do you think Satan's worried about?"

"There's no telling. It could be as big as the church you're building, or it could be one special person, even a child, who will be reached by what you're going to do there. It could be how this experience will impact your life in the future. You have to keep your heart, eyes and ears open for every opportunity. And be on the alert. Something tells me it is *big*."

We fell silent and looked again at the vista spreading out in the valley before us. The silence was complete, broken occasionally by birds flying in groups overhead.

"Charles, Bob said I can be sure now that I'm walking in God's will. Do you agree with that?"

"Yes, I do. But you have to be careful. Right now you're in God's favor. He's happy with you and has blessed you with this opportunity."

"I totally get that, but why do I have to be careful?"

"It would be easy to be proud of that and think you're special. You are special, we all are, but you have to always remember that it's all about Him. Just as quickly as you please the Lord, you can displease Him. Remember what happened to Moses?"

Moses had been God's faithful servant from the time God called him from the burning bush. He had led the people of Israel out of Egypt, through the wilderness, as God directed him. The people were astonishingly ungrateful. Every time they were the least bit uncomfortable, they started whining. They seemed to have a hard time remembering what God had done for them. One particular time, they began whining that they were thirsty, saying it would have been better if they had just stayed slaves in Egypt. Moses was understandably frustrated with them.

God told him to speak to a stone and water would come forth. Moses went to the stone and struck it with his hiking stick as he spoke to it, and water did come forth. But for his disobedience, he was not allowed to go into the Promised Land that God had promised the people of Israel. He got to see it from a distance, but his feet never touched it.

"I remember," I said. "I always thought that was a little harsh."

"Careful. We have all had that thought, but it's not for us to question God. He demands obedience, and it's absolutely imperative that you remember that. If you know you're supposed to do something, then you had better do it. No waffling.

"Also remember to always give Him the glory for everything. When you finish that church building, tell an interesting Bible story, even just do a good deed, give Him the glory and the credit. Remember that it wasn't you at all. It was God through you. Obey Him, and give Him all the glory, and you'll be just fine.

"Mark, repeat after me—It's all about Him."

"It's all about Him."

"Again. This is important. It's all about Him."

"It's all about Him," I repeated with more volume and feeling.

"I want you to say that any time someone says something good about you and your work. It is the most important lesson you may ever learn. You've heard that God hates pride, and pride cometh before a fall? It's all Scriptural and true."

With that piece of advice, we rose from our spot by the river and started the long walk back to the truck. We spent the trip back to Anchorage laughing, relaxing, and talking about anything and everything. When we got back to the Chandlers' house, Patsy had supper waiting. Charles was right—it was the Dall sheep he'd brought home before. I would have never thought I'd eat, and love, a sheep steak. It was one of the best things I've ever put in my mouth.

Then, after a week of living with, and being ministered to, by the wonderful Chandlers, I was on my way back to Nome.

18

Now, as I pick up my story, I was back in Nome. Will had met me at the airport and had dropped a bomb on me. The job I'd come back to Nome for had gone away. I had no money to go anywhere else or do anything else. And, I found myself miles from town, on top of the highest peak in the area, dressed only in a thin shirt and jeans, with an arctic storm blowing in. I was minutes from hypothermia and too cold even to pray. I had wedged myself into a crack in Anvil Rock to get away from the wind. And I knew no more.

*   *   *

Some time later, I had no idea how long, I opened my eyes and felt my face. Everything was warm. Was I dreaming? No, the storm was still howling, but now it was dark. I had been asleep for several hours.

I realized God had just saved my life again. It was like He had covered that opening in the cleft of the rock with His warm and mighty hand. I remembered the story of Moses. He had asked God to show Himself to him. The passage from Exodus reads:

"'You cannot see My face, for no man can see Me and live. Behold, there is a place by Me, and you shall stand there on the rock; and it will come about, while My glory is passing by, that I will put you in the cleft of the rock and cover you with My hand until I have passed by. Then I will take My hand away and you shall see My back, but My face shall not be seen.'"

Now here I was, in the cleft of this mighty rock. I felt very much as if I were witnessing the glory and majesty of God. Had He sent the storm? I didn't know, but even if He hadn't, He was definitely using it. Before, I had felt fear, embarrassment, complete disillusionment, anger and panic. Now, I felt peace, protection, and an astonishingly real and humbling connection with the Almighty. I realized in a whole new way that the God of the universe, who'd created all the majesty around me, cared about Mark. He loved me—small, insignificant me—completely and deeply. I'd known it before, but I felt it now in waves washing warm over me. It was deep and unmistakable, and I cried new tears that didn't freeze. I got the message clearly, from deep in my spirit, that I was indeed supposed to be here. There was work to do, lives to touch. It wasn't going to be easy, but God would be with me. And if it was His will, I would still find a way to serve Him, even though this job had gone away.

Another story came to mind, this one from the first chapter of Joshua. Before Moses died, God chose Joshua to take over the leadership of Israel and lead the people to the Promised Land. Joshua was understandably nervous and hesitant. Moses was a much-loved leader, who had led the Israelites out of slavery, through the wilderness, and to the doorstep of Canaan. He had communed with the Lord and had worked miracles in His name. Now he was about to die. It must have felt like a tall order to be the one selected to replace him. But God told Joshua, "Just as I have been with Moses, I will be with you; I will not fail you or forsake you. Be strong and courageous. Do not tremble or be dismayed, for the Lord your God is with you wherever you go."

I felt those words speaking to me now. When the storm passed and I crawled out of my cleft, I was still warm. My clothes were dry, no longer soaked with sweat. And I knew that I'd been protected. I could pray just fine now. I turned my body over so that my face was on the rock and cried, "Lord, thank You for seeing me here safely. I'm sorry I questioned You and doubted You. I'll stay here, and work hard, and look for ways to serve You. Thy will be done. Amen."

I suddenly realized I'd been gone for hours, and people were probably wondering where I was. I set out down the mountain, but it was pitch dark, and it took me quite some time to find my way. When I got about halfway down, a group of bright lights came into view and guided me the rest of the way.

As I got closer, I saw that the lights were car headlights. There were several four-wheel-drive vehicles parked in front of the group home, with men about to load up. When they saw me, they stopped short. Denise West emerged from the middle of the group, ran toward me, and hit me hard on the chest. Twice. Then she collapsed in my arms in tears.

"Don't you ever do that again!" she shouted, and beat on my chest some more. "You scared me to death!"

The group of men was a search party, about to come after me. No one knew where I was, but little Prissy had seen me coming in this direction and had somehow communicated to Mona Sanders. The search party had been waiting for the storm to pass before coming to find me. No one had much hope that I'd be found alive because of the ferocity of the storm and how I was dressed.

Denise cried in my arms for a few more minutes, then wiped her tears and pulled away. "I'm sorry." She sniffled. "You just scared us so bad."

"I'm sorry too. Will's news just hit me pretty hard."

When I got back to the Wests' house, we had a more in-depth talk about my situation over the welcome meal of moose steaks Denise had prepared.

"The good news is that you're still a semester missionary, with your room and board paid until the end of the year," Will said as he ate. "We still need you to do all the things you came here to do. You just won't have a salary."

"The salary was pretty important." I forked up another bite. "It was going to pay my tuition at seminary."

"I understand that. But don't forget, if you are being called to the ministry, God will find a way for you to do it."

"That's what I was doing on the mountain. I was thinking all that through, and I realized that I was putting way too much focus on the money. That's nothing to God. He'll provide if that's what He wants me to do. In the meantime, this is where I'm supposed to be, and I need to figure out how I'm going to support myself for the next nine months."

"There's plenty of work here," Denise said. "You just have to go out and find it."

19

For the next month, I took Denise's words to heart and discovered that there was indeed work to be had here in Nome, if I was willing. Will gave me wide latitude to use this month, while I was being paid, to get myself situated with work to do and a place to live.

I started with a vengeance the first day. I reconnected with Jack Barker, who had gone back to California to tie up loose ends there and was now back in Nome, courting Connie Vaughn in earnest. He'd found a job at the airport and a tiny apartment a few blocks from the church. It cost two hundred dollars a month. He was happy to have someone to split the rent with. Sight unseen, I accepted the opportunity.

I looked at the want ads in the *Nome Nugget* and applied for several jobs, including one as a dump truck driver. I'd never driven a dump truck, but I was confident that I could figure it out. Denise suggested going to the central school district office and seeing what might be available there. I did that, and came away with a small job driving a school bus. I also registered as a substitute teacher, figuring that even if I was just twenty, I had a high school diploma and two years of college. I certainly knew more than these kids did.

But these jobs still wouldn't be enough. Walking back to the Wests' after my visit to the school district office, I racked my brain. *Think, Mark.* I remembered how I built my customer base for my lawn business, and ended up with twenty-two lawns and other projects at the age of sixteen. I didn't wait for business to come to me. I went after it. But what could I do here? There were no lawns to mow or bushes to trim. What, then? What kind of skill did I have that I could offer these people?

I thought it through. I had come here with a good basic knowledge of fixing things and building things from a lifetime of helping my father with projects around the house. Maybe call myself a handy man and post some flyers? I discarded that thought. People here either fixed it themselves or bought new. Or, if they were poor, they went without.

But I could build. Yes, I could. After building the church, I could do pretty much any project like that. And as I walked, I began to notice something. Not all houses here had the arctic entryways that Will said were essential to life in Alaska. Many of these were the "temporary" houses that were erected after the big storm decades before. They were never intended to be permanent, and they weren't equipped with arctic entryways. I could just knock on doors, like I did with my lawn business, and offer my services.

How much to charge? When I had bid on jobs before, I had figured out how much the supplies would cost, and had simply doubled that amount for my time and effort. That seemed like a good formula here. If three of us had worked as fast as we had on the church, I should be able to build an arctic entryway by myself in a week or two. I had no idea how much supplies would cost or how much I'd earn, but it would be something.

I was tempted to start knocking on doors right now, but I wanted to bounce this idea off of Will first. Full of enthusiasm now, I jogged back to the Wests'.

Denise was running the vacuum and didn't hear me come in. I crept up behind her, poked her in the back and said, "Boo!" She shrieked and jumped so high she threw the vacuum across the room. I knew it was time to duck and run. She came after me. We dodged and weaved around the house for the next few minutes until we both collapsed, laughing hysterically. She poked me in the stomach. "Don't you ever do that again!"

"Yes, ma'am."

"What put you in such a good mood?" She retrieved the vacuum and put it in the front closet.

"I had a good morning. I got a job as a school bus driver, and I registered to be a substitute teacher. And, I applied for a job as a dump truck driver."

"Can you drive a dump truck?"

"How hard can it be? I'm comfortable driving pretty much anything." I told her about the first time I'd driven a stick shift. My parents had gone somewhere in the one automatic car we had, and the only thing in the driveway was a manual transmission pickup truck. I had never in my life driven a stick shift, but I had an appointment so I had no choice. After some jolting starts, I got the hang of it and everything was fine until I was on my way home and had to stop on a steep, long hill. I had to roll all the way back down the hill to a flat spot and get a running start.

"You taught yourself to drive a stick shift in just a few minutes?"

"Yes."

"Then I'd say you should be fine."

"I had another idea." I began to tell her my idea about arctic entryways, then had to start over when Will walked in the door.

"How much would you charge?" he asked in his quiet way when I got to the end of my explanation.

"When I did projects before, I figured out how much the materials would cost, and I doubled that."

"Sounds reasonable." He lit his pipe.

"So, what do you think?"

"I think it's a great idea. People definitely need those entryways, and they would pay for themselves in lower heating costs within a couple of years at most."

"I can put together some flyers for you if you want," said Denise, "and I can talk it up for you at church. Even put something about it in the church bulletin."

"That would be great. Any help getting the word out would be appreciated."

"In the meantime," said Will, "how about we go over to the church and then swing by the group home? What am I paying you for, anyway?" He gave me a grin. I knew he felt bad about the lost job, but it wasn't his fault. I was excited now to be back and doing whatever I could.

20

When we pulled up to the church, I felt vaguely disappointed. The roof was finished, but other than that, it really didn't look any different. Will interpreted my silence correctly.

"Doesn't look like a big difference, does it?"

"No, not really."

"Let me show you."

We got out of the Bronco and went in, and I began to see. Where the walls had been just wooden beams, now a network of wiring and piping snaked throughout the building. I could see now that an immense amount of work had been done. It looked as if the plumbing and electric work was complete.

"Wow," I said.

"We've been busy. First a roofer came and put on the roof so we were working under cover. Then we had some local contractors in here, and they've finished the plumbing and electrical work. Heating and air is next, and that will be this week. Then we start putting the walls up."

I went closer for a better look. My dad and I had done some of this kind of work as well, so I had an idea of what I was looking at. "They did a really good job. They didn't cut any corners. It looks like they did it right."

"You have to do it right here, or it won't hold together in the cold."

As we walked through the church and Will showed me the work that had been done in my absence, I told him more about my experience on the mountain, hoping for some insight as to why God would work a miracle like this for me. "I knew when I got to the top that I was in trouble. It was already windy and sleeting, and then another storm was coming in from another direction. I wasn't dressed for that kind of cold, and I was soaked in sweat. There was no way I was going to make it down the mountain, not on my own."

"And then God took over."

"He absolutely did. There's no doubt in my mind. I crawled in that cleft and fell asleep, or passed out, I'm not sure which. But when I woke up it was dark and I was warm and dry. And I knew I was supposed to do whatever it took to stay here. Satan wants me to leave, but I'm not going to. I don't know why God did this for me, but He must have had a reason."

"There are several Psalms that talk about the protection of God. Do you remember any of them?"

"I was thinking about Psalm 46 when I was in that cleft. 'God is our refuge and strength, a very present help in trouble. Therefore we will not fear, though the earth should change and though the mountains slip into the heart of the sea.'"

"That's a good one." He paused, then seemed to consider his words. "Mark, I think you were without a doubt protected on that mountain. I also think there's something important that you're supposed to do, here or in the future, or both. But you need to be careful of something, and please listen carefully. We are indeed all special, and God has plans for us all. But none of us is indispensable. God saved you from your own foolhardiness this time, but you need to make smarter decisions. Generally, when we do stupid things, He doesn't bail us out. He lets events run their natural course and then gets His work done some other way. Do you understand what I'm telling you?"

"Yes, I understand. I know what I did was stupid. God saved me and used the situation so that I'd have a powerful testimony, but He does expect me to use the brain He gave me. I'll be smarter from now on."

We moved on through the church, taking stock of what still needed to be done, and the crew began to arrive to install the heating and air conditioning ductwork. Will said he expected that to be done by the end of the week, and we could start on the walls next week.

As we walked through the church, I noticed a man coming up to the building. He moved in the classic shuffle of the inebriated native. It was a walk I'd come to recognize since I'd been here. This man didn't look familiar, though.

"Will, who's that?" I pointed to the man. Will looked and sighed.

"That's Robert Wallace. You know that my major focus here is helping alcoholics and trying to get their life turned around, right? And you know I never give up on anybody."

"Sure, Will, I know that."

"Well, Robert has taught me a new lesson. No matter how hard you try, there are some people who just won't be helped. Robert is one of those."

"Tell me about him."

"I don't know that much. I just know about my own dealings with him. He's a native, of course. Does artwork on animal skins. He's really talented. For a while I thought I could help him use that talent as a way to a new life. I even bought some of his work. I helped him and encouraged him, even gave him a place to stay so he could be secure and warm and dry. He just uses the money for booze and goes back out on the street. Every time. Then he'll do more artwork and sell it, and the process starts all over again."

I watched Robert as he approached. "That's sad."

"It is sad. I really wanted to help him, but he has to want it, too. My advice to you is to steer clear of him. If you can't avoid him, be nice, but remember what I told you."

"I will."

*   *   *

Our next stop was at the group home. As soon as we pulled up, a boiling mass of kids exploded out the door. I quickly found myself tackled and on the ground.

"Mark! Mark!"

"Hey, y'all!" I was laughing uncontrollably on the bottom of the pile. I retaliated by tickling whoever was in reach. This resulted in delighted shrieks, and the kids started rolling off of me. "How's everybody?" I got to my feet, with Prissy already attached to my back.

"We're good," said Darren, as always the spokesman for the group. "Welcome back."

"It's good to be back." We moved toward the house. I looked the kids over and counted ten, one fewer than when I left. "Who's missing?"

Mona mentioned one of the older boys, named David. His grandparents had come from a nearby town and taken him to live with them.

"That's good, right?"

"Maybe." She wiped her hands on her apron. "At least here we knew what kind of life he had. He's a smart kid. We were making some headway with him, and getting him to see he really had some gifts to offer. Now, who knows? We just hope and pray that he's being taken care of. It's out of our hands."

Will spoke up. "You know, Mark, you weren't the only one affected by the funding cut."

"Who else?"

"The Sanders. We can't pay them, either, after this month."

I looked at Mona with horror. The home wouldn't be the same without the Sanders. "What are y'all going to do?"

"I have no idea," she said. "I do know we love it here and we're going to stay. We'll just have to find something else to do."

"Who's going to take care of these kids?"

"Remember the couple who came up with the California crew? Leo and Jo Roberts?"

"I think so. I saw them, but didn't really meet them."

"They're good people. They loved it here and decided to stay, and they're retired and don't need the income. They're going to come on board as houseparents."

"They're already here," said Mona. "We're showing them the ropes. They'll take over at the end of the month."

"I'm sorry you can't stay at the group home, but I'm glad you aren't leaving Nome," I said.

"Nome's home now. We couldn't leave. We won't be strangers

around this place, either. These are our kids."

The kids were grouped around me, hanging onto whatever body part they could reach. Prissy still clung to my back. Darren had one arm and Paul the other. The others hung close, trying to get my attention. Thinking of how I'd missed them all while I was gone, I could understand the Sanders' decision to stay here.

"So, guess what I'm going to be doing now," I said to them.

"Working on the church?" Paul guessed.

"Yes, but that's not all."

"Helping at the Lighthouse?" Darren asked.

"Yes, but that's not all."

Others made guesses that were only partially right. I now wore an ear-to-ear grin. "Give up?"

"We give up!" They chorused.

"I'm going to be one of your houseparents," I said, and earned a cheer.

"Really?" asked a small boy named Ernie.

"Really. I'm going to be here two afternoons a week and on the weekends to give your houseparents a break. Think we can find something to do?"

The kids were all full of ideas, and I knew that wouldn't be a problem. We'd find plenty to get into. And I knew again I'd made the right choice to come back.

21

My last stop of the day was at the apartment I'd agreed to share with Jack Barker. He'd been working all day, and we had set it up for me to come by right before supper.

I passed by the apartment several times before zeroing in on it. It was a long, narrow, nondescript wooden structure that took up only about twenty feet along the street, but went about fifty feet deep. Its roof had a one-way vertical slant, which I learned later was to keep the snow off. The building was divided into three apartments. One was on the back of the lot, one in the middle, and one on the front. Jack lived in the front one, and he came to the door immediately when I knocked.

"Hey Mark, good to see you!"

"It's great to be back. Thanks for letting me move in with you."

"It'll be good to have the company, and the help with expenses." He stood aside to let me in. "Let me show you around."

"Showing me around" took about twelve seconds. The furnished apartment consisted of a sleeping area with two twin beds set against the walls in an L shape; a kitchen area with an old refrigerator, a small stove, and a tiny table with two rickety chairs; and a small bathroom with a toilet, a sink and a shower. Jack evidently slept on one bed and used the other as a storage space.

Jack warned me about the water situation. "Although we do have running water, we really don't. The insulation isn't any good, and once we start getting deep freezes, everything will be frozen solid until we thaw out in the spring. No running water, no toilet, no showers.

We'll have to melt and boil snow for drinking water."

I stood looking at the place that would be my home for the next nine months. To call it rustic was a stretch. "Wow," was all I could say. For this I was paying one hundred dollars a month. "What's the heating situation?"

"I'm already having issues that that." He explained that there was one heating unit, and it was at the opposite end of the building. The man in that apartment had the controls and we were to try and stay on good terms with him for obvious reasons. He stayed too hot and lived in shorts while at home, while the person in the middle apartment was just right. We, on the other hand, would be much cooler and susceptible to some deep freezing. I was getting a glimpse of the future right now, as I could hear the wind whistling through what I assumed were cracks in the boards. I could feel the draft. The place already felt like an igloo.

"There has to be a bright side," I said a little desperately. "Tell me about the bright side."

He thought for a moment. "It's close to everywhere we have to go. It's right on the road so we won't have to shovel much snow. And it's cheap."

I looked at my new roommate. "Good enough. When do I move in?"

22

Things were falling into place. I had an apartment, and I began moving in immediately. Jack wasn't home very much, as the Vaughns' house had plenty of food, hot running water, and Connie. One person had hired me to build an arctic entryway, and I'd be netting about two thousand dollars for that job. I hoped word of mouth would get me more work. I had my job driving a school bus, which took up the early mornings and the mid-afternoons. I also began driving dump trucks, which entailed picking up junk at a given location in town and hauling it out of town to a landfill. Sometimes I also helped out with the bulldozers at the landfill. About once a week, I got a call to substitute teach at Nome's tiny high school. It was usually math or science, which was easy, but it was occasionally English. That had never been my strength, but I still knew more than the kids did. And I was back to feeding and exercising Will's dogs for him. This was more fun now that snow was actually on the ground.

Will had a license to bring home one moose each year, and the dogs were a big asset for him during that hunting trip. He left one Monday in October and was gone for several days, taking the team so he could venture farther than snowmobiles could. I was beginning to worry about him when Thursday came and he still wasn't home, but Denise had been through this before and said Will could take care of himself. Sure enough, on Friday I was working at the church when he came into view. First came the dogs, pulling hard against their harnesses. Then came Will, walking rather than riding. Finally came the carcass of a giant moose with enormous antlers, being dragged on the sled behind the dog team. Will encouraged them at every step and helped push the moose over bumps himself. He waved, and the little procession passed the church and down to the pastorium. I knew that every bit of that moose would be used, and the meat would feed him and Denise until next summer with plenty left over.

The jobs were bringing in enough money for now, but I wasn't sure how I'd eat and pay the rent when my semester missionary status ran out at the end of the year. Eating was already hard enough. Food was expensive here, and the stipend I received from the Mission Board was small. Spam and huge biscuits made from Bisquick were dietary mainstays. Jack called them cathead biscuits. My mother sent occasional care packages containing staples like egg noodles and instant potatoes, and her homemade butterscotch cookies that were, to me, the ultimate comfort food. The Wests shared their moose with us. People at the church took pity on their poor missionary and brought us food, which Jack and I stored in a fifty-gallon barrel outside our door. The weather was already cold enough that food was safe there indefinitely. We supplemented our diet by hunting and fishing. Jack, as a trapper, knew how to cook our catch so it was pretty tasty. He borrowed the Vaughns' snowmobile or else we went on foot. We used his one gun and hunted arctic hares; ptarmigan, which is the Alaska state bird and is a member of the grouse family; and whatever else we could find. Since we weren't natives, we couldn't go for large game. Occasionally we bagged a muskrat, which we ate and Jack skinned for a little extra income.

We had to be extra careful of moose and polar bears. For dog teams, moose are the most dangerous animal to encounter because they use the same trails, and moose associate dogs with wolves and react accordingly. Many good dogs have gone down under their deadly hooves. Polar bears are deadly predators, because they are patient and calculating. They follow dog teams on hunts and bide their time. When they see a hunter make a kill, especially a big one, they move in and take the food.

The cold was another issue. It was literally breathtaking. Snow was on the ground to stay now, and it just got colder and colder. It had taken its toll on the Nome population. Now the only people here were the natives and a few whites. Miners and most other white people had headed south for the winter. This was already beyond anything I'd ever experienced, and I was being told that I hadn't seen anything yet. But I didn't have the choice of staying indoors. I had to work to survive.

The thing I found most rewarding was what I wasn't getting paid for, which was the work at the church and with the kids. I still relieved Leo and Jo Roberts—everyone called them Mr. and Mrs. Leo—on the weekends and two afternoons per week. At the church, we were putting up the interior walls. Twelve-foot-long wall boards are a bear to handle, and it was now just Will and me, and sometimes Jack. James Vaughn was there as often as he could take time away from his job, and occasionally we had other volunteer help. This wasn't something the kids could help with.

George Allen was again a lifesaver. Our church had become one of his personal projects, and he often showed up to see how things were going. If we mentioned that we had a particularly tough job coming up, someone would be there to help. Often we didn't even have to say it. George seemed able to judge these things for himself.

As October gave way to November, the church began to take shape. We put the outside walls up first, and soon we were working in a completely enclosed building. It was just in time. A day in the thirties was a warm day, but the temperature was usually in the teens. Nights got down to single digits. I was very happy that the Chandlers had insisted on outfitting me with warm clothing. The things I'd brought from Tennessee would definitely not have been warm enough.

23

I was getting involved in more aspects of Will's ministry. He'd had me do the devotion on the radio again, and one Sunday after church he waylaid me with another opportunity.

"Mark, hang on a second, would you?" He was putting his coat on after the service, ready to head home. "I need to ask you something."

"Sure." I waited while he put on his coat and locked up the federal building, where we were still holding services until we finished our church. We walked to the car together.

"You know I do a church service for the guys in the jail at two o'clock on Sunday afternoons."

"Yes, I think that's great."

"Today something has come up with one of the alcoholics I'm counseling. He's having a pretty big crisis and needs me to come. Can you handle the church service?"

I wasn't sure how to respond. *Conduct a church service singlehandedly? In jail?* I felt completely unequipped. I had been with a group back home when they visited the local prison, but this was way different. But then I remembered my commitment to make the most of every opportunity, so I didn't see much choice.

"Sure, Will. I'll take care of it for you. Did you have anything already prepared?"

"I had some Scripture and hymns picked out and some thoughts jotted down." He handed me a folder. "You can use what I have or come up with something on your own. You have a couple of hours before you have to be there. Good luck and thanks."

A couple of hours. Fantastic. This was not at all how I'd imagined my first sermon. I flew to my apartment, praying as I went, and spent that time with Will's notes and my Bible. After an hour, I had a skeleton of a plan, but I still felt anxious. At one-thirty, I sank to my knees again.

"Father, it's all about You. Please help me make the most of this opportunity. This is Your Word and Your people, and I am Your messenger. Help me know what to say and how to say it, so it's meaningful to these men. Speak through me to get Your message to these men the best way. Protect me and help me serve You. In Christ's name, amen."

Then I took a deep breath, got to my feet, gathered up my Bible and my notes, and walked out.

The jail was four blocks from my apartment, on the Bering Sea side of Front Street. The single door was sandwiched between two saloons, and there was no sign indicating what it was. If you didn't know it was there, you wouldn't be able to spot it. I walked in the street door and down a hall to another, stronger door, then down two flights of stairs. The jail itself was underground, stretching for about one hundred feet under the Nome waterfront area. People in the saloons usually had no idea there were inmates under their feet. Ironic, I thought, that the drunks upstairs had no idea they could easily end up downstairs. And many did.

I went in the jail's main door. At a desk behind a thick glass window was a burly guard who looked up when I walked in. His nametag said Hendrix. He picked up a microphone.

"Can I help you?"

"My name's Mark Smith. I'm here to do the Sunday church service."

He looked me over. "Where's the reverend?"

"He had an emergency and asked me to fill in."

"Okay then." He punched a button, there was a loud buzz and the sounds of heavy locks releasing. A door to the right of his window opened. "Come on in. I'll let them know."

I went through the door and into a security checkpoint. Everything in my pockets came out. I was allowed to keep only my notes and my Bible. Then I was led down a long hall and into a small room where eight men waited on cheap folding chairs placed haphazardly about the room. A warped metal podium stood in one corner. The guard left and shut the door behind me. I heard the lock clang into place. It was one of the most frightening noises I'd ever heard. Charles' words were repeating over and over in my mind: "It's all about Him."

Trying to find some spiritual balance, hoping for inspiration, I walked slowly to the podium and faced my small congregation. Will had told me that everyone in the jail who wasn't drunk would be here. These were the long-term inmates, not the ones who were in and out after a few hours. The jail was home to them, and the other inmates their family. They were happy to have the lodging and three square meals a day. If they got out, they usually did something to get back in—to come "home." They all looked like natives, with the characteristic black hair and tip-tilted dark eyes. Natives don't usually get very big, but one of these guys was a monster. He sat on two chairs, and had a mustache, bulging muscles, and some impressive tattoos. The others were more typical sizes. They had a wiry build that bespoke latent strength.

I had absolutely no idea what to say to get things started. My notes blurred on the page and seemed completely worthless anyway. My brain froze. I knew this was an opportunity to reach these men, but I couldn't formulate a thought. What if they didn't even speak English?

The huge guy spoke up in a gravelly, heavily accented voice. "Let's sing a song, then just talk to us, brother!" It knocked me out of my stupor. We began with a song of their choosing, which turned out to be "Amazing Grace." They sang it in their language, to the classic tune I knew. I sang along with them in English.

Amazing grace, how sweet the sound
That saved a wretch like me
I once was lost, but now am found
Was blind, but now I see.

Through many dangers, toils and snares
I have already come

'Tis grace has brought me safe thus far
And grace will lead me home.

Together, in two languages, we stood and sang with enthusiasm the beloved old hymn, our voices reverberating off the reinforced concrete around us. We sang all five verses without hymnbooks. We didn't need them.

When we've been there ten thousand years
Bright shining as the sun
We've no less days to sing God's praise
Than when we first begun.

It was a bonding moment, and I suddenly knew everything was going to be all right. The message of the Gospel is universal, crossing all lines of culture and race.

The singing died down. The men sat down, settled in, and looked at me expectantly. I put my notes down, knowing now that I didn't need them. I would just speak to them from the heart and say whatever I was led to say.

"Hi guys. My name's Mark Smith, and I'm a missionary working with Brother Will. I know you were expecting to see him today, but he had an emergency and asked me if I would come do the service for you."

I told them a little about myself, my Tennessee origins, and how I came to be in Nome.

"Just a couple of years ago, I was a freshman at the University of Tennessee, just sailing along, studying to be a doctor. When I was ten years old, I knew I was a sinner and needed Christ. I asked Him to come into my life and take charge. I was baptized and formally joined a church.

"I'm sorry to say I didn't act much different at first. Mostly I just went along doing things like I'd always done them. I was saved, but there was not much change. I had no real fire in me.

"Then I started going to a new church with a friend on the weekends, and everything changed. People there seemed to have a fire and excitement in their lives that I didn't have. My friend, who I'd known for years, acted like a different person. He was happier and more positive and encouraging.

"Suddenly I knew what I'd been doing wasn't enough. I told Jesus I wanted His fire in me like I saw in those other folks. I started spending more time in the Bible, and suddenly the things I had heard and read started to make sense like never before. When I prayed, I realized God was actually listening to me. I started seeing the Bible as an instruction book full of stories of guys like us who all messed up at some point, but wanted to do better. When you do something that is not His way and you don't really care, it puts up a kind of wall between you and God. Well, I quit doing things my own way and when I did mess up, I told Him I was sorry and asked Him to help me not do those things over and over. He did.

"I was at a retreat with that same friend, Doug, when the real turning point came. I have to admit, I went to the retreat because there was a tennis tournament, but it changed my life. I went home knowing I wanted to do something to serve God, and that's how I came to be here. I helped build a church with Brother Will as a summer mission project. Now that has turned into staying here for an entire year.

"I promised God when I came here that I would take whatever opportunities He gave me and do my best with them. When Brother Will asked me to do this today, I had a moment of panic. I'm just twenty years old. I haven't been trained to preach or be in the ministry. What could I possibly say that you guys would want or need to hear? But I prayed and asked God to speak through me, and that's my hope and wish today.

"How many of you know beyond a doubt that you'd go to heaven if you died right now?"

Seven hands went up.

"That's amazing. That's great. How many of you got saved here, at the jail?"

All the hands stayed up. My respect and admiration for Will West went up another notch. How terrific it must be to be the vessel God uses to save souls.

I gestured to the one person who hadn't raised his hand. He was a small, grizzled-looking man. "What's your name?"

"Jasper."

"Jasper, would you mind sharing with us what you believe?"

He looked me up and down for a moment. "I believe in the ancient ways." He proudly looked around at the other inmates.

"What are the ancient ways?"

He explained briefly. "Everything has a spirit. Spirits are everywhere. We must keep all the spirits happy or we will have bad weather or will not able to catch animals for food and shelter. We have rituals that we must follow every day, and our shamans interpret signs and events for us so we know what to do."

"That's interesting," I said. My knowledge of Eskimo religion was sketchy at best. I needed to learn more before I could have an intelligent conversation with Jasper. In the meantime, I didn't want to offend or alienate him. He was here, and for now that was enough. "I'm glad you came today. If you'd like to talk more after the service, I'd be happy to stay around.

"For those of you who are already Christians, let's spend a little time talking about where you go from here. It's great that you're saved, but that's not the end of it. That's the lesson I had to learn. If you want God's fire in you, if you want to know what He wants from you, you have to read His Word and ask Him to show you."

I turned in my Bible to the familiar story of Daniel.

"Most of you guys have probably heard the story of Daniel and the lions' den, but did you know that Daniel was set up? Years earlier his country was conquered. His family became slaves in a foreign land. They had a different language and different customs, but the king was smart and looked for talented kids. Daniel and three of his friends got singled out as special. They learned the native language and God helped Daniel interpret peoples' dreams. He got promotions and special gifts from the king.

"Then he was framed, set up by two other guys who were jealous. He was one of three commissioners who were in charge of the entire kingdom, which was ruled by a man named King Darius. Daniel was by far the best of the three commissioners and the king was planning to appoint him over the entire kingdom. The Bible says Daniel had 'an extraordinary spirit.' The other commissioners started looking for ways to bring him down. They couldn't find any evidence of corruption, or negligence, or anything related to how he ran the government.

"They knew Daniel was devoted to his God. They had passed by his house and knew that he asked God to help him do his job. They convinced the king to make a law that said anyone who asked any god or man other than King Darius for help would be cast into the lions' den. If you broke that law there would be no fines, no prison time, they just chucked you in a pit with hungry lions. No second chances, and in that country when they wrote a law, and the king signed it, that was it. Nobody could change it—not even the king. They knew Daniel would have his daily prayer and Bible study time, and the trap was set.

"Daniel knew about the law, but he continued kneeling three times a day and praying to God as he always had. He had windows open to the city, and he prayed in plain sight of all. They didn't have air conditioning, and he wasn't about to hide his faith in God, right? Sure enough, some of the guys who set him up just 'happened' to be passing by at his normal prayer time and made sure to pause at his window to see and hear him. Daniel was asking God for help running the country. They went straight to the king and reminded him about the law. The accusers then told him they'd seen Daniel breaking the law by praying to God.

"The king realized he'd been tricked by these guys because they were jealous. It broke his heart so he tried everything he could to save Daniel, but there were no loopholes in the law he himself had signed. At the end of the day, the king had no choice but enforce his law and have Daniel thrown into the lions' den. He told Daniel, 'Your God whom you constantly serve will deliver you.' Daniel was put into the den and a stone was put over the entry so no one could disturb it.

"The king was so upset that he spent the night alone. He couldn't eat or sleep and just cried like a baby till morning. Well, he was already up at the break of dawn and ran to the lions' den. When he got close, he called out to Daniel, asking if he had survived the night.

Daniel called back, 'No problem, king. My God sent His angel and shut the lions' mouths and they have not harmed me, and besides, I am innocent toward you and my God.'

"Daniel came out of the den literally without a scratch, because he had trusted God. The king was way past happy, he was ecstatic. Then he looked around and saw the guys that had set both of them up to get Daniel killed. They were standing there with their mouths wide open. The king now had a better idea. He told his guards to take the accusers, their wives, and their children and throw them into the lions' den. The Bible says they hadn't even reached the bottom of the den before they were torn limb from limb. Completely devoured.

"King Darius wasn't finished. He gave some more orders, this time to the whole nation. He made a decree that everyone in his kingdom was to fear and tremble before the God of Daniel—the only true God. And Daniel had success under Darius and even the next king, Cyrus the Persian."

I paused. The men were hanging on every word.

"So Daniel took a bad situation, where by all reason he should have been torn limb from limb, and came out blessed because he trusted in the Lord. What's more, the king came to believe in the true God, and the Lord was glorified throughout this foreign land. All because Daniel trusted God and allowed Him to work through this bad situation. Imagine what would have happened otherwise. If the king had come back that morning and found a greasy spot on the den floor, we wouldn't be talking about this today. The entire history of his people, Israel, would be different."

"Aaaa-men, brotha," said the big guy with the tats.

"What's your name?" I asked him.

"Hank."

"Hank, what's your story? Do you mind sharing?"

"About like everybody else, I guess. I was into some bad stuff. Going after liquor finally got me. I'd do anything to get a drink, then another and another. I here 'cause I put a gun to the wrong guy's head for money to buy more. I was half drunk at the time, and they got me down before I got to the end of the block. It's a good thing, 'cause Brother Will got ahold of me in here and now I'm saved."

"God got ahold of you," I said. "He just used Brother Will to do it."

"That's right!" added a small man in the back.

One by one, each man told his story. They were remarkably similar. Will was right to target alcoholism in his ministry, because it was at the core of all the issues in this room. It was also clear that every man here thought that since he was saved, he had nothing more to worry about or anything else to do. In a flash, I knew why I was here.

"Are you guys grateful to God for saving you?" I asked.

"Hallelujah!" several of them exclaimed.

"Do you want to do something for Him?"

"Just tell us what," Hank said.

"There's plenty you can do for Him right here. Let me show you some examples from the Bible."

I showed them stories in Acts where the apostles were in prison and used the experience to win people to God. Peter and John were the first to be arrested for preaching the Gospel.

"Peter was one of the great apostles. And John went on to write the book of Revelation from an Alcatraz-like prison in the middle of the Mediterranean.

"Joseph, in the Old Testament, was a victim of a woman's lies. His boss's wife tried to romance him for days. He always said no, but one day there was nobody else around and she got physical. She grabbed him by his shirt and begged him to take her to bed. He ran out, leaving his shirt behind, but she screamed rape. He really was innocent, but he got tossed in jail for a long time, but he stayed faithful to God. He kept an eye out for opportunities to serve, and they came along eventually with the other inmates and guards—even the chief guard."

About that time we heard the latches unlocking the door. A few seconds later a guard appeared. I wondered if I was supposed to be done by now. "Everything okay?" he asked. "It's about time for you to wrap it up." Then I understood the guards were listening on some kind of intercom in their main office.

"It's my first time with these men, so do you mind if I take a little longer?" The door shut loudly, clicks and locks back in place. I jumped right back into my stories.

"Then there was Paul, and he's the main example I want to tell you about. At first he helped track down Jesus' followers and have them killed until God did a work in his own heart.

Hank interrupted, "The big blinding light out of the sky, right?"

"Bingo. Then Paul was constantly on the move, telling about Jesus and preaching the Gospel. He could speak several languages and traveled all over the world as it was known at that time. He organized new believers into groups in these new cities and trained guys to be in charge. Along the way he wound up in prison several times and sometimes stayed there for quite a while.

"Once, he and his partner, Silas, were beaten and thrown into jail in a place called Philippi. They were put in the inner prison and put on major lockdown and were even fitted with ankle cuffs. About midnight they were praying and singing hymns, and the other prisoners were listening. Then an earthquake came, and the whole jailhouse was shaken. All the doors were opened, and everyone's chains were unfastened. The jailer woke and saw all the doors opened and drew his sword to kill himself, because he was sure everyone had escaped. Paul called to him and told him not to harm himself, that everyone was there. The jailer and his family became believers and were saved that night, and probably some of the prisoners too.

"Another time, Paul was in jail in Rome for more than two years. He had places to go and people to see, so I'm sure he was frustrated. He had all these churches to attend to and people to counsel. He didn't have time to be in prison.

"But if he hadn't, we wouldn't have a good chunk of the New Testament. The books of Ephesians, Colossians, Philippians and Philemon were written while Paul was in prison. Those were letters to those churches he'd helped establish. They contain specific instructions to the people he trained and left in charge on how to teach the Gospel and how to live life as a Christian. He also wrote the books of Timothy and Titus from a prison cell. He couldn't be there in person to teach them, so he wrote them letters. He wrote Timothy when he knew he was about to be executed. It was the last thing he wrote.

"The point is, it's wonderful to be saved, but being saved is just the first step. You're supposed to bloom where you're planted. Wherever you are, God can use you. When new people come into this jail, you have the opportunity to try to reach them. Tell them the Gospel yourself, or bring them to church and let Will or me do it. When you get out of here, there's a whole world waiting for you. While you are in here you can get some good work done for God. You have a powerful testimony. Let God use you.

"Let's end with a prayer."

I knelt with those eight men, and we held hands and said a heartfelt prayer together. When we finished, we all stood up. Then it occurred to me that these men, as new Christians, needed to be able to read the Word.

"Do you guys read the Bible?" I asked.

"There's just one Bible here, and it's in the library," Hank answered. "It's hard to understand. It's written in English, but weird-like." I knew then it was a King James Version, which could be hard to read.

I handed Hank my Bible. "This is my Bible. It's the one I've been reading and studying for the past two years. You'll find some of my favorite verses underlined in here. I think you'll find this one easier to read and understand.

"I want you guys to pass it around and take turns reading it over the next week. Read Acts. It has some of the stories I just told you about. Read Judges. There are some stories you'd all like in there. I'll ask Will if I can do the service for you again next week, and we'll talk about what you read. Hank, I hold you responsible for safekeeping. You guys can all use it this week."

Hank handled the Bible as if it were gold, and I knew it was safe with him. "Thanks, brother," he said. "We'd like it if you come back next week."

I left with the best feeling I'd had in some time. These men had the power and the opportunity to do good things, and I believed they were now fired up to let God use them.

24

I arrived at the church the next day full of fire and conviction. There were new Christians at the jail who didn't have access to Bibles. Surely there was something we could do about that. We were a mission, after all.

"Hey, Will!" I trotted into the building.

He looked up from the wall board he was measuring. "Hi there. How'd it go yesterday?"

"Incredible. Much better than I ever could have expected."

"Did you use what I gave you?"

"No. We started talking and one thing led to another, and we went in a different direction."

"Okay, then I can use my stuff this week."

"About that." I grabbed a pencil to help Will measure the wall board. "Is it all right with you if I do the jail service this week, too?"

"It must have really gone well."

"It did." I marked a measurement on the board. "There were seven new Christians in the service I did, but they don't really have access to Bibles. I left mine with Hank and told him I'd try to come back this week and pick it up." I told Will how I'd piqued their curiosity with some meaty Bible stories they could relate to. "They need to be able to read the Word."

"I completely agree." We each took an end of the wall board and lifted it into place. "I've tried to get the jail to provide more Bibles, but they have a very tight budget."

That seemed like a copout. "Surely we can make that happen.

Don't we have some Bibles I can take to the jail on Sunday?"

He gave me his full attention for the first time. "You're really pumped up about this."

"It was an incredible experience. You helped them get saved. Now I want to help them grow."

"All right then. You know we don't have Bibles to spare at the church, but there are some boxes that just came in from the mission. I haven't had time to go through them. There are usually Bibles in those donation boxes. If there are, you can take them to the jail."

That week, I unpacked the boxes, inventoried the contents, and put them away for Will. Among the donated items were a dozen dog-eared Bibles in the New American Standard Version, which was much easier to understand than the King James. They'd obviously been well studied and read, but as I looked through them at the underlined verses I realized that someone else's diligence would now benefit these men. They wouldn't have to start from square one. Here were excellent memory verses, already picked out for them.

I couldn't wait to get back to the jail.

25

Jack had often asked me about dog mushing. Several times, he'd gone with me to feed the dogs so they'd get to know him. He'd ridden along with me a few times as well, so they could get used to his voice, but he hadn't yet gone on the snow. This week, the opportunity came up for him to go with me and drive the sled, and we hoped to bag ourselves something to eat while we were out. We were nearing the bottom of our food barrel.

A fresh blanket of snow had fallen the night before, and the ground was pristine and white. We made new tracks as we crunched toward the area where the dogs were chained. It was the coldest day so far, with the temperature dipping below zero. The sun shone brightly on the new snow.

Jack was wearing his most prized possession, a hat of beaver skin. He'd trapped the animal himself when he'd first arrived back here, and a native woman had made the pelt into a native-style hat for him. It came down snugly over his forehead and ears. Beaver skin was the best thing in the world to keep the cold out. With a ski mask that covered his nose and mouth, along with a pair of dark sunglasses, Jack was set for the day.

I wore all my warm clothing the Chandlers had bought for me, plus a wool skull cap and some glasses I'd rigged to protect my eyes while mushing the dogs. My rigged glasses were regular sunglasses with electrical tape over the top and bottom of each lens, just leaving a horizontal slit in the middle to see through.

We trudged up to the area where the dogs were chained, and saw nothing but a level blanket of white. I grinned. Jack looked confused. He was in for a surprise.

"Ya!" I shouted. At once the ground started moving and dogs erupted, barking deliriously, from under the snow. Sled dogs don't mind the cold at all. They simply use the snow as insulation, and curl up and let it drift over them. I mixed their food quickly to prevent it from freezing on the spot, then poured the gooey mess into their bowls. They inhaled it and looked at me with bright eyes. They knew what was coming next. I rubbed the lead dog, Snickers, between her ears and talked to her. She seemed to know exactly what I was saying, which I think she did. She was a beautiful dog, with thick brown and white fur and blue eyes. She nuzzled my hand and looked eager to get into the traces.

"You ready to go, Snickers?" I whispered to her. She yipped excitedly and headed for the harnesses.

These dogs weren't huskies, although many of them had some husky blood. They were bred from multiple breeds for characteristics that were important for the work they had to do. They needed intelligence, strength, stamina, ability to withstand cold, and also specific physical traits that varied depending on their job. A lead dog needed to be smarter, while a wheel dog needed to be stronger. All needed to be able to understand and follow instructions. Will's team looked like a collection of misfits, but they worked well together—so well that he now planned to run them in the 1981 Iditarod. Teamwork was the single most important thing. The best dog wasn't any good to a musher if he or she couldn't fit in with the team.

I carefully harnessed all eleven dogs, checking each of their harnesses as I went. They had to be tight enough to be secure, but not too tight. Snickers, the leader, would be alone at the front. The other ten would be in pairs, side by side. The wheel dogs, Sitka and Silver, who had to actually start the sled in motion, were directly in front of the sled.

Jack stepped into place on the runners, and I climbed into the basket on the sled and signaled him to go whenever he was ready. I wanted the dogs to hear his voice only, so they wouldn't get confused. He had been waiting a long time for this, so he didn't hesitate. He pulled up the anchor, which was sunk into the snow. "Hike!" he shouted. The dogs lunged forward, and the sled was instantly in motion.

Drivers use no reins, or ropes, or anything other than their voices to guide dogs. We had no casual conversation, because the dogs were listening to our voices for instruction. As we went, Jack guided them through the snowdrifts and other obstacles with an occasional "Gee" or "Haw."

It was a beautiful afternoon, and we intended to enjoy it. Each day we lost ten minutes of daylight. The area would quickly go from the long hours of light in the summer to almost complete darkness in the winter. But for now, the sun was shining brightly on the white snow, and for the first time I fully understood Charles Chandler's warnings about snow blindness.

We went for a long time, stopping occasionally to hunt and let the dogs rest. We bagged a ptarmigan and an arctic hare and were happy that we had our supper and some extra meat for the barrel. I relaxed in the basket, enjoying the sensation of being pulled without having to do the driving myself. Farther and faster we went. I could hear the dogs' happy panting as they lunged on through the snow. Now and then, Jack gave them some direction, but mostly we just glided across the open tundra. I had no idea where we were, and I didn't really care.

Suddenly I was tossed into the air. Dogs, jerked by the impact, came to a skidding stop. I landed in a snowdrift and poked my head up. I could see the dogs still standing where they were, looking back with a *what-on-earth-are-you-thinking* look on their faces. Jack was somewhere behind me. When I went flying, he did too.

"Jack! Jack?"

"I'm over here," he said from behind a big rock that had evidently caused the accident.

"You okay?"

"I don't think so."

"What's the matter?" I made my way over to him. He looked okay. No broken bones or any other physical problems that I could see. But he looked panicked. He took his glasses off and squinted.

'I can't see," he said.

"What do you mean, you can't see?"

"I mean I can't see. It all looks the same—everything!" His voice began to get louder and more panicked.

"Okay, okay, just stay calm. What kind of sunglasses are those?"

"Just regular UV sunglasses. Why?

Regular sunglasses. Not glasses built for the bright arctic tundra. Jack had snow blindness. I racked my brain. Charles Chandler had told me how to avoid snow blindness, but what had he told me I should do if I actually got it? Little by little, my brain unfroze and I began to remember. Snow blindness, Charles had said, is actually sunburn, maybe even small blisters, on the corneas. You begin to feel it hours after you're exposed, just like sunburn. Jack probably wouldn't have lasting damage, but he'd be in pain for a couple of days. His recovery depended on how severe his case was. Charles had told me some simple first aid, and there were a few things I could do here.

"Jack, don't rub your eyes," I said. That was rule number one. Second, wet compresses. I felt steadier now. I looked around for something I could use and found a rag in the sled. I ripped it in two and melted some snow in my hands to soak the pieces. I gently placed the compresses on Jack's eyes. Now I'd done all I could here. I had to get him home.

Therein lay another problem. Where was home? I hadn't been paying any attention to the direction we were going, and I had no idea where we were.

"Jack, where are we?"

But he'd lost track too, and since he couldn't see, he couldn't help.

I spent a few minutes getting Jack settled in the sled basket and checking the dogs. They all seemed okay, and their harnesses were intact. I untangled them, soothed them, and gave them all some water. My mind was racing. How to get home? And what to do if we couldn't make it? The sun was already low.

The answer was simple. Jack had to have help, so we had to make it. Then, in a flash, it came to me. Snickers knew a command that Will had told me about when I first started working with his dogs. I'd never used it, but it would save us now.

I double checked everything, then climbed onto the sled runners. The dogs waited expectantly.

"Snickers, home! Home, Snickers!" I shouted.

Immediately the team lunged against their traces, and Snickers turned her beautiful nose toward the east. I would have never thought home was in that direction. I was very grateful that Will had taught Snickers that command, and that I'd remembered it. For the next two hours we whizzed over the snow. It was fully dark now, and more snow had begun to fall. It caked on my glasses. The freezing wind whipped against our faces, and I kept making sure all skin was covered on both of us. Now I couldn't even see where we were going, but Snickers knew. On and on we went. When I could tell by the terrain that we were almost back to Nome, I said "Easy" to slow the team.

Snickers led us into the clearing where the dogs lived. Stiffly I climbed off the sled and helped Jack out, then spent the time necessary to get the dogs unharnessed and settled comfortably for the night. I gave them an extra treat. They'd earned it.

"Mark, I think I need some help," Jack said plaintively. "Can't you take care of the dogs later?"

"Just another minute. Keep those compresses on. How does it feel?"

"Like my eyes are full of sand."

"Don't rub them. We're going home now."

"I'd rather go to the Vaughns'," he whined.

"Home is closer. Let's get you settled, and I'll go get Lily and Connie if you want."

We began the walk home, with me keeping a firm grip on Jack's arm to guide him and keep him from falling. It was a slow process, but finally our apartment came into view. We stumbled through the door.

The next step was pain killer and gauze bandages. Both were in my Boy Scout first aid kit, which was in my trunk.

"Do you have a whole store in there?" Jack asked in amazement as I rummaged.

"I'm a Boy Scout, remember?" I joked. "We're always prepared." I fed him some ibuprofen, laid the gauze pads on his lids, taped them loosely into place, and set out for the Vaughns' house. All three Vaughns insisted on coming back with me, and soon we were back at our apartment in their truck. They rushed into the apartment, full of concern. Lily, who was a registered nurse, took the lead and examined

Jack. She gently took off the pads, then carefully looked at his lids and his corneas. She replaced the pads and sat back.

"There's not a thing I can do for him that you haven't already done, Mark. You did just right."

"I need to remember to thank Charles Chandler. He told me everything to do."

"It's good you were listening. If you hadn't done everything you did, he could have had permanent damage in those eyes."

"Thank you, Mark," said Connie tearfully, then gave me a big hug.

I pattered her back awkwardly as she clung to me. It felt good to be thanked and to get the credit, but I knew I didn't deserve it. I'd felt completely unprepared and unable out there, but somehow training had kicked in, and I ended up doing the right thing. And then I remembered Charles's admonition to always give the Lord the credit and the glory, and I realized that he and Will had been put into my life, and had told me the things they had, for a reason. Dr. Stanley, the First Baptist Atlanta pastor who'd inspired me to come here, taught that the Lord works in all sorts of ways, and one of those ways is through mentors. Charles and Will had served that purpose, and they'd taught me what I needed to know to help Jack and get us home. Panic had not taken over. The right thoughts came at the right time.

"I can't take the credit," I said. "I was scared to death, especially when I realized it was so late and we didn't even know how to get home. God helped me stay calm and made me remember all the things Charles and Will told me."

"Really?" Connie looked up at me.

"Really."

"That's amazing."

"I know. It really is important to listen to our elders. This time it saved both of us."

Lily wiped her eyes. "Jack, do you want to come home with us?"

"No, I have work tomorrow. I'll stay here."

"You can stay here, but you do not have work tomorrow," she said sternly. "You'll be somewhere, either here or at our house, with those bandages on your eyes. You have to keep them covered. You can't let any light at all get in."

"You should go with them," I said. "You need someone to check on your eyes regularly, and I won't be here."

So Jack went home with the Vaughns, and I was alone with my thoughts. Again, the Lord had stepped in, in a new way this time. I felt humble and unworthy.

"Lord," I prayed. "Thank You for rescuing us. If You hadn't made sure I knew what to do, I'm pretty sure things would have turned out badly today. Thank You for Your help and your guidance. And help me to be worthy of it. In Christ's name, amen."

I opened a can of Spam and ate it cold, then fell into bed. Snuggled deep in my warm sleeping bag, I fell asleep.

26

When I made my return trip to the jail with a dozen Bibles in hand, it was a completely different feeling than the first time. I was excited and full of anticipation. I couldn't wait to hear what the guys had learned from my Bible.

I went through the same stout door and faced the same doubtful guard, but this time he opened the door without comment. I went through security without trepidation and this time, when the door shut and locked behind me and left me alone with the men, I was not nervous at all.

This time ten men sat in the makeshift sanctuary, including the eight from last week. "Hi guys," I said. "I brought you something." I opened the box with the precious Bibles. "Believers should be able to read the Word whenever they can. Hank, would you help me give these to anyone who wants them?"

Hank handed me back my Bible and looked into the box. "Thanks, man." He chose one for himself. "There was some good stuff in there." He fanned the books out in both big hands and offered them to the other men.

"I want to hear all about it from everyone," I said. "But let's open with a hymn."

Again, they chose "Amazing Grace," as I'd hoped they would. I had a surprise for them. I had heard that only about 15 percent of natives choose to ever speak English at all. Here in Nome that number had to be even less. I'd worked hard this past week to learn part of this song in their language, and they looked at me with astonishment as I sang the first verse in horrible, Southern-accented Inupiaq. The guttural clicks and sounds that were a big part of their language were way beyond me, but I did my best.

"Man, that's cool," said one of the men.

"What's your name?" I asked him.

"Sandor."

"Sandor, let's start with you. Did you have a chance to read my Bible this week?"

"Yeah, man. We all did. There's some wild stuff in there."

"Tell me your favorite."

He thought for a minute. "My favorite was the chick who killed the dude by driving—what was it?—a tent peg into his head."

I nodded at the succinct summation of the story of Jael in the book of Judges. She conquered her husband's enemy, Sisera, by inviting him to take shelter in her tent and then driving a tent peg through his temple while he slept.

"Yeah, that was cool," said Hank. "My favorite was in Acts. Paul was preaching until late at night, and they were on the third story, and a kid was sitting by the upstairs window. He fell asleep and fell out the window and died. Paul brought him back to life."

I pointed to the next man. "How about you?"

"My name's Sam, and I went back to the beginning of the Bible. My favorite story was when God was mad at this guy for going somewhere, and He sent an angel to stop him. The guy couldn't see the angel, but his donkey could, and it was scared and kept turning around. The guy was getting all mad and beating the donkey, and then the donkey talked back to him and asked him why he kept beating him. He didn't even act like it was crazy that the donkey was talking out loud. He said if he had a sword that donkey would be dead. Then the guy could see the angel, and the angel said if the donkey hadn't turned around he would have killed the guy and let the donkey live."

Everyone was staring, and I could tell not many of them had gotten into the book of Numbers to read the story of Balaam. I was impressed. There was some tedious reading in Exodus, Leviticus and Numbers, but Sam had found a gold morsel.

Hank spoke up. "How about the long-haired guy who killed a

bunch of people with the jawbone of a donkey?"

"That was pretty incredible, wasn't it?" I said. "That was Samson. What did you think of what happened to him?"

"Women," he snorted. "He shouldn'ta trusted her to begin with. I also liked the one where the guy walked into a king's palace bold as anything with a big sword hidden under his cloak. He told the king he had a secret message, so the king would send everyone away. Then he stuck that sword in him. I'm not sure, but I think it said his guts came out."

"That's exactly what it said," I said. "That was Ehud. Do you remember how he got away?"

"It looked like he just walked right out."

"He sure did, and the guards didn't check on the king because they thought he was using the bathroom."

They all hooted. The dam was broken, and they shared story after story they'd discovered. They were amazed by David; he'd had many chances to kill Saul, who'd tried time after time to kill him, but always let him go. They couldn't believe the nerve of Gideon, who was visited by an angel and was spoken to by God, but still doubted enough to ask for proof not once, not twice, but three times before he did as God asked him. They laughed at Abimelech, who was in battle when a woman threw a big rock from a wall onto his head. While he was dying, he told one of the men to draw his sword and kill him so it wouldn't be said that he died at the hand of a woman.

Another man had discovered Song of Solomon. "Man, who'd have thought I could read how to please a woman in the Bible!" he chortled. "It talks out in the open about this chick's breasts and stuff, and what this guy wants to do to them."

"That was Solomon, and the woman was his wife," I explained. "Song of Solomon is one long love song, and the point is to show how a marriage is supposed to be. The words are a little different than any we'd use today, though. When I get married, I won't be telling my wife she looks like a horse. I'd probably be sleeping on the couch."

An hour came and went, and no one showed the slightest inclination to leave. They were all excited to share what they'd discovered in the Bible.

I noticed that the two newcomers and Jasper, who believed in the ancient ways, were listening intently. One of the new men looked familiar.

'What's your name?" I asked him.

"Robert." Then it hit me why he looked familiar. This was the man I'd seen walking by the church, the one Will said did drawings on animal skins. It was the one person I'd ever heard Will say was beyond help, simply because he didn't want to be helped. Maybe this once, Will was wrong.

"Robert, when did you get here?"

"Three days ago."

"What did you get arrested for?"

"Got in a fight in the saloon. Didn't have the money to get out. I get to see the judge tomorrow."

"Are you saved?"

"Nope, the pastor tried to talk me into it but I'm still thinkin' about it."

"When you get out, you come see me anytime you want, and we'll talk about it."

"I might do that."

I moved on to Jasper. "What do you think of these stories?"

"They're pretty interestin'. Might like to read that book for myself."

"I brought twelve of them," I said. "Read it whenever you want, and if you want to talk just let me know and I'll be here."

I moved back to the front of the room and addressed the whole group.

"You're all taking big steps now. Being a Christian means learning more about God, and His ways. The Bible is like our how-to book. There are some great stories in there. Some are sad, some are funny, but they are about real live people who lived, loved, and learned. Everything we need to know to live our life God's way is in there. I brought enough so you each can have one of your own."

"I'm going to read the whole thing," one of the men said. "We have lots of time in here. By the time I get out, I'll have it memorized."

"You're probably kidding, but it's a good idea to memorize some of your favorite parts," I said. "That way, whenever you have tough things happen to you in life, you won't have to go find your Bible to read your favorite verses. You have them in your head."

"Makes sense," the man said. "I'll do that."

"I'm not sure who's going to be here next week, Will or me. But whoever it is, we'll ask you about what you've read. I suggest spending some time in Psalms and Proverbs over the next week. There's some amazing stuff in there, too. David wrote most of Psalms, and Solomon wrote Proverbs. If you have time after that, start on Matthew, Mark, Luke or John. Any of those will tell you all about Jesus' life."

We closed with a prayer, and I left the jail satisfied with the afternoon, and with hope that perhaps Robert Wallace wasn't beyond help after all.

27

Life was an unending adventure here in Nome. As the year got older, the weather got colder, and the snow got deeper. Things I took for granted at home were not so simple here. The snow drifted over cars and up to rooflines. Kids jumped from roof to roof and built snow caves in the snow between the houses. Just getting from place to place was a challenge. If you stayed on the trampled path you were safe, but sometimes you couldn't tell where the path was. You'd be walking along just fine, and suddenly find yourself buried in snow because you'd unknowingly stepped off the path and into a deep pile of soft snow. Once you did that, you had to scratch and claw and dig yourself out.

One day some members of the Nome Fire Department pulled up in their big truck at the field behind the church. I happened to be looking out the window, so I went down to check it out. Where was the fire? I saw no fire. Then the men pulled out their hoses, hooked them up to the hydrants, and doused the ball field with water. As fast as the water covered the field, it froze. Kids were standing by excitedly, ice skates over their shoulders, and when the field froze they attacked it with whoops of glee. The field stayed an ice rink all winter, and we constantly heard kids' shrieks as we worked in the church.

Jack's beaver skin hat protected him well, but only if he wore it correctly. One day he walked to the Vaughns' house, which was only fifteen minutes away, but he made the mistake of leaving the lowest tips of his ear lobes exposed. When he arrived they were red. A couple of days later they turned black. Finally they fell off. He'd lost the tips of his ears to frostbite and learned a valuable lesson about the Nome cold.

People stayed indoors as much as they could, but that was not an option for people who had jobs. Jack and I had to work to survive, and we had to be safe in the bitter cold. Our eyes got crusty, as the moisture in them froze. We learned to breathe without freezing our lungs by inhaling through our mouths and out through our noses. Even then, icicles formed around our mouths. We had to keep our mouths covered to keep our teeth from freezing and falling out. Many Eskimos had no front teeth for this very reason.

Our apartment was so cold, we had to leave the oven on with the door open at night. Jack got tiny icicles in the whiskers around his mouth when he slept. He shaved every day, sometimes more than once a day, to try to keep the whiskers at bay and cut down on the frost. I didn't have much of a problem with that. At twenty years old, I barely had to shave because of a small fraction of native American blood in my veins. It had been a source of frustration as I grew up because I had less facial and body hair than other young men. Now, though, as I watched Jack struggle, I blessed my heritage.

Food was another adventure. Jack and I fed ourselves pretty well with what we caught and what generous church members donated to us. This was fortunate, because food was otherwise scarce. Restaurants, even if we'd wanted to walk to them, were closed in the winter. Stores had only nonperishables; they were hideously expensive, but at least Jack and I were able to keep Bisquick and Spam in the house. Jack spent a lot of time at the Vaughns' house and ate many meals with them. I sometimes got invited to eat with some of the locals, who knew of the starving missionary and took pity on him. I quickly learned to be careful of those invitations, though. I would rather eat Bisquick and Spam three meals a day, every day, than partake of some native delicacies. I learned that lesson painfully when one family invited me for supper and proudly fed me a meal that featured whale blubber and rancid seal oil. My Southern system rebelled and I was ill for several days. After that, I pleaded a hectic work schedule and politely asked if I could just pick up a plate of food and eat it when I could. That way I could either eat it or stealthily dispose of it.

28

One day in November, the week after my second visit to the jail, I was walking to the Lighthouse when I realized something was missing. After a few minutes, I finally realized what it was. The Bering Sea was usually a source of constant background noise with its whooshing and sighing. Sometimes it was soothing, sometimes it was scary. Always, it was noisy. Now it was silent. I ventured closer and stared. Where just yesterday the sea had been water with ice chunks, now it was frozen solid. People were already walking and driving on it. The ice was already about six feet thick and, I'd been told, would extend nearly to the bottom of the sea by mid-winter.

I walked on to the Lighthouse, planning my lesson in my head. I tried to come up with real-life lessons from the Bible to teach these kids, and there was no shortage of material. I just had to choose. This time, I had noticed some kids making fun of other kids, and I had the perfect story.

I walked into the entryway, shook off the snow and took off my gear, then entered the main house. As usual, the kids shrieked and launched themselves at me. Prissy immediately climbed onto my back. I noticed with pleasure that Atka was there. He and I had developed a strong relationship since that day on the riverbank. Since his father was somewhere on the streets of Nome, and his mother looked to him as the oldest male in the house, I tried to be someone he could talk to and count on.

"Hey, Atka," I greeted him.

"Hey, Mark!" He hugged me. He wasn't old enough to outgrow

hugging yet, and for this I was grateful.

"How's it going?"

"Good. Guess what?"

"What?"

His voice dropped to a whisper. "I'm eight today."

"Today's your birthday? For real?"

He nodded.

"Why are you whispering?"

"My baby brother is really sick and my mom forgot what day it is. She'll feel really bad if she remembers, so I didn't want anyone else to find out."

I didn't know what to say to that. An eight-year-old boy deserves a birthday, but he was being sympathetic to his overworked, worried mother. I had to respect that.

"I'm sure she'll remember sometime today. I bet when you get home she'll say happy birthday."

"You think so?"

"I absolutely think so. Is it okay if we sing to you and have a snack?"

"If you really think she'll remember. I don't want her to feel bad."

I knew Atka's mother, and I knew her to be a good, loving mom. I couldn't imagine that she'd completely forget.

"I think it will be fine," I said.

I made the announcement about Atka's special day and we all made him feel special, then we settled in for our Bible story. I spun Prissy around to sit on my lap, and she snuggled in.

"Today's story is about how to treat others."

"We know how to treat others," interjected a young girl named Kim. "You already told us. We're supposed to love each other."

"That's right. It is easy to love people who are being nice to you, but how many of us really do that all the time? Do you ever act mean or ugly when you know you shouldn't? Do you ever join in what your friends are doing even when you know it is wrong?"

"You mean we're supposed to love everyone?" a small boy named Thomas asked.

"That's what Jesus says."

"I don't love everyone."

"Most of us have problems with that," I assured him. "The thing is, we can't do it by ourselves. We have to let Jesus give us the love He wants us to have for everyone. He will, if we ask Him."

I was getting off the point I wanted to make. I circled back.

"If you have ever been mean to someone who really didn't deserve it, raise your hand."

All hands went up, including mine.

"In the days long ago, before Jesus was born, God had some rules. He protected the people who did things according to His rules, and He punished the people who didn't. One time there was a man called Elisha. He did things God's way. In fact he was God's main prophet, which means he was the one who listened to God and told everyone else what God wanted them to know. He spoke for God to the people—sometimes even to very important people like the king who ran the whole country.

"Anyway, Elisha had just lost his best friend, and he had started this brand new job, and he had some really big shoes to fill. He had a lot on his mind. He was walking from one city to another . . ."

"He wasn't riding his donkey?" Kim wanted to know.

"No, he wasn't riding. He was walking. And while he was walking, a bunch of young people came out and starting teasing him and making fun of his bald head, which was bald because he'd shaved it for the Lord. They called him baldy and were just really mean to him. Now, what do you think Elisha did?"

"Just went on?"

"Nope."

"Stopped and talked to them?"

"Nope."

They all looked at me.

"Give up?"

"We give up!" they chorused.

"He cursed them in the name of the Lord," I said.

They looked at me with wide eyes. "What does that mean?" asked Thomas.

"He basically asked God to take care of the situation for him. It meant that they were about to answer to God for how they treated him."

"What did God do?"

"He sent two big female bears out from the woods, and the bears killed forty-two of those people. The Bible says the bears tore them up."

They stared at me open-mouthed. I somehow kept a straight face. This was absolutely a true story, taken straight from 2 Kings, chapter two. I couldn't laugh, but their faces were priceless.

"He did?" Kim whispered.

"He did. He protected His people then, and He still does today. So be careful how you treat other people. You never know what might happen when you're mean to the wrong person."

This was the end of the Bible lesson. When I was finally on my way home, safely away from the Lighthouse and the kids' watchful eyes, only then did I allow myself to laugh. Hopefully the story had struck a chord with the kids and they would think twice before they were cruel to others.

29

I was back at the Lighthouse the next day to take care of Thomas while Will was counseling his father. My work with the kids, an add-on to Will's work with their parents, had turned into a side ministry of its own.

Most of the Lighthouse kids lived at the group home and went to the Lighthouse after school. Thomas, Atka and Kim were among the few who lived at home. Thomas was a small native boy, six years old, with bright eyes and a bubbling curiosity that reminded me of myself at that age. Yesterday I'd noticed that he was quieter than usual and held his right arm with care, as if it hurt. I wanted to get to the bottom of that today if I could. If he'd trust me enough.

I greeted him warmly and took out a jigsaw puzzle with large pieces. It featured shepherds, sheep, camels, wise men, angels, Mary and Joseph, the infant Messiah, and a bright star over it all. This seemed appropriate because Christmas was in just a few weeks, and I wanted to give him something to do that would force him to use, or compensate for, his sore right arm. Either way, it would give me an opportunity to bring it up.

We sat on the floor, spread the puzzle out, and began organizing the pieces. Corners in one pile, outside pieces in another, center pieces in another. Thomas quickly became engrossed in the task. And sure enough, although he was right-handed, he held his right arm against his side and worked with his left. Soon we had all the corners in place and were halfway done with the frame, and I saw my chance.

"Thomas, would you hand me that piece over there?" I pointed to a piece to his extreme right, which would force him to either use his sore arm or reach all the way across his body with his left hand. Unthinking, he started to use his right arm but winced with pain and used his left instead. He got the piece and handed it to me

"What's the matter with your arm?" I asked casually as I put the piece in place.

"Nothing." He didn't look at me.

"You're not using your right arm today."

"It's sore, that's all."

"Did you do something unusual?"

"Not really."

"How did you hurt it?"

"I don't remember."

We worked in silence for a moment, than I spoke again.

"Would you let me look at it? I'm pretty good with things like that. Did you know I'm studying to be a doctor?" Sort of. A dentist was a kind of doctor, and I really had completed two years in the pre-med track at UT.

"It's nothing, *see?*" He spun his arm in a circle, then cried out in pain and grabbed his shoulder.

"Thomas, let me look at it." He didn't protest this time as I eased the shirt off his right side. He grimaced in pain as my fingers gently probed his shoulder. There were no bruises, and nothing felt out of place, but I'd bet that very recently, this shoulder had been pulled out of its socket.

"I knew a boy back home whose arm hurt just like yours," I told him.

"Really?" Thomas looked at me with eyes afraid to hope.

"Really. He was on a hike and fell down a hill. He grabbed a root as he fell and it pulled his shoulder so hard it came out of its socket. We were out in the middle of nowhere, and we were lucky that a doctor was one of the dads. He put the shoulder back in place. The kid's arm was really sore for a long time."

"Was he okay?"

"Eventually. But it hurt for a few days. Did that happen to you? Is that why your arm hurts?"

He nodded.

"How did it come out?"

He hesitated a long time and finally said, "My dad was playing with me and accidentally pulled it out. He felt really bad and took me to the hospital for them to put it back in."

Having gotten this much out of the boy, I wasn't about to push it farther. I knew it was no accident, that Thomas' father had pulled his son's arm out of its socket in a drunken rage. But for now, it was enough that Thomas had trusted me this much.

"I'm glad he got you taken care of," I said. "Your arm should get better really fast now."

We spent the rest of the time completing the puzzle and talking about Jesus' birth, and finally Will showed up with Thomas' father. Father and son bundled up and left for home. Will and I methodically went through the procedure of shutting the Lighthouse up for the night. As we worked, he asked me how it went with Thomas.

"It went fine."

"It looked like he was favoring his right arm when he was putting his coat on."

"He was." I looked at Will and knew he'd seen most everything there was to see here. I was pretty upset and wanted his take on my suspicions. "I'm pretty sure his dad pulled his arm out of its socket."

"You'd be right."

I looked at him in surprise. "You knew?"

"Only because his dad told me in our counseling session tonight. What did Thomas tell you? Anything?"

"He said his dad was playing with him and accidentally pulled it out, and then took him to the hospital to get it fixed."

"That's almost the truth, except he wasn't playing. He got angry when Thomas was too slow to empty the honey pot. He grabbed him up by the arm and pulled his shoulder out."

I looked at Will incredulously. "How can you look so calm? This kid is six years old. Shouldn't we be reporting this to someone?"

"Who? This isn't like the Lower Forty Eight. People take care of their own here."

"Then how do kids get to be at the group home?"

"Those are extreme cases, where the kids literally have no one to look after them. Thomas has parents. It's up to us to teach them how to do better. It's a long road, because they don't see that they're doing anything wrong."

I couldn't believe what I was hearing. Surely there was a Department of Social Services, someone who could go to Thomas' house to investigate if there were evidence of abuse, which there most definitely was. I said as much to Will.

"Yes, there's such a thing, but they're spread so thin that they can't handle anything except the most extreme cases. Thomas' case wouldn't qualify. He's fully functional, walking around, going to school, with two parents who care enough to take him to the hospital when he gets hurt. Like I said, it's up to us to make his life better."

Incredible. But I realized that Will knew what he was talking about. I walked home that night amazed all over again at how much these people needed what we had to offer them.

30

The frozen Bering Sea opened up a new possibility for food—ice fishing. Salmon are wonderful and delicious, but the one time to get them is when they make their run up the river in July. You get as many as you can during that short time, then put them away for the winter. After that, you have to go after other fish.

Now was the best and only time for ice fishing for two reasons. One, you need at least a little daylight to ice fish, and when December rolled around we would be in almost total darkness. Two, it was possible to cut holes in the ice now, but it would be impossible when the ice got thicker.

On Monday of Thanksgiving week, I decided to give it a try. I'd been fishing my whole life. How hard could it be? I got some local wisdom and headed out, equipped with two sticks, a long string, and a silver hook. I was told I didn't need bait. I had no idea why I had two sticks, but I figured I'd watch someone for a few minutes and I'd be fine.

Straight out on the Bering Sea I went, looking for holes that had already been cut. I didn't have the equipment to cut a new one. As I walked along I noticed several holes in the ice. They were all about a foot wide and looked like they had water, not ice, at the bottom. That was a good sign, but I wanted to be near someone else so I could have some confidence that there were really fish down there and that I was doing this right.

It was bitterly cold that day, about twenty degrees below zero, and it felt even colder out on the unprotected sea. Wind whipped around me, making me very glad for my cold weather gear. Again, as I had numerous times before, I blessed the Chandlers.

On I walked, scanning the ice for other fishermen. It must have been too cold for all except the hardiest souls, because the area was deserted. Finally, after walking for about fifteen minutes, I spotted a small figure far out on the ice. I sighed in relief, stamped my feet and walked faster. As I got closer, I saw that the figure was not a small adult, as I'd assumed, but a child. A little boy of maybe ten years old was standing over a hole in the ice, pulling out fish after fish. No sooner did he drop his line than he snared another fish and hauled it to the surface. The fish were all slim and cigar-shaped, about eight or nine inches long. Even better, there was another hole about ten feet away. Excellent! If a ten-year-old could do it, of course I could too.

I watched him for a few minutes before putting together my own rig. He had a hook on a string, like mine. He dropped the hook down into the hole and fed out the string until the hook was about twelve feet deep. Then he maneuvered his sticks, one on top of the other, to gently and gradually pull the hook up through the water. As the hook rose, it flashed in the light and attracted the fishes' attention, or so I'd been told. It seemed to work, because his hook always emerged with a wriggling fish on it. As he pulled each fish out, he whacked it on the head and dropped it on the ice at his feet, then resumed fishing.

This was going to be easy. Jack and I would be having fresh fish for supper tonight. With high confidence I assembled my rig and positioned myself at the nearby hole. I fed the hook and line down through the ice as I'd seen the little boy do, and waited. Nothing. I gently raised and lowered the hook to catch the attention of nearby fish. Still nothing. I stood there for several minutes, raising and lowering the string in the water with my sticks.

Maybe I'd lost the hook. That would be bad, because I only had one. I slowly and carefully lifted the string until the hook emerged from the water. It looked fine. I retied it to be safe, then lowered it back into the water. Still nothing. I tried it for about fifteen minutes to no avail, while the little native boy stood several feet away and caught fish after fish.

I pulled up my rig and went to another hole a little farther away and went through the whole thing again. Lower the hook into the water. Gently raise and lower it. "Here, fishy fishy!" Nothing. Now the little boy was starting to watch me as I was watching him. Finally he started packing up his gear, having evidently caught enough fish. When he finished packing he started to leave the ice, then detoured in my direction. He came to where I was fishing and looked down into my hole. I'd looked into it numerous times and all I could see was dark water.

The little boy got down on his belly, looked intently into the hole, looked at me, and said, "No good. No fish." He went to the other hole that I'd been fishing in, looked in, and shook his head. "No good." He motioned toward his hole and said, "You fish there." And then he walked away, across the ice toward Nome.

I watched him incredulously. His hole was only a few feet from the two I'd used. How could fish be at one hole and not at another just a few feet away? I shrugged. Might as well try it. My luck couldn't get any worse. I lowered my hook down into the little boy's hole and fed out the line. Within seconds, I felt a jerk and hoisted up a wriggling silver fish. I whacked it on the head as I'd seen him do and dropped it into the bag I'd brought along, then lowered the hook into the water again. Again a jerk and a glistening fish.

An hour later, I'd caught fifty fish. I stared down into the hole and shook my head, at a loss for an explanation. It looked just like the other two that I'd fished in. Who cared? Thanks to the little boy, I had plenty of food to restock our barrel. I started packing up my stuff and realized too late that I now had to lug the heavy bag all the way to our apartment. When I got there, I saw with relief that my roommate was home. I banged on the door and shouted that I needed some help. He came out and looked into my bag. His jaw dropped.

"Holy cow, man. This is amazing. How'd you do this?"

"I found an expert on the ice who gave me some pointers." I then relented and told him the whole story while we cleaned the fish and added them to our barrel. He hooted at my being schooled by a ten-year-old. I was accustomed to filleting fish, but these were very bony and didn't lend themselves to filleting. We settled on cutting off their heads and their fins and gutting them, and deemed them ready to cook. Several were left out to serve as our supper.

This time I, as the Tennessee mountain boy, was the expert cook. I prepared them the way my scoutmaster had prepared trout caught in clear mountain streams on campouts, with lemon juice and pepper and then wrapped in foil and roasted. We had no vegetables or potatoes, but the fish were feast enough. We pulled the flaky white meat off the bones, smacked our lips and licked our fingers.

I'd found a new passion, and resolved that every day until the days got too dark and the ice got too thick, I'd be out on the sea putting more food in the barrel.

31

This week, Thanksgiving week, I began to notice marked differences between Nome and back home. In Tennessee, the Christmas season would be well under way. Houses would be draped in festive lights, people would be starting to buy and put up their Christmas trees, and shopping would be in full swing. Street lights would be adorned with lighted snowflakes, poinsettias, and wreaths. Lawns would have manger scenes, snowmen, and Santas with reindeer and sleighs. The newspaper would be full of ads for Christmas specials. Television programs like *A Charlie Brown Christmas*, *Frosty the Snowman*, and *Rudolph the Red-Nosed Reindeer* would be on every night. The Santa countdown would be under way.

Here, I saw very few outward signs that Christmas was just a little over a month away. Everything looked like life as usual, except that it was getting colder and colder and darker and darker. Snow fell constantly, and the incessant wind blew it sideways. The temperature had dropped to forty below; the constant wind made it feel like eighty below. People were beginning to hunker down for the winter. The only reindeer in evidence were grazing on the tundra.

I wondered about this until I had a chance to bring it up at the Wests' house on Thanksgiving. The Wests, the Vaughns, Jack, and I sat at a packed kitchen table and ate succulent roast moose, gravy, biscuits, instant potatoes, and canned vegetables. We were well past the time of year when any perishables were available at the store. There was no turkey, hence the moose, and people ate canned vegetables or did without.

The meal was different, but the warmth and holiday cheer were the same. A fire crackled cheerfully in the fireplace. Denise had placed a few Christmas decorations around the house. A boxed Christmas tree sat in the corner. It looked more like home than anything else I'd seen here.

"I've noticed something," I began. "By now at home, I'd be seeing Christmas stuff everywhere. I'm not seeing anything here. No lights, no decorations, not even any ads in the paper. How come?"

"That was hard to get used to," Denise agreed. "You have to remember, natives don't celebrate Christmas at all. The few white people here are the only ones who'd consider December 25 a special day. We do a special Christmas service at the church, but we'll have less than a dozen people there. It's really different from anything you've ever seen before."

"I don't like the commercialism, but I do like the celebration," I said. "Jews don't believe in Jesus, but a lot of them celebrate the holiday in their own way. Maybe we can make our own excitement. We can at least decorate the Lighthouse and tell the kids about Christmas."

"Good luck with that." Will forked up more moose. He helped himself to potatoes and ladled gravy over them generously. "I tried the first year I was here, but then I could see why things are like they are. Besides the fact that natives don't celebrate Christmas, people just aren't in the mood to celebrate in December. It gets really dark and depressing. People hunker down. Hardly anyone will be on the streets, and the ones you do see won't look you in the eye. Suicides will be way up.

"You'll understand better when you experience it for yourself. December and January are just months we have to get through, and it's not much better in February."

We ate pies and cakes for dessert, then sat around groaning until we were able to bundle up and roll ourselves out the door. Jack and I took leftovers home with us to eat for our evening meal.

"The whole Christmas thing is kind of sad, isn't it?" Jack said as we walked home. "I'm with you. I miss it too."

"Yeah. I'm not sure what we can do about it on a big scale, but I'm going to at least work with the kids. They love any reason to celebrate, and I know they'd like presents."

The next day I found a cookie recipe on our Bisquick box and spent the afternoon trying to come up with something palatable for the kids. It was my first attempt at cooking anything, other than over a campfire, but finally I came up with something I thought the kids would like. Armed with knowledge and ingredients, I packed my stuff and headed for the group home for the weekend.

I met Mr. and Mrs. Leo on the front porch. They had seen me coming and were on their way out. Mrs. Leo waved. "Hi Mark! We're going to get an early start on our weekend. Y'all have a good time!"

"You too!" I said and went inside. I'd have warmth and running water for the weekend, which was now a luxury. As I hung up my gear in the arctic entryway, the kids thundered in and tackled me.

"Hey!" I said as Darren tried to pin me to the floor. I still remembered my high school wrestling, so I used one of my favorite maneuvers and flipped him around. To his surprise, now he was the one on the bottom. Then he grinned. "Teach me to do that."

For the next thirty minutes I gave the kids some impromptu wrestling lessons, which ended up with all of us rolling on the floor hysterically. Then I got serious.

"Do you know what time of year this is?"

"Yeah. It's the cold and dark time," said Paul.

"Yes, but besides that. Is it special in any way?"

"I hate it," piped up little Ernie. "There's nothing to do but stay inside, and people get in really bad moods."

"It's not like that where I come from." I described how things would be now at home. I described the decorating, shopping, baking, and all the other things that make Christmas special. "But the most important thing, is that it's Jesus' birthday. He was born in Bethlehem nearly two thousand years ago. That's the whole reason why we have Christmas."

"Jesus' birthday is coming up?" asked Darren.

"Yep. It's December 25. I brought some stuff over so we could make some Christmas goodies."

We spent the evening in the kitchen using the recipe I'd found to make and decorate Christmas cookies, which we had for dessert after I fed the kids leftovers from Mrs. Leo's Thanksgiving dinner. For the rest of the weekend, I took every opportunity I could find to interject holiday cheer and educate the kids on what Christmas is really all about. We cut branches from willow bushes near the house, tied ribbons around them, and decorated the house. Each child wanted to do one and put it in his or her sleeping area.

Saturday night before bed, I gathered them all in the living room and opened the Bible to the nativity story.

"Here's where our faith began. There was a teen-aged girl named Mary. She was about fifteen years old. We're not really sure exactly how old, but that's about the age when girls got married in those days. She was engaged to a young man named Joseph, and they were planning their wedding. They were good people and had decided to wait until after they were married to be together.

"One day Mary was going about her business and heard a knock at her door. She went to answer it and found a man standing there. He was an angel. He greeted her in a very different way. He said 'Hail, favored one! The Lord is with you.' It scared her a little until the angel explained that she was going to have a baby, and that her child's father was going to be God Himself.

"Now, think about this. One minute this young girl's life was going along as normal. She was planning her wedding to a nice young man and the future was bright. Then, all of a sudden, everything changed. She didn't understand it yet, and maybe never really did, but the entire history of the world changed in that moment. That baby was going to be Jesus, God's Son, who had come to save all who would believe in Him.

"Joseph didn't believe her, and you can't really blame him. Who'd believe something like that? He knew the baby was not his. He didn't want to embarrass Mary, so he was planning to send her away to have the baby in secret. Then the angel came to see him in a dream, and told him that Mary was telling the truth, that the child's father was the Holy Spirit, and that the child's name should be Jesus."

The kids were looking at me raptly. They looked like they'd never heard this story before. What a blessing that I could be the one to tell them. I doubled my efforts to make it interesting and special for them.

"So Mary and Joseph stayed engaged, and when Mary was about

ready to have her baby, they had to go to a place called Bethlehem. There was a rule that all the people had to be counted at a certain time, so all families had to go to the husband's birthplace. Joseph had been born in Bethlehem. So they packed up their stuff and went, just hoping the baby would wait until they got back to be born.

"That's not how it worked out. They got to Bethlehem, and Mary started hurting. She'd never had a baby before, so she was pretty scared. Joseph was scared too, and tried to find a place for them to stay. All the rooms were already taken, because a lot of people were there for the same reason they were. Think of the Iditarod. It's pretty hard to find a place to stay here in Nome that week, isn't it?"

"Yep," Paul agreed.

"So guess where Mary had to have her baby."

No one had any idea.

"The only place Joseph could find for them to stay was in a stable, with a bunch of animals."

"No way," Ernie said.

"Yes way," I assured him. "Women today, at least the ones where I come from, go to hospitals and have doctors help them have their babies. The mother of our Lord had to have her baby in a stable. The only cradle she had was a little bin that was used to feed the animals. So when the baby Jesus was born, she wrapped him in the only cloth she had and laid him in that bin. It was called a manger."

"What happened next?" Prissy asked. I looked at her, startled. Since I'd known her, I could count on one hand the number of words I'd heard her say. Now she looked up at me with those big dark brown eyes, absorbed in the story.

"Mary and Joseph and the baby were tired and were resting, but the excitement wasn't over for the night. A little distance away, shepherds were in a field watching their sheep. It was a pretty boring night for them, but then the sky lit up and an angel was there. Think how you'd feel. That must have been a little scary. The Bible says they were terrified. The angel told them that the Son of God had been born in the city of David, which was Bethlehem. He said they should look for a baby wrapped in a cloth and lying in a manger. Then the whole sky lit up and a bunch more angels appeared and started singing. You guys have seen the

Northern Lights, right? Well, think of that times a thousand.

"When the angels went away, the shepherds looked at each other. I can just imagine the conversation. I bet they said, 'Did you see that?' When they realized it had really happened, they went to Bethlehem and found Mary and Joseph and the child. The shepherds told them what had happened, and worshiped the new baby.

"That night, three men a long way away saw a new star in the heavens and knew a new king had been born. They gathered gifts and got on their camels to come and worship. They were so far away, it took them two years to get there. They found Him by following the star until it stood over Mary and Joseph's house in a town called Nazareth. They gave Him presents, and that's where we get that tradition today."

"What tradition?" Darren wanted to know.

"You know," I said. "People give gifts to the people they care about at Christmas."

The kids all looked at each other. Clearly, this was news to them. I vowed to myself that these kids would get gifts this Christmas. I had the weekends to make this happen for them.

"Never mind," I said. "So Jesus came to earth as a little baby, and grew up just like any other kid. He had brothers and sisters and a mother and father, and they raised Him with the rest of their kids, but He was different than anyone. Did you know that He never did anything wrong? It makes you wonder what His brothers and sisters thought."

"I think they knew He was special," said Ernie. "I think He was so special everybody couldn't help but love Him."

"I think so too," I said. "Anyway, that's what Christmas is all about. And we celebrate that on December 25. We can talk more about it later."

I tucked the kids into bed, vowing that this Christmas was going to be special for them. I was going to see to it.

32

The next week, Jack and I were busy trying to get as much food as possible put away in this last week of November, while we still had a little daylight. We were down to about three hours of twilight every day, and the rest of the time was total darkness. Jack hunted, trapped, and worked, while I fished and worked all my jobs. I'd finished one entryway and was well under way with a second. And all week, whenever I was around, Will kept looking at me with a weird look in his eye, a kind of shrewd sparkle. I had come to know that look, but this looked even more ominous. He was either keeping a big secret or had a special request to spring on me. I shrugged and figured he'd tell me whatever was on his mind when he got around to it.

On Tuesday when I arrived at the Lighthouse, Paul and Ernie met me in the entryway as I was taking off my gear.

"Mark, what's a sheep?" Ernie asked.

"And what's a stable?" Paul asked.

I hung my stuff up and went with them into the warm house, marveling. I'd taken such pains to tell the story in the simplest way I could, but I'd underestimated the complete difference in culture here. Of course they had no idea what a sheep was. Or a stable. They'd never seen or heard of either here on the Alaskan tundra.

I went in and gathered them together. All the group home kids were there, plus Thomas, Atka, and Kim. Those three had already been thoroughly briefed by the kids from the group home, and all of them had questions.

"What's a king?" Thomas wanted to know.

"And what's a camel?" asked Atka.

"Let's sit down and I'll try to answer all your questions," I said. Then an idea dawned. Surely, somewhere in the Lighthouse, there was a picture book of the nativity story. I detoured to the storage bins in the living room and rummaged. All I could find on the subject was a coloring book, but it would serve. I took it back to where the kids were gathered and sat down cross-legged in the middle of the group. Prissy nestled in my lap.

"So, you guys have questions," I began, and opened the book to a typical nativity picture. "Let's take one at a time. A stable," I pointed at the picture, "is a shelter where animals sleep and eat. It's usually made out of wood. We still have them where I come from."

"It must be a really good shelter," said Darren, "or the animals would freeze."

"No, it's completely different than here. It's usually really hot there. It's what's called a desert, with lots of sand and hot sun. The hottest day here is much colder than the coldest day there."

"Tell us about the animals," demanded Paul. "What do camels and sheeps look like?"

"Sheep," I corrected automatically. "The word 'sheep' is both singular and plural."

They looked at me blankly.

"Never mind," I said, appalled at myself, and thought that Dr. Ferguson at Maryville High would be proud. Something had rubbed off.

"Anyway," I continued, and pointed at the sheep in the picture, "a sheep is an animal about the size of a big dog. There are usually big groups of them called herds, like reindeer, and people called shepherds have to keep them together and protect them because they aren't very smart. They have white fluffy coats, and people shave off their coats to make warm clothes." I showed them my wool sweater and socks. "This stuff came from sheep."

The kids looked at me, horrified. "They shave off their coats?" Kim whispered.

"Yes, but it doesn't hurt," I assured her. "Camels are big animals, bigger than moose, with big humps on their backs." I showed them in the picture. "When people ride in deserts, they ride camels because camels are really strong and don't need much water.

"Thomas, you asked about a king. Does anybody know what a king is?"

"Isn't that, like, the boss of a country?" Darren asked.

"Yes, exactly. In Jesus' case, He's the King of everything, not just one country."

I looked around at everyone. "Did I answer all your questions?"

They all nodded.

"That was a pretty cool story," said Ernie. "I like your stories."

"I'm glad. They're all completely true, straight from the Bible. You can believe every single word that's in there."

For the rest of the afternoon we had snacks and colored pictures from the book I'd found. It contained several pictures of the nativity, which generated more basic questions that I tried to answer in the simplest terms possible. I'd learned my lesson.

33

Within a few days, I found out what Will's secretive looks had been about. He never told me. He showed me.

On Sunday, things were pretty normal. I took the group home kids to church in the home's van, and then back to the home and fed them lunch. My mom had sent me some honey, so I treated all the kids to cathead biscuits with honey. They smacked their lips and licked their fingers over the sweet treat. Mr. and Mrs. Leo came back in the mid-afternoon and relieved me, and I went to the Wests' house to say hi before going home to my apartment.

As I went up the front walk, I sensed something different. It just seemed quieter than usual. My sixth sense kicked in, and the short hairs on the back of my neck tingled. I tentatively put my hand on the doorknob and slowly opened the door. I saw no one. Slowly I hung my gear in the entryway, then eased my way into the living room, craning my neck to see into the kitchen.

And was blindsided. I was tackled at the knees and went sprawling. Then my attacker pressed his advantage and pinned me, face mashed against the floor, arms behind my back. The wrestler in me kicked in and I wriggled, gained some leverage, and flipped my attacker off. I was about to pin his throat to the floor when I saw the grinning face of my best friend.

"Doug?" I said stupidly.

"Hi, Mark," he grinned.

I collapsed on the floor beside him. I'd almost hurt my best friend, thinking he was an intruder. Then it hit me. I rolled over, grabbed him and hugged him. "Doug!"

Will and Denise came into the room, howling hysterically, wiping tears from their faces.

"You should have seen your face," Denise gasped. "It was priceless. I wish I had a movie camera."

"Yeah, well, Doug was almost a greasy spot on the floor. I thought he was an intruder."

"I knew you wouldn't hurt me," my friend said confidently. "And I pinned you!"

"In your dreams. Man, I'm glad to see you. What are you doing here?"

"Seeing you, idiot. Why should you get to have all the fun?"

We chattered away and I learned that my parents, Doug's parents, and the Wests had cooked up this surprise for me. Doug's parents were living in Perth, Australia, where his father was working at the Alcoa aluminum plant. Doug was going to spend the Christmas holidays with them, and had broached the idea with his parents of taking a week's detour to Alaska on his way to Australia. Will had sneaked to the airport to pick him up while I was working at the home this afternoon.

Going to Australia by way of Nome, Alaska, sounded like a heck of a detour to me, but I wasn't complaining. Doug was here!

"You have the week off your church work, Mark," Will said. "I know you want to spend time with your friend."

"Then I'm taking the week off of everything."

"I'd like to see what you're doing up here," Doug put in.

"Then I'll show you."

Denise had figured correctly that Doug had never eaten moose, so she'd planned a supper of moose steaks for him. He took a bite and looked at her, amazed. "This is moose?"

She nodded.

"It just tastes like the best steak I've ever put in my mouth."

She smiled, pleased as always when someone enjoyed her cooking. "I'm glad you like it."

We stayed at the Wests' for a while longer then left for the short walk home.

"Man, I can't tell you how glad I am to see you," I said as we walked. "I have so much to show you. How long are you here for?"

"I fly out on Saturday. I'll get to Perth on Monday."

"I bet it's a long trip."

"Nome to Anchorage, Anchorage to Seattle, Seattle to Los Angeles, Los Angeles to Sydney, Sydney to Perth. It's a total of twenty-eight hours in the air, plus all the layovers. Brutal. And from what I understand, I'll be seeing a temperature swing of about one hundred forty degrees between here and there."

"That's right, it's summer in Australia right now."

"Yep. And let me tell you, when I walked out of that airport and felt how cold it really is here . . ." he shook his head. "It's a whole different world. And it's even colder now."

"It is. I hope you brought some really warm stuff to wear."

We walked in silence. It was pretty amazing that he was willing to do all that just so he could spend some time here with me. I was touched, but of course guys never say stuff like that. I punched him in the arm instead.

We passed the church, and I pointed it out. "That's what I spent my whole summer doing. We're doing the inside work now."

"Can we go in?"

"We could, but I'd rather take you back tomorrow when we can see. I'm pretty proud of it."

We walked on, and I pointed out some of the Nome landmarks. It was dark now, so we couldn't see much. Then we drew near to the apartment, and I figured I better warn him what life was going to be like for the next week. Doug was used to having things pretty easy. I was wondering where he'd sleep.

"Doug, this isn't going to be like anything you've ever seen before."

"I know."

"I mean, really."

"I know, Mark. I want to see how you're living and what you're doing. All of it."

"Okay then." And I grasped the doorknob and opened the door.

Of course, it was dark at first. I groped for the light and flipped it on, then sneaked a glance at Doug's face. I tried to put myself in his shoes and see this place like I'd seen it for the first time.

To wash our clothes, Jack and I had to thaw snow and heat water. Then we hung them to dry on lines draped across the room. Yesterday had been laundry day, so Doug's first glimpse of my home was a maze of laundry. Our two twin beds bore rumpled sleeping bags and punched-up pillows. Leftovers from Jack's breakfast remained on the tiny kitchen table. And above it all was the amazing smell of the honey pot, which hadn't been emptied in several days.

On Jack's bed was a note.

"Mark," it said, "have fun with your friend this week. I'm looking forward to meeting him. I'm staying at the Vaughns' so he can have my bed. See you later. Jack."

"Well, that's one problem solved. I was wondering where you would sleep."

Doug studied the note. "That was nice of him."

"His girlfriend's there, and he gets good meals and hot running water for the next few days."

"Oh."

I grinned. "Yeah, it was nice of him."

I showed Doug around, which didn't take very long.

"What is that incredible smell?" he asked.

"That's the honey pot. It's exactly what you think it is. The pipes are frozen all winter, so we have no running water. The honey pot is how we go to the bathroom. It freezes about as fast as we use it, and we dump it in the snow outside when it's full."

Doug's face was incredulous. "How much do you pay for this?" he asked, shivering. I turned on the oven and opened the door.

"A hundred dollars a month."

"Wow."

"I know. But that's actually cheap for Nome, and it's within walking distance to everywhere we need to go."

"What do you eat?"

"We hunt and fish, and people invite us to eat and bring us stuff. I'm still a semester missionary, so I get a little food money that we use for staples. We eat a lot of Bisquick and Spam. We put fresh food in the barrel outside the door." I opened the front door and showed him. "It freezes pretty quick, so it's good for quite a while."

"This is amazing." He peered into the barrel. "You said you hunt. What do you hunt? How do you go?"

"Either we walk, or we take Will's dog team, or Jack borrows the Vaughns' snowmobile."

"Cool," was all Doug could think to say.

We spent the next hour talking and settling in, and I caught up with what was going on in his life.

"Georgia Tech is a bear, man," he said. "I thought after I survived the first year, it would get easier. But it just gets harder and harder, and I'm halfway through my junior year now. When I get out I'll be a heck of an engineer, though."

I smiled at his pun of the Georgia Tech fight song. "Are you seeing anybody?"

"Now that you ask . . ." He gave me a grin. "There is somebody. I met her at church, and she goes to Georgia Tech too. I think she might be special."

"Really?" This was a new thought. "How special?"

"Pretty special. Thinking about rings, special."

"Whoa."

"Yeah, it's pretty scary. But not scary at the same time. You know?"

"Not really. I don't really think about that right now. There are no white girls my age here, for one. They're all native."

"How about Connie?"

"She doesn't count. She belongs to Jack. For another thing, I still think of girls like I thought of the ones in our group in high school. You know, how we all ran around as friends."

"Yeah, I know. That'll change. You'll know when it happens. There'll be no doubt."

I couldn't even imagine yet. All my energies were devoted to my work here and growing spiritually. Girls and dating were the farthest thing from my mind.

Finally, the euphoria wore off and Doug's long trip caught up with him. We turned in early.

I lay in bed thinking, and thanking God for bringing my best friend. I hadn't realized how lonely I was until I saw that familiar face from home. Until now I hadn't really been looking much past tomorrow, then tomorrow, then tomorrow. Now I realized that I still had a very long way to go here, and the roughest time was still ahead. After a week with Doug, I thought I'd be rejuvenated and could get through the next few months just fine.

Over the next few days, Doug got a true taste of Nome life. I took him out on the tundra in the dog sled, out on the Bering Sea to ice fish, and to the group home and the Lighthouse to meet the kids. I showed him the church I'd helped build, the radio station where I sometimes did devotions, and the high school where I taught from time to time. I couldn't get time off from my bus driving job, but I took Doug with me. And, after clearing it with Will, I took Doug to the jail to meet the men who had by now become real friends.

I told him about the work I'd been doing and the way I'd been trying to relate to the people I came in contact with. I described my radio devotion and my prison sermons, and how it felt to relate to the children stories that we took for granted but that were new to them. And I told him about my experience in the cleft of Anvil Rock.

His experience on the airplane into Nome was unique. He'd never flown on such a small plane before, and he'd never landed on snow. He also found out how it felt to breathe icicles, and to throw water out the door and have it freeze before it hit the ground.

He learned how to use a honey pot and empty it in the snowdrifts outside, and he helped me scrape mystery foods out of the barrel for our meals.

We also did things with Jack and Connie. One day we went four-wheeling on the icy streets, with the four-wheeler pulling two people behind it, like a boat pulls tandem skiers. Jack and I were skiing, and Doug drove. After all my driving experience here, I could tell when fast became too fast, and I signaled him to slow down. Unfortunately, he mistook the "slow down" signal for the "speed up" signal, and I ended up bailing out in a snowdrift right before I would have crashed into a buried car. Jack wasn't fast enough. He crashed and burned.

The kids loved Doug. Before the week was over, they were attacking him almost as enthusiastically as they attacked me. When he went to say goodbye to them on Friday, some of them actually cried.

And we laughed. We laughed like I'd not laughed since I'd left home. My life here in Nome was rewarding and good in ways that I'd never experienced before. But it could not be called easy or joyful. After this week, I had my joy back.

As we walked back to the apartment on Doug's last night in Nome, I decided that I had to be honest with him and forget macho stuff. He needed to know how much it meant to me that he'd come here.

"Doug, I have to tell you. I thought I was getting along just fine. I was doing what I had to do, and reaching people when and where I could, and I was okay. But spending time with you, and knowing you came all this way just for me . . . well, I want you to know it means a lot to me. I'm happier now than I've been since I got here. I just want to thank you."

"You don't need to thank me." He was uncomfortable with the way this was going. "You're my best friend. That's what best friends do. I missed you."

We shared an awkward hug and spent our last evening together in companionable conversation and natural silence. We talked, ate, and played chess. Doug was the only one I knew who could give me a real chess game.

"I think I'm making a difference here," I told him over a meal of Bering Sea fish. "You should see the faces of the kids, and even the guys at the jail, when they realize for the first time that God loves them. I can't even describe how it feels to be the one to tell them."

"I can't imagine. This is really good," he added, gesturing with his fork toward his plate. "I'm impressed."

"Thanks. All the kids here have been brought up in what they call the 'ancient ways.' They believe in the spirit world. When they hear the Gospel, and believe it, and accept Jesus, it's just amazing."

"How do their parents feel about that?"

"If they're at the group home, their parents aren't a factor. But for the Lighthouse kids, like Atka and Thomas, we talk to the parents before we let the kid make a commitment."

"And I can't believe you actually built a church."

"We couldn't have done it without God's help." I described the assistance we'd gotten from George Allen and our oil millionaire from Texas. "They were moved to help us, and it wouldn't have gotten done otherwise."

He studied me. "You've changed."

"I think so. Something like this would change anyone. I've pretty much decided that I don't want to be a dentist. I want to go into the ministry, somewhere, somehow. I'm not sure of the details yet, but I don't have to be at this point. God will lead me."

"Let's pray, brother," Doug said. So we did what we'd been doing since we began growing under the teaching of Dr. Charles Stanley. We knelt, side by side, and prayed aloud. We prayed for protection and guidance, for wisdom and discernment. We prayed that we would know and have the strength to follow the will of our Father. And we thanked Him for everything in our lives, both good and bad, for we knew that even bad things are allowed to be in our lives for a reason. When we opened our eyes we looked at each other and smiled, completely at peace.

Then the conversation grew less serious, and finally we looked at the clock and realized that Doug had to get to bed. He had some rough travel days ahead of him. We turned the oven on for warmth and opened the door, and snuggled down in our sub-zero sleeping bags.

"Night, Mark."

"Night, Doug." I patted the top of his head and drifted off.

34

I borrowed the Wests' Bronco and took Doug to the airport the next day. I watched his plane take off with a bittersweet smile. It had been a great week, but now it was time to get back to work.

Rejuvenated, I drove back to the Wests' and parked the Bronco in the driveway. When I went in and dropped the keys on the kitchen counter, I heard Denise's voice from the back.

"Mark, is that you?"

"Yes."

"Hang on a second. Something came in the mail for you."

Getting mail was a big deal. The Postal Service only delivered in Nome perhaps once a week, and I seldom got anything. Within a couple of minutes she emerged from the back dragging a large box. It looked heavy.

"Whoa." I rushed to her. "Let me help you with that." I took the box from her and lugged it into the living room.

"That's heavy," she said. "You need to take the car to get it home."

"I appreciate it. I'll bring it right back." I knew why the box was so heavy. This had to be my Christmas presents. My mother had asked me what I wanted, and I'd said food and books. Both could be heavy. I could hardly wait to open it.

I loaded the box into the Bronco, drove home and unloaded it, then took the Bronco back to the Wests' and ran home. My mother does a fantastic job of taping boxes shut so they don't come open in transit—in fact, she does such a good job it can be challenging to open one. I wrestled and mumbled and finally tore the box open to see several wrapped gifts with an envelope on top. I opened the envelope and pulled out a letter. It was, of course, from my mom.

Dear Mark:

I'm so proud of you, we all are, and I hope these gifts find you well and healthy. Wait until Christmas to open them, do you hear?

I hope you enjoyed Doug's visit. It was fun planning that with his parents and the Wests. I hope it was a good surprise for you.

We all watch the Alaska weather every day, and it looks really cold there. All we can see is Anchorage, but it's all pretty much the same, isn't it? I hope you have enough warm clothes and you're taking care of yourself.

We love you, and we are already looking forward to you coming home in a few months. Merry Christmas.

With much love,
Mom

Wait until Christmas? I considered it for a half of a split second. Christmas was more than two weeks away, and I have never been one to wait. If there's dessert on the table, I'll eat it first. If I find presents ahead of time, I open them. I find my chocolate bunnies before Easter, eat the ears off, and put them back into the package. Planning ahead is not one of my strong points. I didn't even hesitate before tearing into the gifts.

There were books from my dad that I'd asked for because I knew that soon I wouldn't be able to get out as much. I'd specifically asked for books on the book of Revelation, because I was finding it difficult to read and interpret. He'd sent some of his own collection, as well as others that had been recommended to him. Also in the box was an exhaustive concordance of the entire Bible. I remembered that Bob Hall recommended using a concordance to help with difficult passages, and I nodded, smiling.

My mother knew I was cooking for myself. She had sent my favorite treats, wrapped up tight to survive the trip. There were candies, cookies, honey, and other things I could use to spice up my food here. And, God bless her soul, butterscotch cookies. She'd also sent down mittens, which were wonderful since my entryway construction work required me to be outdoors. The gloves I had here weren't nearly warm enough, and were wearing out besides. Mittens were much better in cold like this.

My grandfather's gift was a prize. It was a big, sharp hunting knife and sharpener. I recognized it as one from his collection. He was the one who'd taught me to fish, shoot, and hunt. He'd always said he'd give me this knife when I was old enough. I guessed this was his way of saying I was grown up now. There was no note. He knew I'd understand.

A little choked up, I sat back and surveyed my booty. Everything I'd asked for and more. My family knew me well. I felt the love and care of family that came with each and every one.

I made some cathead biscuits, slathered them with honey, opened one of my dad's books, and settled in contentedly for the evening. The wind howled outside, but snuggled in my warm sleeping bag next to the stove, I couldn't complain about anything.

35

The next morning was a usual Sunday until I got to church and went into the Sunday school class I still taught. To my surprise, a white girl sat in my class. She was slim with shoulder-length light brown hair and freckles scattered across her nose and cheeks. She stood up and smiled when she saw me. Her eyes looked familiar,

"You must be Mark," she said. "I'm Janice King, Denise's sister." That was why her eyes looked familiar. I saw them whenever I looked at Denise.

"Nice to meet you." I shook her hand. She was just a little shorter than me. Denise's sixteen-year-old sister, Allie, had spent the summer here but this was the first time I'd met Janice. I knew from Denise that she was about my age. "I didn't know you were coming."

"It was kind of a last-minute thing." She explained that she was a junior at the University of Wyoming. She hadn't been here before and wanted to see her big sister over her Christmas holiday. She'd be staying for two weeks, then going home in time to spend Christmas with her parents and little sister. "Maybe you can show me around?"

"Sure. I work a lot, but there should be plenty of time."

It was time to start Sunday school, so I cut the conversation short and began the class. After church, Denise invited me to eat Sunday supper with them that night. I spent an enjoyable evening eating Denise's cooking and getting to know Janice better. These two sisters were cut from the same cloth. They were delightful with their bubbly personalities, wit and sarcasm, and emotions wide open for all to see and enjoy.

It was refreshing to see a white face my age. For two whole weeks there'd be someone to hang around with, talk to, and do things with. It was something to look forward to in these dark days of December.

Janice went with me at some point on all my jobs, even to work on my current entryway. We talked nonstop, at the Wests' house, at my apartment, anywhere and everywhere. The kids loved her, both at the school and the Lighthouse. I showed her all the things I'd just showed Doug. We went ice fishing, snowmobiling, dog sledding, and walking. We teamed up with Jack and Connie and did things with them. Playing cards and listening to records were so much more enjoyable with company.

She was very interested in the details of my spiritual journey, and I was more than willing to share. She was a Christian but had grown very little spiritually since her own commitment at a young age; she reminded me of myself before God got hold of me through Dr. Stanley. I shared with her some of the things that had made a difference to me, and hoped they would also speak to her. Maybe God had put her in my path for a reason, and I could help her grow as I'd been helped. I hoped so.

By the time she left, three days before Christmas, I felt that we had developed a really solid friendship—the kind that makes you want to stay in touch from time to time down the road. I was off from the group home that weekend, so I went with Will and Denise to take her to the airport. She took my hand and looked at me with tears in her eyes, and then she kissed me on the cheek and pressed something into my other hand.

"I'll miss you, Mark."

"I'll miss you too." It had been nice to have someone my age to talk to for the past three weeks, one with Doug and two with Janice.

"Maybe I'll come back."

"I hope you do," I said, thinking of her spring break from school. If she came back for a week in the spring, there would be a lot more to do. Maybe it would even be Iditarod week.

"See ya," she said.

"Later tater," I said as she turned to go.

When her plane took off and we were back in the Bronco, I

opened my left hand. She'd given me a picture of herself. On the back she'd written: "To Mark. Janice E. King, December 1979."

"This is a really good picture." I showed it to Will and Denise. They exchanged glances, but I thought nothing of it.

36

After we got back to the Wests', I borrowed the Bronco and made a short visit to the group home. I'd been working since Thanksgiving on gifts for the kids. My grandfather's knife and the experience I'd gained earning my wood carving merit badge had come in handy over the past month.

I went in the entryway and shed my gear, being careful to keep the small bag I carried out of sight. Then I went in the front door.

"Anybody home?"

No one was expecting me, and soon I heard shrieks of surprised delight. All ten kids came barreling into the room and leaped on me. Prissy wordlessly climbed on my back and wrapped her legs around my waist and her thin arms around my neck. "My Mark," she whispered in my ear.

"Mark! Mark!" the others chanted.

"Hi everybody!"

Mrs. Leo followed them into the room, drying her hands on a dishtowel. She was a miniature version of her husband of forty years. Both were trim, had white hair, twinkling blue eyes, and laugh lines around their eyes and mouth. He was tall; she was short. They adored each other. She was called Mrs. Leo because that was the way she wanted it. She was the other half of him.

"Hey, you," she said. "The kids missed you this weekend."

"I missed them too, and since Christmas is just two days away, I had to come see them.

"I brought you guys something," I said to the children.

"You did?" Paul asked.

"I told you that people give gifts to those they care about at Christmas time. Well, I care about you guys. Want to see what I got you?"

With wonder in their eyes, they all nodded their heads. This was completely unexpected and unusual in their lives.

I'd spent the last few weeks gathering driftwood from the frozen beach and carving it into figures. Very specific figures. I'd gone through a lot of driftwood getting everything just like I wanted it. Each one was wrapped individually, with one of the children's names on it. I handed them out one at a time. They reverently peeled the paper off.

Inside were wooden figures that, together, made a complete nativity scene. There were thirteen in all, ten for the kids here and three for the Lighthouse regulars. I planned to walk to each of their houses this afternoon and give them theirs. There were two shepherds, one wise man, two sheep, two donkeys, two camels, Mary, Joseph, the baby Jesus in a manger, and an angel. Each had the name of the child it belonged to engraved on its feet. Jesus' engraving was on the bottom of the manger in which He lay.

The kids understood immediately. They looked at their gifts, then up at me. Mrs. Leo, looking on, started sniffling. "Did you make those yourself, Mark?"

"Yes ma'am. I've never tried anything on this scale before. It helped that some of the driftwood resembled what I was carving."

"It's absolutely beautiful, and so special." She wiped big tears that now cascaded from her eyes. "Let me clear off a place to put it."

Before long the entire nativity scene was arranged in the traditional style on a table in the living room. One donkey, one camel and one sheep, still in my bag, would go to Thomas, Kim and Atka. Prissy's angel was the last figure to be added. She put it in place as we showed her, then kissed me on the cheek and whispered, "Thanks."

As we stood looking at the completed scene, Prissy in my arms, I knew that all the work had been worth it, and so much more.

37

I got home that night to an unusually cold and dark apartment. I hit the lights, and our one dim lamp flickered feebly to fight the thick darkness. The tenant at the other end of the building must not be home yet, because the heat wasn't on. Shivering, I went to the oven, turned it on high, and opened the door to get some warmth.

Looking around, I spied a note on Jack's bed. I crossed the room and picked it up with my mittened hands.

"Mark," it said, "I'm at Connie's for the holidays. Hope you have a good Christmas. See you Wednesday. Jack."

Today was December 23. Tomorrow was Christmas Eve, and I was having an early supper with the Wests. Then we were holding a special Christmas Eve service at their house. I didn't know yet where I'd be for Christmas Day, but I assumed I'd be at either the Wests', the Vaughns', or the group home. That gave me tonight to be quiet, read, and rest. It had been a long, busy month.

It was suppertime but I wasn't in the mood to cook anything, so I opened some Spam and ate it from the can while I read one of my father's books. Caught up in the interpretation of Revelation, I read into the night. I didn't even realize when fatigue overtook me and I drifted off.

*　　*　　*

The thing about the far north is that you never have any idea what time it is. I was used to figuring time by the sun, but when there's no sun, you have nothing to judge by. I opened my eyes the next morning . . . or was it morning? . . . to find total darkness as usual. My watch informed me that it was indeed morning, and I'd actually slept in. The man in the end apartment must have come home at some point, because there was a hint of heat in the room. I could still see my breath, though, so I got up and turned on the oven. My mother's Christmas candy served as my breakfast. I sat and ate it while looking out our one window at the blackness and the few flakes that fell close to the window. We took pains to keep one pane free of snow so we could see outside, for what it was worth.

One arctic entryway was nearly finished and three others were contracted. Today I planned to put the finishing touches on the one that was nearly done, and spend the month of January building the other three. I'd need the money, as my status as a semester missionary would run out in one week and there would be food to buy and rent to pay.

I packed myself a lunch, bundled up, and stepped outside. The cold made me catch my breath, and I had to remember how to breathe safely. When the air is that cold, it literally hurts. The air feels like daggers when you breathe it in. Lungs can freeze. Noses can freeze. Mouths can freeze. Everything has to be done very carefully, and all body parts have to stay covered. The advice from Charles Chandler continued to be golden.

By early afternoon, this entryway was finished. I collected the last of my money from the native family who'd hired me and headed for the Wests'. The walk seemed longer than usual because this felt like the coldest day we'd had so far. I was very grateful when their house came into view. I opened the door, shed my gear, and stepped into the house. My entire body began to relax, muscle by muscle, and I began to be warm for the first time since I'd left the group home yesterday. I sighed in relief and went into the kitchen.

"Hey, Mark," Denise greeted me as she stirred something that smelled wonderful.

"Hey, Denise. Merry Christmas."

"Merry Christmas to you."

I peered over her shoulder. In a huge pot was a concoction that looked like vegetable beef soup, although I knew the beef was probably moose. The smell of fresh sourdough bread wafted from the oven. I knew that this, to her, was a simple pre-church meal, but to me it was a feast. Before long the three of us were sitting down to a hearty, warm meal and discussing the upcoming service. It would be held here, in the Wests' home, and it would be the first real Christmas Eve service they'd done. From word of mouth, we expected a good turnout.

We weren't disappointed. All the people we were accustomed to seeing on Sundays were there. There were the Leos and all the group home kids, the Vaughns, and several other families. Surprise attendees were Atka and his family, and Thomas and his dad. We began the service and then got the biggest surprise of all. In came George Allen, who'd helped us so much with the church building. We'd been inviting him to come to services, but until now he hadn't accepted. Will greeted him warmly when he came in the door.

This simple service was perhaps the most heartfelt I'd ever attended. We ended with everyone lighting a candle in honor of the birth of the baby Jesus, and singing "Silent Night." The quiet reverence carried over after the service. Denise gifted each family with a small container of her soup and a hunk of bread, and everyone bundled up and went out into the night. To do what, I had no idea. I was certain that the kinds of Christmas Eve activities I was used to would not be happening in any of these households. I reminded myself to take Will's advice and choose my battles. We were already doing good things here, and it would only get better as time went on.

38

The next day I woke up knowing it was Christmas. I said out loud, "Merry Christmas." The silence screamed. Then it dawned on me. I was alone. What a strange, depressing realization on what should have been a happy, joyful day. Everyone seemed to think I was spending the holiday with someone else, and I had not been invited anywhere. I knew I could probably just show up at the group home, or the Wests', or the Vaughns', but that did not seem right. They were having family time, and I didn't want to intrude. So I resigned myself to spending Christmas alone.

Now I wished I hadn't opened all my presents. There was nothing left to open, no outward sign in this lonely apartment that this was a special day at all. Well, I could certainly do something about that.

Nome's latitude was above the tree line, so no one had a fresh Christmas tree because there were no trees. It didn't seem like Christmas without a tree. I hadn't worried about it too much before, because I was never home. Now, though, facing this special day by myself, the lack of a tree suddenly seemed intolerable. Surely I could find something that would serve. A big bush, anything. I knew I couldn't do much until the two precious hours of twilight, which were still hours away.

I busied myself until it was almost sunrise. I ate some Christmas candy, then scraped something that looked like a moose steak out of the food barrel and put it in the kitchen to thaw. It would serve as my Christmas dinner.

Finally, unable to wait any longer, I bundled up and stepped outside. In Nome there were only houses with pitiful, bare yards now buried in feet of snow, but I remembered the small willow branches the kids and I had used to decorate the group home. I wanted more than branches, but perhaps I could unearth a whole bush. Across the street from the Lighthouse, almost at the end of town, was a hollow with some big willow bushes. This was only about six blocks away, but six blocks is a long way when you're slogging through knee-high snow. I trudged along slowly, knowing twilight was near now. And about the time I got to the Lighthouse, the edge of the sun peeked above the horizon. That was as good as it was going to get.

The hollow looked like a level expanse of white, but I knew that under the snow were big willow bushes. I hoped I wouldn't have to go too far to find one. I stepped off the road and immediately sank through the fragile crust into hip-deep snow. I kept going tentatively, and with each step, the snow got a little deeper. By the time I got to the area where I knew the bushes were, I was chest deep. I kicked out, hoping to find a bush. Sure enough, my foot hit something solid. I began to dig in that area, and soon my hand felt a branch. I tugged with all my strength. It did not budge. I tried again. Nothing.

There was no way I would be able to get the whole bush. It was down too far, its roots were too strong, the snow was too deep, and it was just too cold. I needed to finish this quickly or they'd find my frozen corpse in the spring thaw. Using the knife my grandfather had sent me, I cut off as many big branches as I could reach. When I had gotten all I could, I dragged them up and out of the snow and began to retrace my steps, which were now already almost filled with fresh snow. It took three trips to get all my branches out of the hollow.

Finally standing back on the street again, shivering and wet, I surveyed my situation. My twilight time was nearly gone. Having worked so hard to get the branches, I was not about to leave any of them behind. But home was six blocks away, and I could not make that trip more than once. I would have to drag the branches home in one trip.

By the time I got home, it was pitch dark and I was half frozen. But I had all the branches. I dragged them inside and checked them out in the light. It would be the weirdest Christmas tree ever, but it would be mine.

I took the branches and lashed them tightly together with a shoe-lace, then shoved the bunch into a bucket and packed rocks around it to hold it up. I stood back and looked at my work. It looked good, almost like a real tree. But a real Christmas tree needed decorations, and I had none. Looking around, my gaze lit on the socks I had hanging up to dry.

I took the most colorful one and used my new knife to cut the yarn at the end. Slowly, painstakingly, I unraveled the entire sock until I had a colorful strand that should make a serviceable garland. I draped it around the willow branches. Then I took some of the rejected carvings from when I was working on the children's gifts and placed them in the branches. Then I rewrapped some of the gifts my family had sent me and placed them under the tree. Standing back, I was satisfied that I'd done the best I could. I had a tree, I had supper thawing, and I had presents, even though I'd opened them all already.

The good feeling did not last long. When I went to cook what I'd scraped out of the barrel, I saw it wasn't a moose steak at all, but a mystery meal given to me by one of the native families. I thought the lady said it was walrus. This was the first and last time I'd ever eat walrus, I promised myself. Thankfully, it was already cooked. Starving now, I warmed it in the oven and determinedly downed it, trying not to think about what I was eating.

Now what? I had a tree, I'd had Christmas dinner, and I'd already opened all my presents. And it was still—I checked my watch—only six o'clock.

Depression and despair hit me hard. I imagined what was going on at home, with the holiday meal, the decorations, the gifts, the togetherness, the love. With a physical pain in my heart, I missed my parents and my sisters. Yes, even my sisters. I missed my brother, Doug. I even missed Janice, although I barely knew her. With no phone, I couldn't even call any of them and hear their voices. And the hours of aloneness and loneliness seemed to stretch out endlessly before me, dark and menacing.

Suddenly it was too much. I collapsed in the floor, sobbing, my head on the bed beside me and my legs curled up under me. I cried like a baby until there were no more tears inside me, then kept sobbing in hiccups for a while. Finally I rested, drained and exhausted. My eyes hurt. My head hurt. I knew that for my entire life, I'd look back on today as the worst, most depressing, loneliest day of my life.

Then it hit me. Hard. Like a two-by-four to the head. I sat straight up. I'd been reading one chapter from Proverbs each day, and one verse now screamed into my brain. Proverbs 18:24 says, "A man of too many friends comes to ruin, but there is a *Friend* who sticks closer than a brother."

I was behaving like a spoiled brat, putting way too much emphasis on the outward trappings of Christmas. So what if my tree was a bunch of willow branches that I'd nearly frozen to death to get, and unraveled a sock to decorate? So what if I had no presents? So what if I was alone? So what if I'd had walrus for supper? The point of Christmas wasn't any of those things. I wasn't alone and never would be. The Friend referred to in Proverbs was Jesus Himself. I had the gift of an entire day, which happened to be one of the most important days in the Christian faith, of solitude to thank Him and commune with Him. It was a glorious gift and I'd almost missed it in my selfishness.

I collapsed with my face to the floor. "Father," I prayed, "please forgive me. You gave me a tremendous gift and I nearly missed it. I'm sorry I was selfish. I could have enjoyed this whole day with You, but I was too busy thinking only of Mark. I would love to spend the rest of this most wonderful and special day with You. Please open my heart and mind now. I'd love to hear what You have to say. In Christ's name, amen. Oh, and by the way, happy birthday!"

I dove into my Bible, and it was like those first days of Dr. Stanley's teaching. It seemed that every verse spoke straight to my heart. Every Proverb had real meaning. Every Psalm sang. Each of Jesus' parables spoke to me in a new way. I spent hours in the Word, crying and thanking God for His hand on me, His personal teaching, and the gift of His Son. By the time I went to bed that night, alone but not alone, my heart was light and my spirit soaring.

The last passage I read was Matthew 11:28-30. "Come to me, all who are weary and heavy-laden, and I will give you rest. Take my yoke upon you and learn from Me, for I am gentle and humble in heart, and you will find rest for your souls. For My yoke is easy and My burden is light."

I had never felt more content in my life. I only had a few more days as a semester missionary, and I didn't know what my future held after that. I did know that it would work out, because I was supposed to be here. God would provide some other way for me to support myself. I fell asleep confident in the future, with my Bible on my chest and a smile on my face.

PART 3:
WINTER

39

I rose the day after Christmas with a sparkle in my eyes and an extra spring in my step. I planned to get started on my third entryway and get serious about looking for a steady job to begin in January.

I worked all day and got a good start on the entryway, then arrived at the Wests' in plenty of time for Wednesday night service. As usual, Denise invited me to eat supper with them before church started, and I knew the conversation would turn to what we'd done for Christmas. I headed it off.

"What did y'all do yesterday?" I asked as we sat around the table and ate moose. Denise was skilled at finding different ways to prepare moose meat, which was good because they had so much of it.

"Just had a quiet day," Will said as he ate. "It was strange just having two people in the house. Usually we have foster kids here or something going on. It was kind of nice actually."

"What did you do, Mark?" Denise asked. "Were you at the Vaughns' with Jack?"

"No." I'd already debated how I would tell someone I'd been alone. I didn't want any pity. As it turned out, it had been the best thing that could have happened. The Lord knew what He was doing, all right. I figured simplest was best. "I spent a quiet day at home, too."

They stopped eating and looked at me, alarmed. Denise spoke first.

"Alone?" She was horrified, her hand over her open mouth.

"Yes."

"Oh, honey. I didn't know. Why didn't you come here?"

"I didn't know what you guys were doing. It was okay, Denise, really it was. It was how God wanted it. I ended up getting closer to Him in ways I never would have otherwise. It turned out how it was supposed to."

"You had the gifts from your family, though, right?"

"No way. I opened those the day I got them."

"Oh, honey! No presents on Christmas?"

"Let him talk, Denise," Will said in his quiet voice. He could see there was more I wanted to say.

I described my day, leaving nothing out. I told them about the willow branches, the walrus meal, the despair, and finally the Scriptural illumination and the elation. When I finished, Will nodded his head. His expression had gone from serious look to a very broad grin as I talked.

"It was tough, but you made of it what God wanted you to," he said approvingly. "I'm not sure I would've done as well."

"I know I wouldn't have." Denise was still upset. "I hope your mama never finds out I let you be alone on Christmas. She'd never forgive me, and I wouldn't blame her."

"It's okay, Denise," I said calmly. "Do I look upset?"

She had to admit I didn't, but she wasn't done. "Just for the record, Mark—you can always, always come here, no matter what we're doing. Remember that."

Then people started to arrive for the church service and conversation time was over. Denise still had tears in her eyes as she stared at the light over the kitchen table.

My prayer was answered during church that night. I'd been praying for work, for some way to support myself after my semester missionary status went away in five days. At the moment, I had no idea how I was going to pay the rent that would be due on January 1. I knew I'd be provided for, so I wasn't worried exactly, but I did wonder how this was going to be worked out.

The answer started to come that night. After the service was over, Denise was in a group talking to several women and summoned me over.

"Here he is," she said to one of the ladies, who looked familiar, but I didn't think I'd ever actually met her. "This is Mark."

"Hi," I said to her. "Nice to meet you."

"This is Belinda Morris," Denise said. "She knows of a job that's open at the hospital that you might be interested in."

"I don't know much," the lady said apologetically. "I just know their bookkeeper just quit and they're looking for someone to replace her. They need someone right away, if you're interested."

My mind started racing. I'd kept books for a lumber company while I was a UT student. It had been my main part-time job, just a five-minute drive from campus. I'd always been good at math and had found that I also had a knack for keeping accurate books and making numbers match.

"Yes, I'm interested," I said. "Who do I talk to?"

"Her name is Susan, and her office is just inside the emergency room entrance of the hospital," Belinda said. "I'd go see her tomorrow if I were you. Good luck."

40

That night in my apartment, I debated. How to go about getting this job? I had no typewriter, no computer, no way to do a resume. All I had was my wits and my experience. My only option was to go see Susan and convince her that I was the person for the job. If this was the door God wanted me to walk through, then He would open it. "Thy will be done," I prayed.

Real cleanliness wasn't even an option. A shower was impossible. The best I could do was to heat snow and scrub myself with a rag. I dressed in the best clothes I had with me, bundled up, and walked to the hospital. The streets were empty. No cars, no snowmobiles, no real sign of life. As I got closer I noticed several pairs of snowshoes at the door, so I knew people were here. Hopefully Susan was one of them.

I walked in the emergency entrance door, shed my gear, and looked at the nameplates on the office doors in the hallway. I found Susan's name, along with a "Wanted: Bookkeeper" sign on the second office door. Beside the door was a glass wall. Through it I could see a desk, at which sat a heavy-set, forty-ish woman with red hair cut just below her ears, right hand poised above a calculator. She wore black-rimmed glasses low on her nose.

This suddenly seemed like a very big moment. Taking a deep breath, sending up a quick prayer, I knocked.

"You may enter," came a distracted female voice, sounding almost perturbed.

I opened the door and poked my head in. The woman peered at me over her glasses.

"Hello," I said to her. "Are you Susan?"

"That's right." She looked me up and down impatiently. "What can I help you with?"

Susan was different than anyone I had met in Nome. She had an aristocratic way about her as if she had to look a long way down her long nose to the rest of society as uneducated, rough-edged, semi-barbaric ruffians.

I stepped to her desk and held out my hand. She did not offer her hand in return. "My name's Mark Smith." I pointed at the sign. "I'd like to apply for the job."

She leaned back in her chair and looked at me with new interest.

"You have really good timing. I just put that sign up. My book-keeper quit yesterday." She rolled her eyes. "What are you doing in Nome?"

"I've been working with Will West since the summer, but now my missionary status has run out and I'm looking for a job."

"Will West, huh? Do you have a resume?"

"No ma'am, I didn't have a typewriter here."

"Have you ever done bookkeeping?"

"Yes ma'am, I was bookkeeper for a lumber business in Knoxville, Tennessee."

"Can you handle a ten-key?"

Thankfully, I knew what she was talking about. A ten-key was a basic calculator with a tape. We'd used them at the lumber business, and I could make that thing sing.

"Yes ma'am." I had a stroke of inspiration. "I can show you, if you like."

"Ohhh-kaaay." She smirked as she pushed her calculator across the desk and motioned me to sit down. "Calculate this: 742 times 8,878, divided by 25, times 43, plus 2,300, times 79. Then 12 percent of that."

My fingers flew across the calculator as she spoke, but my eyes stayed intent on her face. When she rattled off the last number, I looked down.

"107,634,152.66."

She held out her hand. "You're hired. Can you start January 2?"

I shook her hand. "I can start right now if you need me."

"I appreciate that, but January 2 will do. Be here at eight o'clock sharp."

"I'll be here. Thank you for the opportunity. I won't let you down."

"I'm not worried. See you next Wednesday. And you can take that sign down on your way out."

I started to leave, then stuck my head back in the door. "Susan?"

She looked back up at me as she pulled her glasses lower on her nose. "Yeeeesss?"

"Just curious . . . what's the salary?"

"Twenty thousand. That okay?"

"Absolutely. Thanks again. See you next week."

I walked down the hall and out of the hospital, a little dazed. That was the quickest job interview I'd ever had. I began to smile. Hired on the spot! Twenty thousand dollars! That, plus the ten thousand I was clearing on the entryways, plus the money I'd managed to save from my other jobs and the Mission Board—I did a quick mental calculation and came up with a number that made me do a little happy dance in the snow. I'd have more than enough to pay for seminary, buy myself a car, and have a little cushion left over. I shook my head, smiling.

"Lord," I prayed silently as I walked along, "thank You for providing. It's more than I imagined and more than I deserve. Please give me the wisdom and discernment to keep seeing and walking in Your will. In Christ's name, amen." I remembered a verse in Ephesians that I had recently memorized, "Now to Him who is able to do exceeding abundantly beyond all that we ask or think, according to the power that works within us, to *Him* be the glory in the church and in Christ Jesus to all generations forever and ever. Amen."

41

Over the next few days I worked hard on my third entryway, hoping to get this one done before starting my new job. I planned to fit the other two in on weekends and in the evenings. Since I was on a deadline, Jack helped me out as much as he could and I shared my money with him. On January 1, though, he was celebrating New Year's with the Vaughns. That, as it turned out, was the day I really needed him.

I worked fast and obviously didn't pay enough attention to safety. I thought I was doing enough. Although it was forty below zero, as cold as it gets in Nome, and I was working outdoors, I was covered from head to toe in layer upon layer of the warmest clothing I possessed. The house somewhat sheltered me from the constant wind. And, every so often I took breaks to go inside and get warm.

I should have gotten my first clue when I absently put nails in my mouth. In an instant, I knew I'd made a big mistake. Anyone who's ever touched his tongue to a metal object on a cold day knows what happens. Your mouth freezes instantly to the metal. Normally you use warm water to try to unfreeze the metal from your skin, but I didn't have that option. I had to literally tear the nails loose from my mouth, taking skin off in the process. But I kept working, bleeding, with my blood freezing as fast as it met the frigid air.

I was working on the stoop now, racing the clock, trying to make the most of the two hours of twilight. Faster and faster I worked, putting boards down and nailing them home. I shivered, debated whether to go inside and get warm, and decided to push on until the feeble daylight went away. I dropped a handful of nails and grumbled to myself, then picked them up and continued to work. I blanked for a second. What was I doing? Then I remembered I was finishing the stoop. Suddenly I began to feel warm and sleepy, which would never do. I couldn't go to sleep now. I stripped off my outermost layer and kept working. Maybe the cold would help wake me up. I got sleepier and sleepier, but determinedly kept pushing through it. Then things got hazy and I knew nothing more until I woke on the floor inside the house.

I opened my eyes, grimaced, and closed them again. When I re-opened them, faces began to waver into shape, like a television with bad reception. Above me was the native lady who lived here, along with her young daughter. I knew the lady's husband had died the year before. When they saw me looking at them they shared looks of relief. Then the woman sprang up to get me a warm drink.

"What happened?" I asked as I sipped. But these two spoke almost no English, and communication was impossible. I rested until the older son arrived home, and mother and sister told him in their rapid-fire native tongue what had happened. Although his English was not excellent either, he slowly translated for me.

The hammering had slowed and then finally stopped, and the woman cracked open the door to see if I was still there. She found me in a heap on the unfinished stoop, barely breathing. Alarmed, she and her daughter dragged me inside, took off my wet outerwear, and wrapped me in a seal skin in front of their wood stove. Then they simply watched and waited for me to wake up.

When the boy finished, I looked at him and then at the woman.

"She saved my life," I said to the boy.

He nodded. "Yes."

"What is her name?"

"Kirima."

"Tell Kirima for me that I'm in her debt."

"I not understand."

"Tell her I thank her, and ask her what I can do for her."

He relayed the message, and the woman started shaking her head before he had finished.

"She say she glad you okay. Just please finish job soon. Thanks enough."

That wasn't good enough. The woman had saved my life. "Please tell her she doesn't owe me any more money for the work I do here. The rest of it is free." That was a generous gift, as I had been planning to collect five hundred more dollars before I left here today.

The boy relayed the message. More head shaking. "She say that too much."

"Not to me. She saved my life. I want her to accept this as a gift."

I didn't wait for an answer. I got up, rebundled myself, and went back out to finish the job. When I inspected the work I'd done before I collapsed, I shook my head. Pitiful. I had to rip out some of it before I could pick up where I left off. It was well into the evening before I finished and knocked on the door to tell Kirima I was leaving. She opened the door, smiled at her finished arctic entryway, and admired my work. This was a big moment for her. She now had one of the necessities of life in Nome after years of doing without. Her house would now stay a great deal warmer, and her heating bill would be a lot lower. She pushed a wad of cash at me.

"No, you keep," I said. She shook her head and shoved the money at me again. Finally I accepted it and thanked her.

I walked home, slightly ashamed. Again I had been careless and stupid, and again I'd survived my own foolishness. I silently thanked the Lord for delivering me yet again.

42

I arrived at work the next day promptly at eight o'clock and was given a small office just down the hall from Susan. My office was across the hall from an native woman named Malina and beside another named Tasha, both of whom worked in Benefits. Susan spent five minutes briefing me on my responsibilities, which basically included all aspects of the hospital's finances, including orders and receiving, inventory, billing and payroll. Then she turned me over to Malina for a tour of the hospital.

"Make sure he has everything he needs, would you?" Susan said to Malina distractedly. "Then bring him right back. I need him to get started right away."

As Malina and I turned away, she said, "Let's go to the supply room first. What do you need?"

"I'll figure it out when we get there." These supplies were the kind of thing that came on the barge and might disappear quickly. Who knew what might be left? Thankfully, the supply room held everything I needed. I loaded up with notepads, paper clips, a ledger, sheets to fill it, plenty of pens and pencils, erasers, and a ten-key with extra rolls of tape. I organized everything in my office, then went to Susan's office to get my assignments.

I stayed busy all day and the next two days, getting my arms around my new job. My responsibilities were stiff. I had to keep complete, accurate records for not only the Norton Sound hospital, but also for the organization that owned the hospital—which was the State of Alaska. Everything—every syringe, cotton swab, pencil, mop and broom—had to balance to the penny. If it didn't, Susan got involved. She had a way of finding every stray cent. I hated admitting defeat and taking a problem to her, but I had to do it a couple of times as I was getting immersed in the job. I brought her what I thought were very reasonable, educated questions, and she rolled her eyes, sighed loudly and wrinkled her mouth. Training was not her forte and, thankfully, I was a quick learner.

Positioned as our offices were, just inside the emergency room entrance, we saw most of the people who came in the door for treatment. I could see I was going to learn more about natives and their lifestyle than I'd ever wanted to know.

The second day I was at work, a native woman came in with her husband, both dressed in the usual outfit of head-to-toe sealskin. Until this day, I hadn't known or thought much about what they wore under these fur outfits. This woman came in and unzipped her seal skin halfway down to reveal a baby strapped to her back underneath the fur. To my shock, she was naked underneath the outerwear. She swung the baby around to her front, sat down in the waiting area, and proceeded to nurse the child. Malina observed my open-mouthed shock and laughed quietly.

"You'll get used to it," she said. "We see everything here."

"I see that." I averted my eyes got back to work.

43

Having one full-time, indoor job was a luxury. No more freezing and running from place to place to earn enough money to stay alive. Since I was no longer a semester missionary, all my official work with the church and its ministries had gone away. The group home, the Lighthouse, the prison, and the church building itself, all of which I loved, were no longer part of my official responsibilities. I had gladly quit my driving jobs and had told the school I was no longer available to substitute teach. I planned to build the other two entryways I'd contracted for, and that money would go straight into my savings account.

We were about to start Saturday mornings at the Lighthouse, and I still planned to go to that on a volunteer basis because I loved the kids. I'd told Will I would still help him with the dogs on the weekends, and that I would pinch hit for him at the radio station and the jail whenever he wanted; these wouldn't interfere with my job.

Sunday evening, several days after I started my hospital job, I was on my way to the Wests' to eat with them before the Sunday night service. I hadn't seen them since I started my new job and was eager to share with them all that had happened this week. There was a spring in my step as I strolled along through the darkness and the deep snow. January and February, I'd heard, were the darkest and toughest months to get through in Nome, but now that I was spending my waking hours indoors, it looked to me as if it were going to be a piece of cake. It all seemed downhill from here. I whistled through my muffler as I scuffed through the snow.

I went up to the house, tapped on the front door, and walked into the entryway. As I shed my gear, I thought I heard a voice that wasn't Will's or Denise's. Curious to see who was joining us for supper, I finished hanging up my gear and went into the living room. No one. I went on into the kitchen and saw another woman helping Denise with the meal. She turned around and gave me a big smile.

"Janice!" This was really icing on my cake. She must have come back for the last couple of weeks of her Christmas break. "You're back!"

She gave me a hug and a kiss on the cheek. "I'm back!" I was so happy that I lifted her off the ground and spun us around twice.

Will and Denise were all smiles as they welcomed me. "We thought this would be a nice surprise for you," Denise said. "You're surprised, aren't you?"

"I'll say. I thought she might come back at spring break, but not this soon."

We all chatted easily about my new job through a supper of salmon steaks. I told them about the native lady who stripped down and fed her baby in the emergency room, and Will and Denise were not surprised at all.

"It's a different culture here, Mark." Will ate his last bite of salmon. "You'll really see it now, in this new job. I bet you'll have stories every time we see you."

Soon it was time for the people to begin arriving for the church service. I sat in my usual spot on the Wests' sofa, and Janice sat next to me. It really was nice to have someone my age to talk to, although I didn't have nearly as much free time in this new job. The hospital wasn't a place I could bring a friend. I wondered how long she could stay before she had to go back to school for spring classes. I leaned over to ask her, but then the service started and there was no chance.

After the service, people were thanking Will and filing out, and Janice and I were in the kitchen cleaning up from the refreshments Denise had served. Will and Denise had conspicuously vanished, and I wondered what was up. I couldn't even hear their footsteps.

"Wonder where your sister went?" I washed a plate and handed it to Janice to dry.

"I think they wanted to give us some time alone."

"Why?"

She looked sideways at me. "Why? Well, because I just got back and they thought we might like some time alone."

Something wasn't computing, but I just shrugged and kept washing dishes. "Okay. So, when do you go back to school?"

She paused until I looked at her. "I'm not going back."

"What?"

"I'm not going back. I'm staying here. I quit school."

"You what?" I stopped washing dishes and stared at her. "Why did you do that? You only have three more semesters and you're done. And I thought you were doing so well in school!"

"I was. I had a three-point-six. But that's not why I quit."

"Then why?"

"You."

"Me?" It still wasn't making sense, and then it hit me with the force of an avalanche. "You didn't come back for me!"

"Of course I did. I felt a connection last month. I know you felt it too, because you told me at the airport you wanted me to come back. I want to be with you."

This was complete news to me. All we'd done was talk. No hand-holding, no kissing, not even any meaningful glances. Not from me anyway. Nothing—just a couple of shoulder rubs. To me, Janice was just another of many friends in my life who happened to be girls. I felt nothing else for her. I certainly didn't feel what I expected to one day feel for my wife. I'd seen how it was supposed to be, with the Chandlers and the Leos, and I wanted nothing less for myself. But now here was this girl, looking at me with the beginnings of tears in her eyes.

"Janice," I said carefully, "tell me how you left things at school."

"There's nothing to tell. I dropped out."

"And your apartment, and your job, and everything else?"

"All gone. I listened to your story and took it to heart. You had a reason for giving up everything to be here, and I did too. You."

Oh, boy. Then it hit me—the house was very quiet, and I could all but hear the pricking of Denise West's ears around the corner. "Janice, let's go for a walk."

"Now?"

"Yes, please."

I helped her on with her gear and we went out the front door.

"Janice, we need to talk."

"Okay, let's talk. About what?"

"This." I waved my arms. "Us."

"At least you admit there is an 'us.' I was starting to get worried."

"That's just it." How to tell her without hurting her feelings? There was no way. I had to be honest. "Remember I told you about all my friends in high school? How some were guys and some were girls, and we all just hung around together?"

"Sure, I remember."

"Well, that's how I think of us. As good friends. I never thought anything else."

"How about all those days we spent lying in the floor of your apartment, talking for hours? And all the stuff we did? And all the time we spent together?"

"All of that was fun. I enjoyed it. It was terrific to have you here to talk to."

"What about the picture I gave you? What about the things we said to each other at the airport? And the shoulder rubs?"

"What about them? We're friends. Friends say and do things like that. I do care about you, Janice."

"You care about me. I dropped everything for you, to move here, to be with you, and you 'care about me.'"

"Yes, I care about you. But I'm not ready to go any farther than that with anyone right now. I have to give all my time and attention to doing what God wants me to do here. That's really all I'm thinking about."

I couldn't put it any more diplomatically than that. It truly wasn't about Janice at all. This just wasn't the time in my life for a serious relationship. That I knew, was the simple truth.

"So, you're saying I gave up everything, I just threw my life away, for nothing."

"We should have talked before you did that. I would have told you not to."

We walked silently back to the house. I could tell she was holding herself together with great difficulty. Her restraint broke the instant we walked into her sister's house. She burst into loud sobs and ran straight into Denise's arms.

"What is it, sweetie?" Denise stroked Janice's hair. "What happened?"

"There was a misunderstanding," I began, but I was cut off.

"He doesn't want me," Janice howled. "He doesn't love me."

"What?" Denise's hand stopped in mid-stroke and her eyes turned to ice as she glared at me. "What's this?"

"Denise, she and I never talked about it. You know I'm not ready for anything like this."

"What I know is what my sister told me. And I know that you led her on, and now you've broken her heart. I am so, so disappointed in you."

"Denise," said Will. "You only know one side of the story."

"One side is enough for me," she snarled, her sobbing sister still held close in her arms. "I want you to leave now," she said to me with steel in her voice. "And I don't want you to ever come back."

"I'm going, I'm going," I said desperately, backing toward the door. "Will, I'll see you."

"No, you will not." She turned to her husband. "Will, I don't want him anywhere around the church, or the Lighthouse, or the group home. Nowhere. You hear me, now. I'm not kidding. Look what he's done to this sweet girl. He's not the person I thought he was, and he's not welcome anymore."

Will looked at me helplessly and wordlessly as I gathered my things and stumbled out the door.

44

For a change, Jack was home when I got there. He saw my shell-shocked look and extracted the whole story from me.

"Whoa," he said. "You had no idea?"

"None."

"How exactly do you feel about her?"

"She's a great girl and a good friend. The kids loved her. We had fun together. That's it."

"Okay. Tell me what she said."

I related everything, as nearly word for word as I could remember it. When I got to the part about the picture and the airport, he held up his hand. "Picture. What picture?"

I rummaged until I found it. "This picture."

Jack took it and looked at it, and read what Janice had written on the back.

"Dude," he said. "You have messed up."

"I have?"

"A girl doesn't give you her picture, and take your hand, and hug and kiss you like that, unless she thinks something."

"I never thought anything about it."

"I can believe that. But I can also see how she misunderstood. You have to make this right. At least apologize."

"Denise won't let me near the house."

"You're a smart guy. Find a way."

*   *   *

Over the next week I tried. I went by the Wests' house before and after work every day, only to be met at the door by a bulldog named Denise who would not let me anywhere near her wounded pup. I tried to tell her I wanted to talk to Janice to explain and apologize, but all I got was, "I'm not giving you the chance to hurt her again. Just let her alone."

Saturday morning, I tried one last time. Denise informed me coldly and triumphantly that Janice had gone back to Wyoming.

"I'd like to write her. Can you give me her address?"

"Absolutely not. You just leave her alone. And the sooner you leave this town, the better I'll like it."

I saw Will that afternoon when I went to feed and exercise the dogs. Denise, I reasoned, had not told me to stay away from the dogs, so I intended to continue working with them. When I approached the dog yard just outside of town, I saw the Bronco and walked up to Will tentatively, unsure of my welcome.

"Hey, Mark." He lit his pipe. "Listen, I'm really sorry about everything, but I have to support Denise in something she feels this strongly about. It will eventually straighten itself out."

"I feel really bad, Will. I never wanted to hurt Janice. It just never crossed my mind that she thought we were more than friends. I've been trying to get to see her and apologize, but Denise wouldn't let me in the door. Now she says Janice's gone."

"That's right. Janice flew out around noon. It's my understanding she's going to try to get back into school and put this behind her." He paused. "I know you never meant to hurt her. Let's just lie low for a while."

"What about church, and the guys at the jail, and the Lighthouse?" I asked in desperation.

"I'd find another church for now if I were you. As for the others, if I don't see you, I can't stop you."

And so I went from being a key person on the staff at the Nome Baptist Family Center to an outcast who was looking for a place to worship. There were several churches in town that I could try, but I was so broken-hearted and upset this first Sunday that I found myself going to the jail.

I'd been back several times since my two sermons, just to visit and check on the new believers. Usually I went with Will on Sunday afternoons. Never had I appeared on Sunday morning. The guard looked surprised to see me.

"Hey," he said. "What's going on?"

"Just thought I'd come see the guys."

"This the usual Sunday service?"

"No, just kind of an unofficial one. Will should be here this afternoon as usual. That okay?"

He shrugged. "Okay by me. I'll let them know."

The usual eight were here, plus Robert Wallace, the animal skin artist. I hadn't seen him since my second visit here, when I invited him to come see me if he had questions. He never had. I thought it was a stroke of good fortune to be able to see him today, as I knew Will considered him a hopeless cause.

"Mark!" Hank came toward me, all rippling muscles and tattoos. He gave me a one-armed hug that took my breath. He was stronger than any linebacker. "Good to see you."

"Good to see you too, brother."

"What you doing here on a Sunday morning?"

"Just thought I'd do my church here today. You guys okay with that?"

They looked at me dubiously, not fooled in the least. I've never been good at hiding my feelings.

"Maybe it's our turn to be there for you this time," said Sam. "Come on, spill it."

The scene that followed was completely unlike anything I would have predicted. There I sat, in the middle of a circle of inmates, telling them of my failure. As I told the story, there were masculine groans and exclamations, much like I'd heard from Jack. They slapped themselves on the knees in hilarity.

"I thought you were smart."

"My dog would have known better than to do that."

"You really screwed up."

"You're stupid about women," Sandor summed it up.

"I guess so. I don't have much experience with them."

"What you going to do now?" asked Hank.

"Not much I can do. She's gone, and I didn't get to talk to her before she left. I wanted to make it right, but now I guess I just have to live with it."

"There ain't no making it right," Sam said. "You embarrassed her and hurt her. She put herself out there and you crushed her. She don't want to see you unless you're crawling on your knees with a ring."

I shuddered at the thought. Denise as a sister-in-law? Then I shook my head as a new realization hit. "I was way too focused on what was right in front of me."

"What was that?" asked Hank.

"I was so focused on finding and acting on God's will that I forgot to act like a human being and a Christian, and I ended up hurting an innocent girl. I have to think if I'd been a little more observant, I could have avoided this."

"Maybe you at least learned something," said Hank.

"I hope so," I said.

As I was preparing to leave, Robert motioned me over. "I been thinking about what you said."

"About what?"

"'Bout becoming a Christian. Can I come talk to you when I get out?"

"Sure. Anytime. When do you think you'll get out?"

"Prob'ly Monday."

I gave him directions to my apartment and told him when I'd be home. Then I left the jail, full of hope that perhaps this whole thing would have a bright side. Will had been wrong to give up on Robert. How wonderful if I could be the one God used to bring him to Christ!

45

Every day that week I hurried home, hoping Robert would come by. I had everything ready to discuss with him and show him in my Bible, with passages marked and points ready to make. This would be the first time I'd presented the Gospel to anyone older than myself, and I didn't want to blow the opportunity.

Monday and Tuesday came and went. Wednesday felt strange. It was the first Wednesday night in my memory that I hadn't been to church. But being home turned out to be a good thing, because about six o'clock I heard a knock. I opened the door to see Robert Wallace standing there in the gloom. He clutched a big black plastic bag.

"Hey Robert," I said enthusiastically. "I'm glad you came."

He awkwardly stepped into the apartment, obviously ill at ease. "You sure it's okay with you?"

"Absolutely. I want to answer any questions I can and help you with this decision."

But after two hours of talking and reading Scripture, Robert didn't seem any closer to a decision. He was still hanging onto the ancient ways, and couldn't make the two belief systems match. That made sense, because they didn't match at all. That meant he would have to abandon the beliefs he'd grown up with and accept something new. I understood that he still had questions to ask and issues to resolve, but I worried that with his lifestyle he might wait too long. How to convey this to him? I had to try.

"Robert, I understand you aren't ready yet, but no one knows how much time we have left. Please don't wait until it's too late. If you die without Christ, you'll go to hell forever. That's a pretty high price to pay."

"Just need to think about it a while longer."

"Okay." Then I asked what I'd been wondering about since he walked in. "What's in the bag?"

"Some skin drawings I'm hoping to sell to make some money to eat."

"Can I see them?"

He pulled them out of the bag and, to my surprise, they were very good. Will had been right when he said Robert could have had a successful career in art. I knew it was a gamble, but I thought it was a gamble worth taking. I pulled out a big skin with a drawing of a walrus on an iceberg.

"I really like this one. How much do you want for it?"

He looked at the skin and considered. "Twenty dollars."

That was a little more than I expected, but my mother would love it. I pulled a twenty dollar bill out of my wallet and gave it to Robert.

"Thanks, man." He pocketed the money. "This will let me eat tonight."

"No problem. You do really good work. Come back soon and let's talk some more. And remember what I said."

"I will." And he was gone.

46

More and more, I was realizing just how much I'd lost now that the Wests were no longer a part of my life. Will had been an encourager, a mentor, a dependable friend that I could always turn to for any issue or question, big or small. He had led me and guided me, and pushed and prodded me into some of the most incredible experiences and realizations of my life.

Denise had been a mother figure. She'd taken care of me, encouraged me in her way, and made sure Jack and I had enough to eat. Besides sending leftovers home with me when I ate at their house, she was always donating salmon and cuts of moose for our food barrel. Because of her, our barrel stayed at least half full whether our hunting expeditions were successful or not.

Jack was gone more and more. He ate and slept at the Vaughns' house nearly every night, so the food problem was becoming mine alone. It became very real on Friday evening when I went to the barrel to get something for supper and found one lonely piece of meat stuck to the bottom. I had no clue what it was. I pried it loose and held it up dubiously in the fading light. Was it even worth cooking, or should I just make some biscuits and open a can of Spam? Biscuits and Spam won over the mystery meat, and I faced the fact that I had to find some way to get food.

Then the problem of food suddenly became very small as it finally hit me, really hit me, just how much I'd lost. I'd depended on the Wests. They were my family here, and their home was mine. I had no other real friends. The Sanders had moved out of Nome onto the tundra. I'd never gotten close to the Leos. The Vaughns were Jack's friends, not mine. There were acquaintances that I'd encountered or worked with, but no one to turn to.

Emptiness and loneliness engulfed me, and I sank to the bed in despair. Just a few days ago I was thinking that I was in the home-stretch and my remaining time here would be a piece of cake. Now five months stretched out endlessly in front of me, including the two months that everyone said were the toughest, and I wondered how I would get through it.

I dragged myself to the kitchen area and slowly made the biscuit batter. It seemed like a huge effort, but I managed to drop the dough in huge dollops on the cookie sheet. After I slid the sheet into the oven, I meandered aimlessly about the apartment while I waited for my biscuits to cook. As I paced, I felt sorrier and sorrier for myself.

For the first time, I truly understood the impact the dark months can have on a person. Some people get very depressed. Others get drunk. Some have to have ultraviolet lamps to compensate for the loss of sunlight. Some kill themselves or beat their family members. Until now I'd had enough outdoor activity that I hadn't experienced any of this. And, I'd been involved in lots of work to keep my mind busy, so I hadn't had time to think about being depressed. Now, it all crashed in. And it was only the first week of January. How on earth would I ever get through it?

The baking biscuits began to fill the apartment with the good smell of fresh bread. I checked on them, waited a few more minutes, and then slid them out of the oven and onto the stovetop. Then, un-able to bear the silent, closed-in apartment another second, I slipped into my gear and trudged out the door into the frigid air.

I needed some open space, and my apartment was only six blocks from the edge of town. What I needed, I reasoned as I walked, was something to occupy my mind when I wasn't working. The critical times were in the evenings, as my daytime hours were full. Until now it hadn't been a problem, but the Wests' rejection had pushed me into a pit of despair and I felt utterly alone.

I shuffled and thought, shoulders hunched, head down, eyes on the ground in front of me. As I got to the end of town and looked up, something caught my eye in the sky. A green wisp started on the far horizon and began to grow and move. Brighter and bigger and more colorful and more amazing it became, becoming an astonishing, swirling show in the night sky as I stood there and watched in wonder and amazement. For the first time, I saw this show in all its splendor.

Of course, I knew it was the Aurora Borealis, also known as the Northern Lights, but the timing was too perfect to be a coincidence. This was a bold depiction of the majesty of God and a reminder that I wasn't alone, would never be alone. I should have learned that lesson at Christmas, but evidently I needed to be reminded. Passages from Job about the absolute grandeur and omniscience of God scrolled across my brain.

"Where were you when I laid the foundation of the earth? ... Have you ever in your life commanded the morning, and caused the dawn to know its place? ... Have you entered into the springs of the sea or walked in the recesses of the deep? ... Can you lift up your voice to the clouds, so that an abundance of water can cover you?"

The passage goes on and on, in which God seemed to have gotten enough of Job's whining and put him in his place. I got the point too. Whatever was going on in my life, God was in control and I had to trust Him and continue to seek Him, no matter what. These long hours every day provided a golden opportunity to immerse myself in the Word and learn more about the Lord. Again, it was a gift I'd nearly missed in my self-absorbed state.

I watched a while longer, tears flowing from my eyes and into my mask. Then I turned and all but ran home.

47

Now I had a new routine. Six hours, I'd determined. During these dark times, I would devote six hours a day to Bible study.

I rose at seven o'clock each morning, ate a hurried breakfast, had my morning devotion, and walked to work. I stayed there until five o'clock, then hurried home and dove into my Bible. I read five psalms and one chapter of Proverbs each day, and began an in-depth study of the New Testament, especially the part after the four Gospels. I studied them word by word, verse by verse, with my concordance open in front of me, going back and forth between them, gleaning every insight I could.

Everyone in the Bible, it seemed, had their time in the wilderness. This was mine. God spoke to me, not audibly, but just as clearly and loudly, through those Scriptures. Bob Hall had told me to find verses that clearly stated God's will. The Ten Commandments were obvious, but Jesus put those in a new perspective in His Sermon on the Mount in the book of Matthew. There, He explained that "Thou shalt not kill" isn't only talking about actual murder. If you call someone a fool, it's just like killing that person. He went on to put other commandments into perspective too, and I realized I'd violated each and every one of them.

Bob had said I'd find other specific examples of God's will for everyone. I searched for them, and found one in 1 Thessalonians 5:18. "In everything give thanks, for this is God's will for you in Christ Jesus." I'd read this verse before, but now it had a new meaning. I was supposed to be thankful not only for blessings and good things. I was supposed to give thanks for trials and tribulations, too, because God would use them for good in my life.

Another passage was Romans 13:1-2. I had always thought that if a law was stupid, it didn't really have to be obeyed. Like using crosswalks, for instance. But here, in God's Word, was proof otherwise. "Let everyone be subject to the governing authorities, for there is no authority except that which God has established. The authorities that exist have been established by God. Consequently, whoever rebels against the authority is rebelling against what God has instituted, and those who do so will bring judgment on themselves." That meant that I had to obey whoever was in authority over me—my parents, my boss, the police, and the government, among others. Even when it didn't make sense.

A third passage, also in Matthew, had me hitting my knees and praying for hours. My concordance led me to Numbers 5:6-7. "Any man or woman who wrongs another in any way and so is unfaithful to the Lord is guilty and must confess the sin they have committed. They must make full restitution for the wrong they have done, add a fifth of the value to it and give it all to the person they have wronged."

I stared at the passage, then thumbed back to Matthew, where Jesus says if someone is angry with you, even if you don't think you've done anything, you have to make it right. And if you've wronged someone, you have to ask that person for forgiveness before asking God. The reference was Matthew 5:23-24. "If therefore you are presenting your offering at the altar, and there remember that your brother has something against you, leave your offering there before the altar, and go your way; first be reconciled to your brother, and then come and present your offering."

I could think of numerous people I'd wronged in my life, all the way back to Bobby Spangler, the mentally challenged man who'd first spurred me to become a Christian. There were my parents, my sisters, some of my teachers, Janice King, and others. And there were, I remembered to my shame, stores in Athens where I thought it was great fun to shoplift small items. Another time, during a family beach vacation, I thought the Cadillac emblem on the front of a car looked really cool, so I ripped it off and hid it in my suitcase.

I knew my sins were already forgiven, and Jesus had paid the price. But I felt I needed to do something tangible. I was being blessed beyond anything I'd ever known before, and I knew that the time had come to make things right with people in my past. For the next several nights, I wrote letters to all these people, telling them I'd wronged them and asking their forgiveness. I smuggled Janice's letter to Will and asked him to see that she got it; this was the best I could do for her.

In Bobby Spangler's case it was too late, and I now felt a mind-numbing regret. After I became a Christian, I'd treated him better, but I'd never apologized for the times I was cruel. Less than two years later, when I was about twelve, his body was found in a field near our home. He had gotten his hands on his mother's pistol and shot himself to death. I'd seen my father sad and upset, but I could count on one hand the number of times I'd seen him weep. This was one of those times. I found out later that Bobby had tried to call my father right before he took his life, but my father was out of town. Bobby's sad end broke something inside my dad, and he was never the same. Now I wished fervently that I'd done more for Bobby, but it was too late. Some things, I realized, are beyond restitution. I could only learn from this experience and try to be a better person.

Making apologies and restitution to the store merchants would be tricky. I called up a mental picture of the town square in Athens. I'd robbed my way around the square. In the end, I sent letters addressed to the manager of each store. I explained that ten years ago I had stolen from them. I asked their forgiveness and enclosed a check for the amount I believed I'd stolen, plus an additional fifth of the value of those items. I added a Bible verse at the end.

I didn't know what to do about the Cadillac emblem. Then I remembered that when we got home from that beach trip, guilt got the better of me and I confessed to my father what I'd done. I wanted him to punish me, but he decided I had punished myself enough. That was somehow the worst possible punishment, because I'd never stopped beating myself up over it.

Hour after hour, night after night, the Word was revealed to me in new and inspiring ways. I couldn't wait to get home every day and dig a little deeper in the well of God's truth. One passage literally explained another. It made sense in a whole new way. I was so glad to have the hours to pore over and over each section. Every day I grew in my faith, my understanding, my spiritual maturity, and my walk with the Lord.

48

Working with Will's dogs gave me something to do on Saturday afternoons. I'd spend the morning at the Lighthouse, then walk directly to the dog yard. I'd pet them, talk to them, feed them, then harness them up and set out across the tundra.

Dog teams can move fast, and they love to run. As long as I was well bundled up, it was invigorating to be out with the team, the wind in my face, the frozen landscape all around me. And there were always adventures. Every trip had at least one.

The dogs always amazed me with their intelligence, but sometimes they had to have human help. More than once they went off the beaten path and broke through the fragile crust of snow. When a person breaks through the crust, he might sink to his hips. When a dog breaks through, he's immediately over his head. There's nothing he can do until a person comes to pull him out. When those times happened, I wished fervently for snow shoes. Without them, I had to lie down on my belly and creep out on the snow to where the dog was sunk in. When I reached the spot, I'd look down to see the dog, bright eyes looking up, waiting expectantly and patiently to be rescued. He'd look up at me sheepishly and wag his tail, as if to say, "Oops. Get me out, would ya?"

Their strength was amazing. One Saturday Jack and I were out with the dogs and came upon a stranded snowmobile. Dogs can venture farther afield than snowmobiles, because snowmobiles need gas. This particular day, we were streaking across the tundra when a motion from the direction of the mountains caught our eye. We veered over to check it out, and found an embarrassed young native who had been out on his snowmobile hunting polar bears. His fuel line had frozen, and now he was stranded.

Jack and I looked at each other. We could get the young man home, but what about his machine? In his broken English, the native indicated that the dogs could pull his machine.

"No way," Jack said. "What do those things weigh?"

"Several hundred pounds at least." Then I remembered that Will routinely took the team out hunting, and they pulled adult moose back to town. Those huge animals had to weigh a lot more than a snowmobile. I'd seen Will walking alongside to decrease the weight.

"He's right," I said. The native nodded vigorously.

So we lashed the snowmobile to the rear of the sled. Jack and I got off and walked.

"Hike!" I shouted.

The dogs lunged against the traces. Slowly the stuck snowmobile, which had been frozen into the snow, began to break free with a series of icy cracks. The dogs strained and dug in harder. Within seconds, the snowmobile was loose and gliding across the snow behind the sled. Jack and I grinned at each other, incredulous. The native didn't seem surprised at all.

We pulled the snowmobile to a house on the outskirts of town, then took the dogs back to their yard and rewarded them with extra food and attention.

Sometimes, I was grateful for the dogs' incredible sense of direction. When snow begins to fall in curtains on the white tundra, it becomes impossible to tell where the sky meets the ground. All around—over, above, and on all sides—is a solid covering of pure white. This condition, appropriately called whiteout, can be very scary unless your team leader knows her way home. I hadn't always been so lucky with whiteouts. Once when I was out with the kids in the group home van, a whiteout struck, and I'd had no idea where I was going. We'd had to stay put until things cleared. With dogs, though, I could just give the "Home" command and relax.

They worked as a team, but there was a hierarchy. Each dog knew his or her place in the chain, and there was only one leader. Will was preparing for next year's Iditarod and had bought a new dog named Red to try out in the wheel position. Red was a middle-aged dog and looked like a champion. He was built for strength and endurance, with big shoulders and sturdy legs. He wasn't a full-blooded husky but his thick, silver fur and bright blue eyes made him look like one.

When I took the dogs out this afternoon, Will warned me of one unfortunate habit of Red's. The other dogs were accustomed to doing their business on the run. Red, however, was determined to stop and squat. This made him unpopular with the other dogs because no sooner would the team reach full speed than Red's meal caught up with him and he stopped in his tracks.

I thought this was hilarious until we got out on the tundra. Just like Will had said, we were about a mile from town when Red stopped dead and squatted. When he stopped, the entire team had to stop. We patiently waited for him to finish. The other dogs glared impatiently, letting out some yips and growls. Then we got going again. Unfortunately, this didn't happen once, or twice, or three times. Red's system seemed upset, and it happened four times.

When Red stopped and squatted the fourth time, Snickers had had enough. She looped back from her position at the head of the team and headed full-speed, still harnessed and pulling the other dogs behind her, directly toward Red. She barreled into him and ripped his throat out. Then she led the others back into place and calmly waited for my command.

I stood on the sled runners and stared, open-mouthed. Surely Snickers hadn't just killed the new wheel dog. But there he was, sprawled in the snow, blood spreading and staining the area around him in a widening pool. I couldn't leave him in the traces to be dragged, and I knew Will would want to see the evidence of what had happened. I slowly climbed off the runners, unhooked Red, rolled his body into a blanket, and dragged it onto the sled. We went straight back to the dog yard instead of having our usual full run.

Will was still at the yard when we pulled up. He looked at us, surprised at our quick return.

"Will, you won't believe what happened," I shouted before we even came to a full stop.

He scanned his team and could tell by the number of dogs in the traces that something had happened to Red.

"Where's Red?"

"Right here." I pointed to the sled. "He stopped to poop one time too many, and Snickers turned around and just ripped his throat out. Literally, ripped his throat out." I still couldn't believe it, and I'd seen it with my own eyes.

He uncovered the dog and examined him. "Well, I'll be dog-goned. I've heard of such, but never thought my dogs would do it."

"You've heard of it?"

"Lead dogs know they are responsible for the team, so when something slows the team down, they do something about it. You just saw it for yourself."

"Holy cow." I was still shook up. "I'm sorry, Will."

"Nothing you could have done to stop it. I'm sorry for poor old Red. He was kind of stupid and stubborn, but he didn't deserve that."

As traumatic and horrible as that was, something else happened a week later that almost made me decide to stop working with the dogs.

Will's dog yard had enough stakes and chains for the entire team, plus one doghouse that was reserved for mothers and their puppies. As soon as he knew one of his girls was expecting, he moved her into the doghouse until the pups were born and weaned. There had been no pregnancies this season. Or so we thought.

The team and I were far out on the tundra in the driving snow. We were at the far end of our loop, hours from home because of the rapidly worsening weather, and were taking a break prior to coming back. Suddenly I noticed Tanner, a young dog who ran near the front, acting strange. She turned in circles, whined, and licked herself. She lay down, whined some more, and looked up at me beseechingly. I had no idea what was wrong. I went to her and sat down next to her.

"What's the matter, girl?" I stroked her head.

She whined and writhed and licked herself some more. This went on and on. The snow was turning to a blizzard, and I knew we had to start back soon. Tanner was in no shape to make the trip. I was about to load her into the sled and start back anyway when she began to pant. She panted and strained, and a small mass gushed out from between her hind legs.

I'd watched plenty of baby animals be born before, so this was nothing new. The shocking part was that we hadn't even known she was pregnant. She hadn't been showing at all. That couldn't be good. The pup must be either premature or deformed.

I watched Tanner and stroked her while she cleaned the puppy and gnawed through the umbilical cord. And I watched the puppy and protected him from the cold while his fur dried. He was tiny but seemed perfectly formed. I placed him near his mother to feed and stay warm. Soon my heart sank. The puppy nosed at his mother but seemed not to know what to do. She licked him and encouraged him, to no avail. I knew the delicately small newborn needed warmth and sustenance, or he wouldn't survive the trip back. Already his nose and the insides of his ears were turning blue, and his movements were noticeably more and more feeble.

Desperately now, I tried to pry his little mouth open and guide Tanner's teat into it. The puppy seemed not to have the strength to suck. He was getting weaker by the minute.

Tanner and I both tried, more and more urgently, to get him to eat. She whined and licked and nosed him, and I tried to stuff the teat into his mouth. He was getting cold, and I massaged him in my mittened hands. He mewled. If we'd been at the dog yard we could have fed him milk in a medicine dropper, but we had no such supplies here. It was now obvious that this little dog wasn't going to make it. He was far too weak, and we were too far from home.

Finally, I couldn't stand to watch his suffering any longer. Crying, I deftly took the knife my grandfather had given me and pressed its razor-sharp blade below the baby's skull and above his shoulder. It was over in a second. Tanner licked the tiny body tenderly then walked away as if she understood there was nothing more to do. The ground was frozen, but I dug down into the snow as far as I could and buried the little dog. The weather was still getting worse and the sun was now gone, but still I sat over the makeshift grave, mourning the puppy who'd never had a chance to live. How had we not known Tanner was pregnant? We could have protected her and this little guy. Maybe he would have been a champion. Now we'd never know.

Slowly I reharnessed the dogs and turned toward home. After

hours of fighting the wind and the snow, we pulled into the dog yard. I unharnessed them and took care of them for the night, giving special attention to Tanner, who looked at me sadly and licked my hand. I stroked her and comforted her, not noticing that my own tears were flowing again and that my hands were stained with the puppy's blood.

This, I knew, would be a story I'd keep to myself.

49

My work days were actually nine hours, rather than eight, because I didn't take a lunch hour. Food was scarce in my apartment since I was getting no contributions from Denise, so I only ate two meals a day. When my mother sent packages, it was usually treats, not real food. When she'd found out I'd opened all my presents before Christmas, she'd sent me a whole batch of butterscotch cookies, tightly packed and safely layered in wax paper. They lasted me a couple of days.

When Malina realized I wasn't eating lunch, she got the story of Janice out of me. I'd come to expect people's reactions of horror, and I wasn't disappointed.

"You did a bad thing," she said. "That poor girl."

"I know, but I really didn't mean to. It just never crossed my mind. I tried to apologize."

"It should have crossed your mind," she said, then relented. "I have extra food in the kitchen. I'll get you some."

From then on, she or Tasha usually brought extra food so I could have lunch. They also brought their own homemade delicacies and pressed them on me to take home. My food barrel began to fill up again, but now it wasn't salmon and moose. I never knew what I'd be getting when I opened the containers, but now I didn't have the option of throwing them away. I had a choice . . . eat what they gave me or exist entirely on Bisquick and Spam. I was getting really tired of Bisquick and Spam.

As time went on, my appreciation for their thoughtfulness and generosity grew, and my palate became less finicky. I even ate walrus and whale blubber, and liked it.

50

I now counted on the quiet hours at home for my Bible study. Jack was almost never home—except when he and Connie were quarreling. They didn't fight much, but when they did, the darkness and frigid cold stranded my roommate in our apartment. I had my studying; he had nothing. He sharpened his knives endlessly. When they were razor sharp, he threw them into a board propped against the wall so their sharp blades stuck tight. When they dulled, he did the whole thing over again.

During those endless days, I became Connie's biggest fan.

Shrraapp. Shrraapp. The blades went over the sharpener, over and over again. I tried to concentrate. *Shrraapp. Shrraapp.*

"Why does she have to act like that?" The question was rhetorical, spoken with heartache in his voice.

I looked up from my book, where I'd read the same passage six times already.

"She's only sixteen. She loves you. Cut her a break."

"I don't understand women."

"I don't either. Obviously. But I do know you've got a good one there, and you need to fix this. Whatever it is."

"She needs to come to me."

"Jack. She's sixteen. You're twenty. Go see her."

The sharpening stopped, but the relief was only temporary. *Thwaacckk. Thwaacckk.* The knives stuck, shuddering the whole wall.

"I didn't do anything. She got mad at me for no reason."

"Everybody gets mad at everybody this time of year. I know she's missing you as much as you're missing her."

"How do you know?"

"I just know. You can see it in her eyes, how much she loves you. If you go see her everything will be fine."

These times usually lasted just a couple of days, but people weren't themselves during these dark days. Once it lasted a week, and I thought I'd lose my mind. I risked my neck to go to the church one Saturday afternoon and seek out James Vaughn. I begged him to please, please invite Jack to supper so they'd have to see each other and fix this. He grinned.

"Jack's driving you crazy?"

"Completely nuts. I don't even know what it's about."

"I do, and it's so stupid you don't want to know. Connie's driving us crazy too. I'll handle it."

That night, Jack was invited to their house for dinner and evidently all was right with the world again because he didn't come home that night. He showed up at our apartment the next afternoon with stars in his eyes.

"I'm getting married," he announced. He looked ecstatic but slightly dazed.

"Dude," I said, stunned. "When did this happen?"

"Last night." He couldn't stop grinning. "It just kind of came out. I realized that I can't live without her. I don't want to live without her, ever."

"Well, that's terrific! Congratulations, man." I gave him a one-armed hug. "Really."

"I have to find her a ring."

"Good luck with that." I couldn't imagine where he'd find an engagement ring in Nome in January. Or where Connie would find a dress.

"We're getting married June 1. That's a Sunday."

"What did her parents say?"

"I asked her dad first, and he gave me his blessing. Then I asked her. Both her parents are really happy. They welcomed me to the family."

"I'm so happy for you, man."

"I've had good friends in my life, but you're the best friend I've ever had. I want you to be my best man."

"I'd be honored." That would be the day before I was due to leave for home, so the timing was perfect.

51

Things got back to normal, and I began to get back into my study routine. That lasted several days, and then there came a knock at the door on Wednesday night.

Robert Wallace had come by several times, but it was becoming obvious that what he really wanted was for me to buy his skins so he could get drunk. I hated thinking that way, but the evidence was right in front of my eyes. I'd share the Gospel with him, he'd look like he might be about to make a decision, and then he'd put it off again. I bought his skins when I had extra cash, which wasn't often. When I did buy one, I saw him staggering down the street the next day and begging from passersby. It became tempting to pretend I wasn't home, but whenever I was tempted to ignore him, one of my memory verses, 2 Timothy 1:7, sprang to mind. "For God has not given us a spirit of timidity, but of power and love and discipline." I always let him in.

"Hey, Robert," I said today when I opened the door. "What's up?"

"Just had a few more questions." He came in with his black plastic bag. "You got a minute?"

"Sure." I knew how this would go. I would do my best to answer his questions, and then he would try to sell me a skin. Today, thankfully, I had no cash with me. It now felt like I was enabling his addiction when I bought his skins, and I had begun to reluctantly accept the thought that Will West had been right all along. Still, I had to try.

"I've got a minute, sure. What questions did you have?"

"It just seems like an awfully permanent thing, dedicating my life

236

to Jesus. What if I have to do something I don't want to do?"

"I can just about guarantee that will happen, in some way." I turned to several passages in the Bible where that had happened. Moses, Gideon, and many others had all asked the same question, Why me? They had all sorts of excuses, but in the end God had gotten the people He wanted to do what He wanted.

"I know a little bit of how they felt," I said. "I never argued with God once I knew what He wanted me to do, but coming here was very scary. Most people aren't asked to do something like that. Most people are just expected to bloom where they're planted."

"What does that mean, bloom where you're planted?"

"Live your faith wherever you are. When people notice the difference in you, and they will, tell them about Jesus. The thing is, you'll want to do whatever He wants you to do, even if it scares you or makes you uncomfortable. You'll be so filled with His Spirit that you will want to please Him."

"I don't know. It sounds awfully permanent."

"It is permanent, but that's a good thing. Once you're a child of God's, you're His child forever. Nothing can be any better than that."

Silence fell, and I knew Robert had exhausted his reason for coming to see me. Next would come the sales pitch. Three, two, one . . .

"Say, I remembered that you've been buying my skins for your family members as souvenirs. Anybody else in your family you'd like to get one for? I brought some new ones for you to look at."

"I appreciate that, but I've gotten them for everyone in my family now. I know they'll love them. Thanks for thinking about me, though."

He sighed. "I hope I can find someone who wants one. I'm fresh out of cash for supper tonight."

"One of the ladies at work gave me a couple of meals today. They're in the barrel outside the door. You're welcome to take one with you, if you want."

"Thanks, man. I appreciate that."

He loitered another minute, then headed out into the cold. And it was cold! Getting outside for even the shortest time took a big dose of courage. When you factored in the wind, and the fact that the actual temperature was forty below, the chill factor was minus eighty-eight. This was the coldest day so far. The natives here were hardy beyond reckoning, but I was worried about Robert.

52

One Saturday morning in early February, I was on my way to the Lighthouse for my weekly time with the kids. It was amazing to me that on a Saturday morning, they chose to roll out of bed and come out in the cold. They loved Bible stories, and we tried to make them as pertinent and realistic as we could. And, this was now the only time of the week I got to spend with the kids. I tried to make it special. Darren had seemed a little down the past couple of times I'd seen him, so this week's story had been chosen especially for him.

It was still completely dark and bitterly cold. I congratulated myself on making it through the month of January. One more month, and I'd be through the hard part. March wasn't bad because it was Iditarod month. Yes, it would still be cold, but there would be excitement in the air and people in the streets as preparations for the famous race began, dogs and sleds left Anchorage, and mushers began to come across the finish line here in Nome more than two weeks and one thousand miles later.

I arrived at the Lighthouse and stomped the snow from my boots, then went inside. After shedding all my gear in the entryway, I stepped into the living room.

"Hey, everybody!" I called and heard a stampede coming from the kitchen.

"Mark!"

"Darren!" I greeted him. As usual, he was in the lead. As the kids zoomed into the room behind him, I counted. All of the group home kids plus the three Lighthouse regulars. Amazing. Prissy came shyly forward and held up her arms to be picked up. I settled her on my hip as Patricia Boston, who had remained at the Lighthouse after the cuts, came into the room. She'd just finished feeding them a snack, and they were ready for their favorite part of the morning.

"Y'all want to hear a story?" I asked rhetorically.

"Yes!" they all chanted. Prissy nodded.

"I picked a special one today. It's about a boy who was about twelve years old when the story starts." I looked directly at Darren. "He eventually turned into one of God's all-time great leaders. He was Jesus' great-great-great-great—that's fourteen greats—grandfather.

"This boy had seven older brothers. The oldest ones were in the king's army, but the boy, his name was David, was always stuck watching the sheep because he was the youngest. He never got to have any fun, and his father and brothers just thought of him as a little boy.

"One day David was watching the sheep when someone came to get him and told him a man named Samuel was at his house to see him. The name didn't mean anything to David, but his dad wanted him to come home, so he went. As soon as he got home, this old man came to him and poured oil on his head. He didn't really understand at the time, but this meant that God had chosen him to be king of Israel when the man who was king at that time died.

"His life didn't change very much for several years, except that he sometimes got called to the king's house to play the harp for him, because the king had trouble sleeping. He probably kind of forgot about the day he had oil poured on him, because it was so long ago.

"Then one day David was with the sheep and his three older brothers were with the army of Israel, fighting a group of really big men called the Philistines. They were trained for war. Israelites were mostly shepherds and farmers. Israel's army was on one hillside, and the Philistines were on another. There was a valley between them.

"One of the Philistines was especially huge. His name was Goliath, and he was about nine feet tall. He had won lots of battles already. Paul, come here."

Paul came, and I lifted him up so he was standing on my shoulders. He had to duck for the ceiling. "This is how tall Goliath was. That's pretty big, isn't it?" They all nodded. I let Paul down.

"He wore a lot of big, heavy shields to protect his body from spears and other weapons. The Philistines had spears and swords made of hard metals like iron, so they had a big advantage. For forty days, twice a day, he came down to the valley, made fun of Israel and their God, and told the Israel army to send someone to fight him. The deal was if the giant won, the Israelites would be their servants. If the Israel soldier won, the Philistines would be Israel's servants."

"What's a servant?" Darren wanted to know. I had to think about that one.

"A servant is someone who works for another person and takes care of his stuff. Some cook, some clean, some take care of houses, some take care of animals, and some take care of people. Some just carry stuff for you.

"Anyway, everybody was scared of this huge guy. No one wanted to fight him, so no one volunteered. Finally the king put out the word that if anyone fought this giant and killed him, that person would be rich, would get a free house, and would have the king's daughter for his wife. Still no one wanted to fight the giant.

"David didn't know about any of this. He was minding his own business tending sheep when his father called for him and gave him some food to take to his brothers and their boss. He also asked David to bring back news of his brothers. So David got someone to watch the sheep and away he went.

"Just as he got there, Goliath came forward and issued his challenge again. David couldn't believe his ears. You see, Israel was God's chosen people. God had fought battles for them for hundreds of years and, of course, their enemies didn't stand a chance. David asked, 'Who is this idiot who dares taunt the army of the living God?'

"His oldest brother heard him and fussed at him pretty bad and accused him of coming just so he could see the battle. Here's David, who's come all this way to bring his brothers food, and his oldest brother jumps on him for asking a question. This is just like brothers and sisters now, don't you think?

"The king, whose name was Saul, heard that David was asking questions, and he sent for him. David told the king to quit worrying, that he'd take care of the giant for him.

"Now picture this. Here's David, who's not much older or bigger than Darren at this point. He's tiny next to the full-grown soldiers, and those soldiers were afraid of Goliath. And he's saying he's going to take care of the giant. Saul tried to be nice. He said David was just a child, while this giant had been fighting since he was a child.

"David made a good point. He said he had been taking care of sheep all his life, and that had meant killing lions and bears with his bare hands. He said, 'The Lord took care of me against the lions and the bears. He'll take care of me against this guy.'

"Saul tried to give David some armor to protect him, but it was way too big and way too heavy. David took it off and went in without it. He had a slingshot in his hand, and grabbed up five rocks from the creek."

All the children, especially Darren, were staring at me raptly. I tried even harder to paint the picture for them. I could see it so clearly in my own mind.

"Imagine what the giant thought when he saw his opponent. He must have thought this was going to be easy. Here's the nine-foot-tall giant in heavy armor, with swords and spears, against a fifteen-year-old boy who had only a slingshot and rocks.

"The giant wasn't very nice to David. He made fun of him. He said, 'Am I a dog, that you come to me with sticks?'

"David wasn't scared at all. He told the giant, 'You come to me with a sword, a spear and a javelin, but I come to you in the name of the Lord of hosts, the God of the armies of Israel, whom you have taunted.'

"David went on to tell the giant that he was going to strike him down and cut off his head, and the birds and the beasts were going to eat his body and the bodies of his army, so that the whole world would know there was a God in Israel.

"I can just see it, can't you? Little David saying this to Goliath the giant."

All the kids nodded, big-eyed.

"Then when David got at the right distance he put a stone in his sling and aimed. When he let it go, it hit the giant in the forehead and he fell. David didn't have a sword, so he took Goliath's sword and cut off his head. I imagine that the armies on both sides were standing there with their mouths wide open when David noticed that the guys in his army weren't moving. He yelled, 'Attack!' The Philistines all ran, but the army of Israel caught them and killed them. And then, just like David said, the birds and the beasts had a big meal.

"David went on to become one of the greatest leaders Israel ever had. He did become king, and his son after him. He served God all the days of his life, and God loved him."

*   *   *

I made a point of having one-on-one time with each child every Saturday morning, now that I didn't get to see them very often. Today most of that time was spent with Darren and Atka. I wanted to find out what was causing that depressed look in Darren's eyes, so I sought him out first. Once we were alone, I worked at getting him to open up.

"You could tell something was wrong?" he asked.

"I could tell, but that's because I know you and I care about you. What's up?"

"Nothing new," he shrugged halfheartedly. "Everybody always gets down this time of year."

"It's more than that."

"Maybe."

"No maybe."

He looked at me, considering. "Why do you care? You'll be out of here soon."

"Who told you that?"

"I heard."

I wished he hadn't heard that. I'd worked so hard at building trust, but it was no use if the walls started going up again. Now that he knew, I'd just have to work with what I had.

"It's true. My time here will be up in June."

"Why can't you stay?" Darren was in tears now.

"God wants me to do something else."

"What about me? What about all of us?"

"What about you? You have plenty of people here who love you. What do you think I could do if I stayed?"

"Be my friend, just like you have been. Be someone I can talk to."

"Darren." I got down on his level and looked him in the eyes. I wiped his tears with my thumbs. "Remember all the stories from the Bible I've told you, about people being expected to do things they didn't think they were ready for? Like the story I just told you?"

"Yes."

"Now it's your turn."

"My turn? To do what?"

"To use that gift of leadership I've always told you about. Someone will have to step up for the other kids when I'm gone. They already love and respect you, so it needs to be you."

He mulled that over. "If I'm there for them, who'll be there for me?"

"That's something we need to pray about. Of course, God will always be there for you. We can pray that He will send a person into your life to help guide and support you, too."

"Do you think He will?"

"I know absolutely that He will do whatever is best for you. If He thinks you need someone, then He'll send someone. But you do have to ask, then trust Him to know what's best."

I pulled out my Bible and read to him from Romans. "'And we know that God causes all things to work together for good to those who love God, to those who are called according to His purpose.' See, Darren, you can be sure that whatever happens, it will be what's best for you."

"I'm scared," he said with tears in his voice, looking and sounding very much like the child he really was.

"I know." I put an arm around him. "It's scary. But I'll be here for a good while longer, so let's not worry about it just yet."

He sniffled and leaned against me. "I love you, Mark."

I felt a sting in my own eyes and tightened my arm around his shoulders. "I love you too, Darren." I began to pray. "And God, I know you see this. You know Darren needs someone to help him when I'm gone. Will you send him a very special person, please? We both ask you right now. Amen."

The other child who really needed my attention today was Atka. There had also been trouble brewing in his eyes. He proved to be an easier nut to crack than Darren. I didn't have to seek him out; he came up and climbed onto my lap.

"Hey, little man." I ruffled his hair.

"Hey."

"What's up?"

"My dad came home last night."

"He did?" This was a surprise. Atka rarely talked about his father. All I knew was that the man was one of the many drunks on the street.

"He does that sometimes. It's no fun when he does."

"What happens?"

"He knocks on the door and begs my mom to take him back. She always says she will when he quits drinking. He says he wants to, but he can't."

"Is that what happened last night?"

"He seemed okay when he got there. He didn't smell or stumble around or anything. He even spent the night."

"That's good, right?"

"I don't know what happened, but my mom was crying this morning and he was gone again. I wish he'd just stay away. We do just fine with him gone. When he comes back, he makes my mom cry."

I knew Missy's life must be stressful, with no husband and three young boys to care for.

"I'm sorry, Atka. I know it's tough. It's even harder because you're the oldest. I wasn't the oldest, but I was the only boy, and my parents, especially my dad, expected different things from me than my two sisters."

"Like what?"

"They expected me to grow up quicker and take care of myself sooner. My dad paid for my sister to go to college, but I had to work and pay my own way. When my sister got picked on by bullies, he went to see the bully's parents. When the same bully beat me up, my dad said I was a sissy if I didn't fight back to protect myself. When I was two years old, he left me alone in a big department store to teach me a lesson because I went up the escalator without them."

"What's an escalator?"

Hmmm. Atka had no real point of reference to help him picture that one. "It's a moving staircase. You stand still and the steps take you up or down without having to walk."

"I hope my mom doesn't do any of those things."

"If she does, it's because she thinks you're ready."

"Sometimes she tells me to do things that don't seem fair."

"Like what?"

"Oh, just stuff. I can't think of anything right now." I was pretty sure it was something like making his bed or helping clean up the supper dishes.

"Atka, your mom is the person God put in your life to take care of you. The Bible says we have to obey those in authority over us. For you, that's your mom. You have to respect and obey her, no matter what. She loves you."

He looked at me with big eyes. "God wants me to do what she says?"

"Absolutely. Every time. He wants you to obey and respect her, and treat her right. Even if what she's saying doesn't seem fair."

"That's gonna stink," he said. I hid a smile.

"You just try not to worry about your dad. Let your mom handle that, and you concentrate on being a good son. That's your job, okay?"

53

My intensive Bible study continued, six hours a day as I had committed weeks before. I always started with a prayer for understanding, and every day I continued to find new golden nuggets of truth and inspiration in the pages of the Scriptures. Sometimes there were passages I felt led to read; other times I simply stumbled onto them. Still other times, my reference materials led me to them. Always, I came away feeling enriched, encouraged, and blessed.

I read of Israel being delivered over and over again from her enemies, often obviously by God Himself. He would turn enemy armies against each other so they destroyed themselves. He would send angels to fight battles for His people and hundreds of thousands of enemy soldiers would be destroyed. He would empower small groups of people to destroy huge armies against all odds. And always, always, His glory would shine through.

Lately, my readings were beginning to take on a new slant. Most of the passages seemed to discuss leadership and ministry.

There was Colossians 3:16-17, which read, "Let the word of Christ richly dwell within you, with all wisdom teaching and admonishing one another with psalms and hymns and spiritual songs, singing with thankfulness in your hearts to God. And whatever you do in word or deed, do all in the name of the Lord Jesus, again giving thanks through Him to God the Father."

There was 1 Timothy 4:15-16: "Take pains with these things; be absorbed in them, so that your progress may be evident to all. Pay close attention to yourself and to your teaching; persevere in these things; for as you do this you will insure salvation both for yourself and for those who hear you."

And Galatians 5:22-23: "But the fruit of the Spirit is love, joy, peace, patience, kindness, goodness, faithfulness, gentleness, self-control; against such things there is no law."

There were others as well, mostly written by the apostle Paul, discussing how to minister to people and correctly preach and teach the Gospel. I felt this was more proof that I was being led into the ministry when I returned home, and I earmarked these passages for the future.

My time in Nome had been so much different than I had thought. My expectations, I realized now, had been unrealistic. I had envisioned coming here and making an immediate impact on the lives of people. I had not reckoned on the conflict between the old ways and the new beliefs we were bringing. Those old ways were thousands of years old, and it had been naïve of me to expect to change people overnight. Nome was indeed a mission field.

I also realized now that there were many good Christians who did just as I had told Robert Wallace. They bloomed where they were planted, and many never see fruit. That's not to say they don't produce fruit, but many of them never see it. They might plant a seed that someone down the road would water, and someone else farther down the road would fertilize. Years later, the seed would actually sprout, and the person who originally planted it might never know. I had a heard a story about a man who explained salvation to a woman and gave her a tract to read. She wasn't interested and tossed it aside. He thought the story ended there. But he found out many years later that someone else, who was listening to him talk to that woman, asked her for that tract and became saved as a result.

I was realizing that while the kind of missionary work I thought I came here to do was important, there were other ways of serving that were just as important. Everyone has gifts to give, and while some people operate much more behind the scenes than others, they are no less important. I thought this was a valuable lesson to share with people, as I got the chance.

There were also passages about dealing with adversity, and these

I read hungrily. The trials and tribulations I'd had since I'd been here were taking on a new significance, in the light of the Scriptures I was reading now.

"All discipline for the moment seems not to be joyful, but sorrowful; yet to those who have been trained by it, afterward it yields the peaceful fruit of righteousness" (Hebrews 12:11). This passage told me that while hard times might be painful, our loving Father has a reason for everything He allows to happen to us.

"Every good thing is bestowed and every perfect gift is from above, coming down from the Father of lights, with whom there is no variation, or shifting shadow" (James 1:17). From this I learned that our Father is perfect, and everything He does is perfect. Everything that happens to us, even things we think are freak coincidences or accidents, are things He allows to happen, and they are all for a reason.

1 Peter 5:6-10, spoke loudly to me: "Humble yourselves, therefore, under the mighty hand of God, that He may exalt you at the proper time, casting all your anxiety upon Him, because He cares about you. Be of sober spirit, be on the alert. Your adversary, the devil, prowls about like a roaring lion, seeking someone to devour. But resist him, firm in your faith, knowing that the same experiences of suffering are being accomplished by your brethren who are in the world. And after you have suffered for a little while, the God of all grace, who called you to His eternal glory in Christ, will Himself perfect, confirm, strengthen, and establish you."

This passage reminded me of what Bob Hall and Charles Chandler had warned me about. Looking back, I could pin many of the bad things that had happened directly on the devil and his forces. They had been trying hard to scare me away or make things so hard for me that I would want to leave. What could little me—insignificant me—have to do that would threaten them so much? Maybe it was something I was supposed to do now or maybe it was fruit that would be borne in the future as a result of what was happening here. I did not know, but I was determined to stay the course and do my part in God's will.

54

Working in the hospital was illuminating. While Will West had told me endlessly about some of the miseries of life here in Nome, I'd not actually seen them firsthand until now. Hospital work brought these miseries to my attention in a new and stark way, and I saw exactly what Will had been talking about since the first day I'd met him.

Every morning an influx of people arrived with various degrees of frostbite. Almost always, they were people who slept on the streets. When a person has a high amount of alcohol in his system, he is protected, to a degree, from freezing to death. That protection does not extend to his extremities. Just as Jack Barker lost the tips of his ears to frostbite, I saw case after case where alcoholics lost hands, feet, even arms and legs.

This time of year was also the worst for abuse. The days were still almost completely dark, except for a very brief period of twilight in the afternoons. People went stir crazy, and their spouses and children paid the price. I saw numerous children with broken bones and bad bruises. Twice, Thomas' father brought him in with new injuries. Thomas continued to maintain that they were accidents. Never could I sway him from that story.

The worst, though, was early one morning at the end of February. I had just arrived at work minutes before, and Malina and Tasha were standing in my doorway saying good morning. I was expressing relief that the two bad months were almost over.

"You got that right," said Malina. "This year was a bad one, but I've seen worse."

"This year was bad?"

"Yes, it was for sure. It was colder, and darker, and windier, and people got crazier."

I shuddered to think what the "worse" winters she'd seen must have been like. Then over Malina's shoulder I saw the emergency room door open and Missy and Atka rush in pushing a wheelchair. They streaked in the other direction, down the opposite hall.

"Excuse me," I said to Malina and ran after them. I caught up just as they reached an examining cubby.

"Hey, Missy, hey Atka," I said breathlessly. "What's going on? Who's hurt or sick?"

"It's my dad," Atka said, tears rolling down his cheeks. "We went looking for him this morning. Something just told us. And . . ." He couldn't continue.

"Missy?" I took both their hands.

"He was so cold and stiff." She sobbed and latched onto my hand as if it were a lifeline. "I can't imagine anyone being that cold and surviving. I feel so bad."

"I work here. Let me get you some help." And with that I dashed off in search of a doctor. Our tiny Nome hospital was good, but it was an outpost and few doctors chose to be here. Even fewer were in the hospital at any given time. After about five minutes, I snagged the only one on duty between patients and persuaded him to see Robert next.

I returned to Missy and found her adjusting the blankets around her husband. I put my arm around her. "He's coming. Can I get you anything?" She shook her head wordlessly, rocking, staring into space. I changed tacks and decided to get her talking.

"What happened? Why did you feel like you needed to go looking for him?"

She took a ragged breath. "He's been coming home and trying to get me to take him back. I always tell him I'll take him back when he stops drinking. I thought that was best for all of us, so I never gave in. He just can't stop, so he goes away again.

"Last night it was worse. He seemed more upset. When he left, it was just different somehow. We were worried about him all night. This morning we decided to go find him. Something just told us he needed us. Maybe if we'd left sooner . . ." She broke down again and buried her face in her hands.

"Missy." She looked up, tears streaming. "You went after him. You found him. If he has a chance now, it's because of you."

She choked back a sob and turned back to the wheelchair, looking lost and helpless. She needed something to do, I decided.

"Come on guys, let's get him on the gurney and start warming him up while we wait for the doctor." We slid the man, covers and all, onto the gurney and began rubbing his arms, legs, feet and hands vigorously. His extremities were, literally, like ice. He would be fortunate to keep them all, if he lived. Little Atka worked hard on his father, looking tearfully relieved to have some way to help.

Then we got to his head, and the cover fell off. No. It couldn't be. The man on the gurney was Robert Wallace. His face was bluish and expressionless, but it was unmistakably Robert.

"This is your husband?" I asked Missy in a choked voice.

"Yes."

"I know him too. He's been coming to see me to ask questions about Jesus and salvation. I've bought some of his artwork."

"Really?" The tears began to stream again. "Really? You've talked to him? You've helped him?"

"I've tried my best. He's important to me too."

The doctor arrived then, and while he examined Robert I took Atka out in the waiting area and sat with him.

"I feel so bad." He leaned against my shoulder. I put an arm around him.

"Why do you feel bad? You found him. You're helping him."

"I said just the other day I wished he'd stay away. I didn't mean it! If we hadn't sent him away, he'd be okay."

"Maybe, for now. But your mom is right. It's way better for everyone if he quits drinking. She's doing all she can do to make him quit, and she's absolutely right."

"Even if it hurts him?"

"Sometimes that's what it takes. Hopefully he'll be okay and this will be a lesson for him, and he'll quit."

"You think so?"

"I don't know, Atka. I don't know how bad it is. Let's just say a prayer for him and for your family."

"And you, too. He is your friend too, Mark."

"Yes, he is. Now let's pray."

"Father," I began, "Atka and his family need You right now. They are hurting, with their husband and dad in bad shape. He is my friend too, and we are all scared. Be with us, Father God. Give us Your strength in this tough time. Be with Robert, and the doctor right now. And help us to see that whatever happens, You are in control and You love us. In Jesus' name, amen."

I hugged Atka closer and sat silently, thinking, tears rolling down my face too. Atka and his mom were beating themselves up, thinking that if they hadn't sent him away last night, he'd be alive. I was having my own guilty pains. Maybe I'd been enabling his alcoholism by buying those skins. I knew now that there was a high probability that he'd bought liquor, not food, with the money I'd given him. Maybe if I hadn't done that, he would have been forced to seek real, sincere help. I added silently to my original prayer, "Dear Lord, please help Robert live. I don't think he's accepted You yet, and I don't want him to go to hell. Please help him live so I can try again to help him. In Christ's name, amen."

Atka and I sat quietly for a few more minutes, then Atka spoke in a voice so soft I could barely hear him. "You were telling my dad about Jesus?"

"Yes."

"How did you meet him?"

"I was doing a service at the jail, and he was there."

"Do you think he listened to you? Do you think he's saved?"

"I really don't know." This was an honest answer, as Robert could have changed his mind and prayed a prayer for salvation at any time. I'd been through it with him, so he knew what to do. He hadn't done it with me, but that didn't mean he hadn't done it. I hoped fervently that he had. "I've spent a good bit of time with him, explaining things and answering his questions."

"I hope he's saved."

"Me too."

Just then the curtain to Robert's cubby was pulled aside, and the doctor came out with Missy. She was crying. That, and the doctor's face, told me all I needed to know. I reached for Atka, but it was too late. He, too, had seen the truth in his mother's tears.

"No!" he screamed and ran into the cubby where his father lay. I ran after him and found him climbing up onto the bed with his father.

"Daddy, Daddy, please wake up," he cried, his tears falling on his father's face. "We'll take better care of you. We'll help you. We'll never send you away again. We'll be a family. Daddy. Daddy!"

I leaned over to put my arms around both of them. The dam broke inside me and I sobbed too, holding Atka and his father. Did I try hard enough? Did I give up too quickly? Was this truly God's will, that Robert never come to Him? No, it wasn't. God doesn't want anyone to be lost. It was the thought that I hadn't done all I could, that I'd somehow missed some opportunity with Robert, that was killing me now. If I was the one who'd been appointed to reach him, I'd failed.

Or maybe Will was right. Maybe some people are just hopeless, lost causes. They have to want to be helped before you can help them. How do you decide when to quit trying? Robert was more interested in getting me to buy a skin so he could have his next drink than he was in really listening to what I had to say and giving his life to the Lord.

Will. My heart sank. I'd never told him about Robert's visits to my apartment and the skins I'd bought from him. I knew he'd be upset that Robert was gone, and he'd also be disappointed that I hadn't heeded his advice. His direction had been crystal clear—steer clear of Robert Wallace. I hadn't listened.

*　　*　　*

The next few days provided an education in a whole new area. I found out what happens in Nome when a person dies.

There was a town cemetery, but you couldn't dig a hole when the ground was frozen. At the edge of town there was a metal box that looked like a box car with the opening at the end. Into that box went all the people who died during the cold months. When the ground thawed in the spring, they would open that box and bury all the corpses that had accumulated there. Robert was the latest addition.

It seemed wrong to simply put his body in the container on top of dozens of others, but that was the way it was done in Nome.

I was right about how Will would react. I saw him at the dog yard the next Saturday and told him about it. He shook his head. "I was afraid of this. I really wish he had let me help him, but he was more concerned with his next drink than his own soul. He didn't want to be helped."

"I tried too," I confessed.

"You did? How?"

"He was at the jail the second time I went, and I thought it was God's way of putting him in my path. I thought I was the one who could help him. I see now that was a prideful, wrong way to think."

"Was that the only time you saw him?" Will's eyes were watching my every movement.

I really did not want to tell him this part, but now I had no choice. I would not lie. "No. I told him he could come by my apartment any time and I'd try to answer his questions."

"Oh, Mark. Didn't you hear anything I said?" Will's normally soft voice came with some volume.

"I heard. But I couldn't not try."

He studied me for a moment and relit his pipe. "I guess I can understand that. I would have felt the same way. Did you learn anything from this?"

"You know how some people in the Bible just won't seem to understand and see what's right in front of them? It's like they don't want to."

"Sure."

"Those passages make a lot more sense now." I told him about the times Robert had come over, and I could predict to the second when he would change the subject and ask me to buy a skin.

"You've learned a valuable lesson," Will said. "Always try, and follow where God leads, but realize that not everyone is going to be saved. That's probably the hardest part of being used by God."

"What is?"

"The ones you can't help."

PART 4:
SPRING

55

Everything I'd heard about March in Nome was true. It was still windy and cold, bitterly cold, but we were getting more daylight every day and now I felt a definite excitement in the air as the Iditarod approached. I learned more and more about the great race as the days went on and people around me talked nonstop about nothing else.

I learned that the race began in 1967 as a fifty-six mile sprint event to celebrate the one hundredth anniversary of Alaska becoming a United States territory. A nine-mile section of the historic Iditarod Trail was cleared for the event, which was held only twice, in 1967 and 1969. The entire trail extended from Anchorage to Nome and passed through dozens of villages. There was an actual gold rush town named Iditarod, which didn't exist anymore. In the days of the gold rush, the trail was the only road, and sled dogs the only means of transportation, through Alaska in the winter. Mail and supplies were carried across this trail, and people used it to get from place to place. Priests, ministers and judges traveled between villages via dog team.

When gold mining began to slack off, people began to go back to where they came from and there was far less travel on the Iditarod Trail. The use of the airplane in the late 1920s signaled the beginning of the end for the dog team as a standard mode of transportation, and of course with the airplane carrying the mail, there was less need for land travel. The final blow to the use of the dog team came with the appearance of snowmobiles and eventually four-wheelers in Alaska.

By the mid-1960s, most people in Alaska didn't even know there was an Iditarod Trail or that dog teams had played a very important part in Alaska's early settlement. Two people named Dorothy Page and Joe Redington didn't want to see history die so easily. They came up with the idea of the sprint race, and expanded it to the modern thousand-mile race beginning in 1973.

The other things I was hearing were hard to believe. In a few days, the tiny town I was used to would be bursting with people. Festivities here would begin when the race started in Anchorage. There would be snowmobile races and various sled-pulling events featuring strong dogs flown in just for this purpose. Local dogs would participate, too, just for the fun of it. There was only one hotel, the Nome Nugget, and it had been booked for years in advance for these two weeks. For everyone else, Nome folks opened their homes to total strangers and people bedded down in every square foot. The Lighthouse would be opened for people to sleep. Churches housed people and handed out hot drinks and soups. The saloons would do an even better business than usual. And the hospital, of course, would be extra busy.

Our goal had been to have the Nome Baptist Family Center finished before the Iditarod events began. We had planned to have our first service the first Sunday in March. I was still honoring Denise's wishes not to go near the church, which for the last six weeks had meant I had to find another place to worship on Sundays. I visited other churches in town and renewed relationships with missionaries at those places, and made some new friends as well. All Christian denominations are slightly different in styles of worship and nuances of their beliefs, but they all share the core belief of salvation. I visited the Bible Baptist Church, the Nome Church of the Nazarene, the Nome Covenant Church, and St. Joseph Catholic Church. Even at the Catholic church, where the style of worship was markedly different, I found like-minded Christians.

Spending time at other churches opened my eyes in ways that wouldn't have happened had I simply gone to our church week after week. It was refreshing to see that on the mission field denominational differences take a back seat to the core message of Jesus and His atonement for man. Again, here was an example of the Lord using what seemed like misfortune for good.

Although I hadn't been inside our church since early January, I couldn't stop myself from walking past every couple of days to see the progress. The church had been looking finished for quite a while. I did not dare go inside to check it out.

The day before the first service was scheduled, I saw Will at the dog yard. When I walked up he was examining Sitka, holding the big dog's feet up one at a time and looking closely at his pads.

"Hey there, Will," I greeted him. "Something wrong with Sitka's feet?"

He put the dog's back left foot back on the ground and patted him on the head. "No, just checking them out. I think I'm going to let him try the dog pull next week."

"Dog pull?"

"That's where they harness wheel dogs up one at a time and have them start big loads moving by themselves. It's something to see."

I rubbed Sitka's ears. "He'll do a good job at that. He's the strongest dog I've ever seen."

"If I'm going to run the Iditarod next year, it's good to know exactly what he can do."

We worked together silently for a few minutes, getting the dogs fed and harnessed for their exercise. I considered and discarded several ways to ask Will what I wanted to know. Finally I decided on the casual approach.

"Say, I noticed the other day that the church looks like it's pretty much finished."

"Yep, it's really close."

"Think it'll be ready on schedule?"

"It won't be quite ready, but we're going to have church there tomorrow anyway." He looked up from harnessing the dogs. "I know it's hard for you."

I abandoned the casual approach. "Will, I'd really like to be there for the first service. You know how hard I worked on that building."

"I know. No one worked any harder than you."

"Does that mean I can come?"

He was silent for so long that I thought he wasn't going to answer. "That's a tough one, Mark. You know how Denise feels, and she will definitely be there. I don't want things to be unpleasant."

"What if I get there late and just stay in the back?"

He thought a while longer. "That might work, especially if you don't come for Sunday school. Denise will be taking care of the kids during the service. If you stay in the back of the worship center, you should be okay."

"Thanks, Will," I said with feeling as I harnessed Snickers. "I'll keep low. I promise. Also, I have an idea about another ministry I want to run past you. Would it help for us to set up a patrol of Front Street where all the saloons are if it is really cold? I'm thinking we might find some guys like Robert staggering or passed out and help them get to shelter for the night."

Will nodded and said that was an excellent idea. Grinning widely, I climbed on the runners and yelled "Hike," and the dogs and I headed off across the tundra. Zipping along with the snow crunching in my ears and the wind in my face, I was so glad I hadn't let the incident with the puppy make me give up mushing the dogs.

This day was perfect. The dogs were happy and the sky was clear. We actually had bright sunshine. Such a huge change from exercising the dogs in those winter days when there was almost no daylight. Tomorrow I'd be attending church in a building I built with my own hands. The actual Iditarod race started one thousand miles away in Anchorage this morning, and festivities would start here next week. They'd continue until the mushers started coming in, and I'd get to see what all the fuss was about. By the time the race was over around the end of March, I'd be down to my last nine weeks here.

The end was in sight. I couldn't wait to see what happened next.

56

It was a surreal experience when I arrived at church. Cars, snowmobiles, and snowshoes were everywhere. It was quite a change from the scene I'd seen here since last summer, with mud and pickup trucks surrounding the building. Now, the church stood bright and new, welcoming worshipers for the first time.

It was eleven o'clock on the dot when I stepped quietly through the front door and slid into a chair at the back. The worship center was one big room with the baptismal tank at the front. Will stood behind a podium to the left of the baptismal and welcomed worshipers to the inaugural service in the new church. He caught sight of me as I edged into a chair and nodded slightly. I glanced around, didn't see Denise, and relaxed a little. Maybe I could actually enjoy the service.

I sat in awe and wonder. I thought back on when I first got here, less than a year ago, and the land where this building now sat was a junky lot full of old decrepit buildings. We'd cleaned those buildings out, torn them down, and put up the skeleton of this place of worship. We'd wondered at times how we were going to get it all done, but God was always there and had someone ready to step in and make it happen. Never had we thought anything else. We knew He would provide, and He had.

My attention sprang back to Will and what he was saying.

"There are so many thanks that go out to everyone who had a part in making this building a reality. First of all, let's give thanks to the Lord, because He has blessed our work and helped us get it finished."

Will went on to thank James Vaughn and his family; Don and

Mona Sanders, who sat near the front, quietly beaming; George Allen, who stood near the back, looking like he'd never been in church before, which perhaps he hadn't; and Matthew Hawkins, the Texas millionaire who'd rescued us when our money ran out. To my surprise, Matthew sat on the front row and accepted Will's thanks with a gracious nod.

"Last, I want to thank the two missionaries who left their families last summer to come up here and help us make our vision a reality. Those two young men were Barry Watkins and Mark Smith. Barry's gone home to Texas now, but Mark is still here and he's sitting on the back row this morning. Mark, thank you."

Shocked, I nodded to all the people who turned around and thanked me. I thought I was supposed to be hiding, here on the back row. What would Denise say about Will's publicly acknowledging me? She was bound to find out. Maybe Will had decided enough was enough, and this was his way of going on from here. I hoped so.

I spent the rest of the service alternately listening to Will and taking a trip down memory lane. I looked at the huge beam crossing the entire length of the church and remembered all the sweat, and extra help, it had taken to get it hoisted into place. I looked at the baptismal and remembered ripping out the front wall while the crane sat with the tank suspended in mid-air, waiting. There were memories associated with every board and nail. Worshiping in a church I'd helped build was one of the most rewarding things I'd ever done.

When Will stepped forward for the invitational at the end of the service, I slipped out the door and started walking home. No sense borrowing trouble, which would certainly happen if Denise finished with the kids and came out to find me there. Much better to leave while I could.

I had only gotten about half a block away when I heard a voice calling my name. I turned to look. It was James Vaughn. He came trotting up to me, as usual in such outstanding shape he wasn't even panting.

"Will asked me to see if you'd hang around for a minute. He's got something he wants to talk to you about."

"Okay. Where does he want me to wait?"

"In his office."

I waited for about fifteen minutes, and Will came in with a smile on his face.

"So, what did you think?"

"I thought it was amazing, and I'm so glad I came. I was surprised you pointed me out, though. I thought I was supposed to be hiding back there. What if Denise finds out?"

"She will, and it's time she got over it. She doesn't have to be around you if she doesn't want to, but I need you."

"You do?"

He sat in his chair, leaned back and steepled his fingers. "We're about to go into the biggest ministry time of the year. Our population here is usually only about two thousand. It will be probably ten thousand over the next couple of weeks. I need people here at the church, others to be at the Lighthouse, others to staff the group home, others on the street handing out food and drinks and inviting people to church, and probably a bunch of other things I'm not even thinking about right now. I need every pair of hands I can get. You, specifically, I need to help head up some of our efforts as a church. I liked your idea of helping drunks off the street. It really could save a life."

"Head it up?" I repeated stupidly. This wasn't something I'd remotely considered.

"Yes. Will you direct the ministry team for the street alcoholics?"

"Of course I will. You'll take care of Denise?"

"I will."

"Then I'll see about working it out at my job. My boss can be pretty unreasonable."

"Susan?"

"Yes."

"I know Susan pretty well. Let me talk to her."

"I do need the money I make at work. I can't take the time off without pay."

"You let me worry about that."

"If you can fix that, then you've got yourself a helper for whatever you need. I am all in."

57

Will was as good as his word. Susan called me into her office the next day and told me gruffly that I now had the next three weeks off with pay to help out her good friend Will West.

"You do a good job for him, you hear?" she said to me, as if I was going to work for someone I didn't know. I held my tongue. Let her think whatever she wanted.

"I will, and thanks for working it out so I could do this. I'm looking forward to seeing what all the fuss is about."

"I just can't wait to hear all about it when you come back." Her voice dripped with sarcasm.

I went immediately to find Will and tell him I was his for three weeks.

I found him in his office, about to head for the Lighthouse.

"Whatever you said to Susan worked, because you've got yourself a full-time helper for the next three weeks. Where do you want me?"

"For now, go over to the town square. You should make it in time for the mayor's welcome. Lily Vaughn is setting up a table to pass out hot drinks. Work with her this morning and come to the Lighthouse after lunch. I have a job in mind for you."

I jogged the short distance to the town square and arrived in time to hear the mayor welcome the crowds. Usually only a couple dozen people, at most, roamed the square. Today hundreds, maybe even thousands, milled about. The mayor, Leo Rasmussen, stood on a stage. He was a robust man with an enthusiastic, booming voice.

"Welcome to Nome!" he thundered. "My wife, Erna, and I welcome you to our town and hope you see nothing but warmth and hospitality during your stay here for The Last Great Race!" He waited for applause to die down before he continued. "It will be hospitality like you've never seen before. We don't have many hotel rooms, but our citizens open their homes to our guests to make them feel welcome. If at any time you don't feel welcome, you come and tell me about it!"

The crowd laughed appreciatively. Mayor Rasmussen went on to explain that the mushers had, hours ago, left Anchorage. In the days to come, while we waited for the teams to arrive, daily events and festivities would take place here in Nome.

"I hope you enjoy yourselves and, again, welcome to our city."

Although I'd lived here since last June, I'd never met the mayor. I stepped to the bottom of the stage.

"Hi, Mayor Rasmussen, I'm Mark Smith." I held out my hand.

"Hello, Mr. Smith. Welcome to Nome. Are you here just for the Iditarod?"

"Not exactly. I've been here since June, working with Will West on the new church. I'll be going back home in June."

He seemed a bit surprised that we had not met. "Where's home?"

"Tennessee."

"Tennessee! Erna, come here." He beckoned to his wife to join him. Slim, dark and petite, she made her way to his side. "This young man is from Tennessee. What was the name of the town we visited a few years ago?"

"Townsend," she supplied in a voice that sang sharply of New Jersey. "The Great Smoky Mountains are beautiful."

What a small world. Townsend was just thirty minutes from Maryville. When I mentioned my home town I always carefully articulate for the benefit of out-of-towners, but she stopped me. "I believe it is pronounced *mur-vul*," she said with a near perfect slow Southern drawl. I was impressed. I spent an enjoyable few minutes talking about East Tennessee with the Rasmussens, then excused myself to find Lily Vaughn. She and Connie were tearing their hair out, handing out hot drinks as fast as they could pour them. I jumped in and helped, and the hours flew by. Finally, the crowd was attracted to the other side of the square when the snowmobile races began, and we all collapsed in exhausted heaps.

I relaxed for a moment on the ground, then checked my watch and leaped back to my feet. "Holy cow, it's nearly noon. I have to go find Will. He has a job for me."

I wove my way through the crowds and headed in the direction of the Lighthouse. For the first time, I understood what everyone had meant when they talked about the crowds of the Iditarod. The slow little town I was used to was now the center of the sports world, and people were everywhere. A walk that usually took me perhaps ten minutes now took me twenty, and I burst through the doors of the Lighthouse about twelve-thirty.

Will looked up from what he was doing. "How was it?"

"Incredible. I understand now what everybody meant about the big crowds."

He grinned. "You haven't seen anything yet. This is only about half as crowded as it will be."

I gawked. "Half?"

"Maybe half. Maybe less. There won't be room to walk."

"Incredible. What job do you have for me?"

He settled himself in his chair and leaned forward. "You know the Iditarod is our biggest ministry time. We hand out hot drinks and soups, give out literature, invite people to church, and put up about a hundred people at the Lighthouse and the church. The backbone of the ministry is the volunteers on the street who do all the face-to-face interactions."

I nodded, and he went on.

"We have fifty volunteers, all really good people. Right now they're scattered to the four winds, all doing their own thing. I need one person to manage their tasks and their schedules. I'd like you to take that on."

"Okay." I nodded again and swallowed hard. "I can handle that. In addition to the street alcoholic ministry?"

"Yes, in addition to that." Will gave me a list of all the volunteers and the jobs that needed to be done. "It's all yours. God help you. I've scheduled a meeting of all the volunteers here at five o'clock. That gives you a few hours to get your arms around it."

"You scheduled a meeting already? You were pretty sure I'd take the job, weren't you?"

"I wasn't worried at all," he said with a grin.

I took the lists and spread them out on the kitchen table. I knew a lot of these people, and Will was right, they were good-hearted Christians who wanted to serve. I matched the people with jobs and posted a preliminary schedule. The volunteers started to straggle in about four-thirty and made themselves comfortable until everyone was there. True to "Alaska time," there were still folks coming in at the very end of our meeting. I introduced myself and told them what my job was.

"You're at the core of this ministry, and it won't work without you. I've made a schedule, and posted it over there." I gestured. "Take a look and see what you think."

The people found their names, jobs, and schedule on the list. Immediately many of them wanted to switch hours or jobs with someone else. That was okay, as long as I knew who was doing what.

"No problem." I sorted all the changes out. "Just give me a minute." I made the changes, then made copies of the new schedules and handed them out. "Now that it's posted, there won't be any more changes unless there's an emergency. If there is, come directly to me. We are counting on every one of you. Thank you for serving in this ministry."

Will had been standing at the back of the room watching all this, and when everyone left he came up to me. "You handled that great. When most everyone wanted to change jobs on the schedule, I would have thrown my hands up."

"That's why I gave them a chance to participate. Now they all have their own copy, and they helped make the schedule. They can't really complain about it now."

He stared at me. "Brilliant."

58

For the next three weeks I was completely immersed in the Iditarod. My fifty volunteers and I had an absolute blast roaming the streets of Nome, relating to people who came to town for this event. We met people from across the globe, all of whom came to our little town to experience "The Last Great Race." Will was right. It was a priceless ministry opportunity and one we absolutely had to take advantage of.

Sixty dog teams left Anchorage, and day by day teams were scratched for a variety of reasons. The course had been cleared, but it might not have stayed cleared. Even if it did, it was rugged arctic wilderness. There could be issues with supplies sent to checkpoints, sleds, dogs' feet, even encounters with moose, bears, and other wildlife. Mushers had to finish the race with the same dogs they started with; no new ones could be added after the race started. They could start with as many as sixteen dogs, but no fewer than twelve. They had to have at least six in the traces at the finish.

Mushers also had to take mandatory breaks. One was twenty-four hours, and this could be taken whenever they wished or needed to take it. Two eight-hour breaks were also required at specific locations.

Since the race began in 1973, times had gotten faster and faster. The first two winners had taken more than twenty days to complete the course. Since then, two had done it in fourteen days. It would be interesting to see what the winning time was this year. The winner would take home a prize of twelve thousand dollars. This race was the number one sport in Alaska and one of the top events in the world.

After the teams left Anchorage, people in Nome amused themselves by shopping, keeping up with the teams' progress and participating in events in town. Front Street turned into an impromptu shopping center, with booths and tables lining the street. Every native in the area had worked for months on crafts and other items to sell to the tourists. Some depended on this as their only income, and they actually did well enough to live on this all year round. Many booths offered figures carved from ivory. Others had smoked and dried salmon. I walked along looking at the offerings and marveling at the natives' creativity. As I walked, I found Atka and his mother at one of the tables.

"Hey, you two. What are you up to?"

Atka gestured to the items on the table. "We found a bunch of Dad's art that he hadn't sold yet. I know what he'd be doing if he were here, so we decided to follow in his footsteps."

"That's a great tribute to him. How's it going?"

"Terrific," Missy said. "There were about two hundred skins, and we've sold all but about twenty. People are paying a good price. I'm going to put the money away for the boys' future—kind of a gift from their dad. I think Robert would have liked that."

"If they're going that fast, I better grab one now," I said. "What do you have left?"

I chose two very large ones with really nice detail work. One pictured a large moose with huge antlers eating on the tundra, while the other had a walrus floating on an iceberg. All the other skins I'd bought were gifts, but these two would be mine to treasure.

My volunteers were very easy to work with. They were mostly church members, all excited to be here and doing important work. At a brief meeting at the Lighthouse each morning, I briefed them on the day ahead, led them in a devotion and prayer, and passed out supplies. We discussed how the race was going, the weather forecast, and whatever other topics the volunteers brought up. Then we scattered for the day's work, roaming the streets and the town square throughout the day. It warmed my heart to see how much my volunteers loved what they were doing.

At first I wondered where we would get all the soups and drinks we were passing out. Will reported that Denise and other ladies were in their kitchens nonstop making soups for the hungry, cold crowds. Their barge order last year had included hundreds of boxes of instant chocolate, coffee, and cider, which made hot drinks easy.

The things I'd heard before the race, about people cramming into every square foot to sleep, turned out to be completely true. The Lighthouse and the church were jammed. The Leos allowed the common areas of the group home to be used for sleeping as well.

Besides the snowmobile races, which went on every day, there were events called "Strongest Dog" pulls. One dog was harnessed to a loaded sled that was stuck in the ice. Sleds had different loads, with varying weights. On command, the dog hurled himself into his traces to break the sled loose from the ice. It often took several tries, with the dog twisting and lunging in different directions and in the air. The dog had to break the sled loose and get it moving. The dog who succeeded with the heaviest load, in the quickest time, won the competition.

I was particularly interested in watching Sitka. Will took a break from his work to come to the square and handle his dog. Sitka was entered in the heaviest weight group, mainly to see how he stacked up against the others. I helped Will hook him up and make sure everything looked right. When it was time for Sitka to compete, I just watched.

Will finished inspecting everything, stepped back, and took a deep breath. "Hike!" he shouted.

Immediately Sitka lunged against the traces. The heavily loaded sled didn't budge. The big dog gathered himself again and leaped into the air, lunging and twisting. Still no movement. The third time he backed up to the sled and bolted to the end of the traces. The sled began to quiver. By the fifth time it began breaking free with shudders and cracks of breaking ice. Then Sitka hunched his shoulders and easily got the sled moving across the snow. He didn't win the competition, but he proved that he stacked up just fine against the best wheel dogs in the world.

I went up to them to congratulate them and found Will talking to a young woman.

"Great job, Sitka!" I scratched his ears.

"Mark, I want you to meet someone," said Will. "This is Mary Shields."

I'd done my homework in recent days, and I knew exactly who Mary Shields was. In 1974, the second year of the race, she'd paved the way for female mushers by becoming the first woman to finish the Iditarod.

"It's an honor to meet you." I held out my hand. "I'm surprised you aren't somewhere between Anchorage and Nome right now."

She laughed and shook my hand. "I'll probably be doing that next year. I didn't have all the dogs I wanted for this year, and that's why I'm here. I was hoping to fill in some gaps on my team. That's what Will and I were just talking about."

The light dawned. Will and Mary were standing near Sitka, looking him over and talking earnestly.

"Are you going to sell Sitka, Will?"

"That's what Mary wanted to know, but no. I'll need him next year. I am willing to breed him to one of her dogs, though. Maybe we could reach an agreement on the puppies."

"I think we could work that out," Mary said. "I'll have to keep looking for an adult dog for my team, but I'd really like to have some Sitka pups."

As the race went on, more and more mushers were scratched. Where sixty had begun, there were only fifty left after the first seven days. Ten more dropped out in the next three days. Ten days in, only forty mushers were still on the course.

Four days later, on Sunday, about nine o'clock at night, Front Street was its usual lively self when the sound of a siren split the air. People looked at each other, startled. The fastest Iditarod time to date had been fourteen days and fourteen hours. This was seven hours quicker than that. We were about to see history. Everyone stampeded to the arch to watch the winner come in. Under the arch they ran, a man bundled in furs, with his tired but valiant dogs pulling his sled at a good steady pace. The dogs' feet were all covered with some kind of protective booties. The public address system announced the winner—Joe May, with a time of fourteen days, seven hours, eleven minutes and fifty-one seconds.

For the next hours and days, the siren went off over and over again. Even after my three weeks ran out and I had to go back to work at the hospital, the sirens continued to sound. The Iditarod was not considered over as long as there was even one musher left on the trail. Whenever one came in, no matter the time of the day or night, the siren sounded and hundreds of people lined the street to welcome and cheer on the new arrival.

Only thirty-three of the original sixty mushers finished the race. The last musher, a Nome woman named Connie Moore, arrived with a time of twenty-four days, nine hours, twenty-five minutes and fourteen seconds. The last person to finish the race each year receives the Red Lantern award, a symbol of toughness and resiliency. When Connie arrived, a lamp known as the Widow's Lamp was extinguished. Traditionally, this lamp is lit on the first day of the race. It remains on the arch, still lit, until the last musher arrives.

The 1980 Iditarod was in the books.

59

The first Monday after the Iditarod was over, I had just arrived home from work and was debating what to have for supper. As I peered into the refrigerator, willing something appetizing to magically appear, I heard a knock at my door. Hoping it was some kind soul with a plate of food, I crossed to the door and opened it. There stood Will West, his ubiquitous hat on his head, his pipe between his teeth, and a steaming bowl in his hands.

"Hi, Mark."

"Hey." I stepped back for him to come in, thinking what a mess the place was. My next thought was that whatever was in the bowl smelled incredible. My stomach growled. Will smiled.

"Brought you something. Mind if we eat it together?"

In short order we were seated at my tiny kitchen table, sopping up moose stew with warm sourdough bread. I nearly whimpered. I hadn't eaten anything this good in weeks, and I knew it could only be Denise's.

"Did you sneak this out for me?" I shoveled in the food nonstop.

"No, she knows." I stared at him, but he kept his eyes on his food and didn't explain further. We ate in silence until we were both stuffed.

"I have something to talk to you about," he began. "Hear me out, please."

"Okay."

"It's been a rough few years for Denise and me. You know it takes a tough person to live here, and even tough people have problems."

I nodded, puzzled.

"The past year and a half or so, it's been even more stressful what with getting ready to build the church and then actually building it. It's been amazing what God has done, but it's been a hard road getting it to this point. Then with Janice and everything else, it's just about broken us. That's a dangerous thing here. You have to stay sharp. I'm losing my focus and being tempted by the very things I'm fighting against."

He sat, hands on his knees, looking at the floor. Then he looked up and into my eyes and took a deep breath.

"Denise and I are burned out, Mark. I'm taking a leave of absence, and we're going away for several weeks."

I didn't know what to say. The silence stretched. "I guess you have to do what you have to do, Will. I hope the break helps."

He looked at me steadily, with a hint of sadness. "You really don't know why I'm telling you this, do you, Mark?"

"No, I don't."

"Someone has to lead the church while I'm gone. I want it to be you. But I wanted to talk to you first, before I mention it to anyone else."

"Me?" I said the first thing that crossed my mind. "I'm not even close to being trained to be a real minister."

"I can recommend anyone I want as interim pastor. The church will appoint a committee and they will make the actual decision, but they'll pick whoever I recommend. It doesn't matter if you're a pastor yet or not. I do have other choices, but I want you."

"Why me?"

"I've been watching you and listening to what people say about you. The kids, the radio station manager, the guys at the jail. Everyone says the same thing. Mark Smith has his heart in the right place, and he's smart as a whip. I gave you two big jobs with the Iditarod to see how you'd handle it. You did amazing. I'm convinced that you saved lives with the street alcoholic ministry, and those volunteers fell right into place and things went smooth as silk."

"This seems completely different."

"It's not. At the core of it, it's dealing with people. You enable them and minister to them however the Lord wants you to. You have that part down pat."

I stared at him, speechless.

"Well? Will you do it? Can I recommend you to the committee?"

I finally untangled my tongue. "When are you leaving?"

"In two weeks. My last Sunday in the pulpit will be April 13. Your first sermon will be April 20."

"Will you help me get up to speed before you leave?"

"Absolutely."

I took a deep breath. What was I getting into? Then I realized clearly that this was another opportunity that the Lord had put into my path for a reason, like the radio station and the jail. I couldn't say no. There would be things He wanted of me in these weeks, things I wouldn't be able to do any other way. And I suddenly knew why I'd recently been led to Scriptures about ministry and leadership. That hadn't been an accident or coincidence.

"Okay," I said. "I'll do it."

60

The next two weeks flew by. Easter Sunday was April 6, the most important day in the Christian faith, and I had something special planned for the Lighthouse kids that Saturday. For weeks, I had been leading up to this day in my Saturday lessons. We'd followed Jesus' ministry in some detail. Using the pictures we could find, we discussed and reenacted some of His miracles and parables. Last week we'd drawn pictures and used felt figures and crayons to illustrate Palm Sunday, when Jesus made His triumphant entry into Jerusalem on the back of a donkey, people laying palm fronds on the ground before Him as He went.

Easter weekend had always affected me differently than most people. For me, Good Friday—why in the world they called it Good Friday was beyond me—was a day of mourning and Easter Sunday a day of celebration. I didn't eat or drink on Good Friday, but stayed inside, meditated and let the dark cloud of despair fully engulf my spirit. Although I knew the day of celebration was coming, I also knew the sin, pride, and worldliness that necessitated our Lord's suffering, punishment, and death. This year I'd had to work, but I'd quietly fasted and prayed in my office.

Today, I wanted to impress on the kids just how important this weekend was. I set the tone as I walked in. I didn't shout for the kids when I came in the door. I shed my gear quietly in the entryway and made my way without fanfare to the kitchen where they were all gathered, having a snack.

"Hi, everyone." They all looked up at me in surprise. Patricia recovered first.

"Well hi, Mark. We didn't hear you come in."

"I was thinking as I came in. I'll tell you all about it when we start our lesson. You ready?"

"Yes!" they chorused.

We sat on the floor in the living room as usual, all the kids in a circle around me and Prissy on my lap.

"Do you guys know what tomorrow is?"

"It's Easter," said Thomas.

"What is Easter? Do you know?"

Darren raised his hand. "It's the day Jesus rose from the dead."

"Good. Let's talk a little more about that, and about what happened before that. Does anybody know what Good Friday is?" No one knew. "Good Friday is the day Christians remember how Jesus suffered and died on the cross. His friends and followers didn't help Him and soldiers drove nails into His wrists and ankles to hang Him on a wooden cross, then they watched Him die. Ernie, come here."

Ernie came forward and I stretched him out on the floor. "They put nails here" . . . I showed them the tender spots on Ernie's wrists where the nails went in . . . "and here." I gently touched the places on Ernie's feet where Jesus let the soldiers nail Him to the cross. "They held Him down, hammered in the nails, and they lifted the cross up so He was hanging by those nails. God was watching from heaven while His Son was being tortured and killed. How hard do you think that was for Him to watch?"

"Pretty hard," said Kim. "My mom can't stand it when I get hurt. She always says she wants to take the pain away."

"I'm pretty sure that's how God felt, too. But He couldn't take the pain away or all of this would have been for nothing. He had sent His only Son to take our punishment. If He'd rescued Him, like I'm sure He wanted to, we still wouldn't have any way to get saved. And the Bible tells us that Jesus could have called angels to help Him whenever He wanted, but He obeyed His Father and let it happen without resisting at all.

"Finally, there came a point when God couldn't stand to watch. There was His Son, hanging on the cross, in so much pain, with a crown of really long, sharp thorns on His head making it bleed. Any parent would want to help. But since He couldn't, He finally turned His face away. Do you know what happened then?"

"What?" I sent Patricia an imperceptible nod, a signal she'd been watching for. And the room went pitch black. The boys gasped. The girls squealed.

"That's what happened. The whole world went dark when God turned His face away from His Son. The world was completely dark for three hours. Jesus cried out to His Father and said, 'My God, My God, why have You forsaken me?' He was asking why His Father had turned away from Him. And then Jesus said, 'It is finished,' and he died. There was a big, thick curtain in the temple. Thirty feet tall, and it all of a sudden ripped completely in two. The earth shook, the rocks split, and all the saints who'd already died came out of their graves and roamed around town.

"Can you imagine?" The lights winked back on. "Can you imagine? Think about it. One person dies here in town, and the sun goes away, and the earth shakes, and the dead people in the cemetery come back to life and start walking around."

"That would be creepy," Atka said. "And scary."

"Think how scary it would be if you were one of the ones who killed Jesus. Some people, including the soldiers who killed Him, realized right then that Jesus really was the Son of God. But by then He was already dead.

"So Jesus died and His body was put into a tomb, which is like a cave made out of rock. They rolled a huge stone in front of the door to keep everybody out. And the police put guards in front of the tomb and put a seal on the stone in front of the door. They wanted to make sure no one stole the body."

"Tell us about when He came back to life," said Paul.

"I'm getting to that. So, all His disciples were pretty sad. They'd been with Him for three years, day and night, and all of a sudden He was gone. After all He'd said to them about how He was going to die and be raised from the dead, they still didn't understand and were very sad.

"Then Sunday morning some women went to the tomb with some spices. After a body has been dead for a while, it starts to smell.

The spices were to cover up the bad smell. But when they got there, they saw that the stone was rolled away from the entrance to the tomb. They went in and saw a young man, wearing a white robe. The place where Jesus' body had been was empty, and the cloths that had covered His body were lying there folded neatly on the bench. The young man turned out to be an angel, and he told them that Jesus had risen from the dead.

"Now, let's imagine. You watch your friend die, so you know he's dead. A couple of days later you go to his grave, and you find that his body isn't there. Some guy tells you your friend has come back from being dead. How would you feel?"

"I'd be happy," Atka said. "If it was my dad, I'd be really happy."

"Uh-unh," said Ernie. "I'd be scared. I'd run. That kind of thing just does not happen."

"That's exactly what the women did. They left the tomb and went back to town, scared to death. They didn't tell anyone. The only one who said anything was Mary Magdalene, and she told the disciples. They didn't believe it until Jesus appeared to them Himself. He stayed around for forty days, suddenly showing up in person to lots of people—hundreds—so there could be no doubt. That's how we know for a fact that He really did rise from the dead. Then He told them to spread the word about Him to all the world, and went up to heaven."

"Why didn't people believe it when He came back from the dead?" asked Darren. "He told them He would, so why didn't they expect it?"

"I've always wondered that myself. I guess it wasn't something people even thought about, for someone to come back from the dead. They watched Him die, and then He was dead and in the grave for days. I'm sure they thought it was all over.

"The point for us is that when Jesus died on that cross, He took the punishment for our sins, all the bad things we do—on Himself. He lived a perfect life. He never had a nasty thought, never did anything wrong. Because He lived a perfect life, He was able to take the punishment for our sins so we don't have to. We all do bad things and deserve to go to hell when we die, but He took that punishment for us. That's how much He loves us. Is there anyone, anyone at all, in this world that you love that much, that you'd go through all of that for them? If we believe in Him and what He did for us we can go to heaven when we die to be with Him forever."

"I believe it," said Paul.

"Me, too," said Thomas.

I looked around. "Does anyone want to pray right now, to tell Jesus you believe in Him and accept Him into your life? I'd be happy to help you."

Paul, Atka, Thomas and Kim all raised their hands. "I don't want to wait too long like my dad did," said Atka. "I want to be a Christian."

"Me too," said Kim.

"I already am a Christian, and Jesus is right here," said Darren, pointing to his heart.

So those four kids and I knelt that day and prayed for salvation: confessing sin and asking Jesus to come in and take control of their lives. Tears dripped from my eyes as I prayed with them, and I thanked God for using me to reach these four little children.

61

I had to put in my hours at work, but I spent every possible minute with Will, asking questions and soaking in information. The day after I'd agreed to act as his interim pastor, he'd called a meeting of the board of deacons and told them he was taking a leave of absence. They immediately appointed a committee, as he'd said they would, to identify his replacement. When that committee was formed, Will recommended me. They also considered Leo Roberts and James Vaughn, but in the end they unanimously appointed me as interim pastor of the Nome Baptist Family Center from April 14 through June 1.

My only real worry was how the congregation would accept me. I was only twenty years old, and I'd had no formal training. That worry went away after a conversation with Dan Sanders. He and Mona had come to town to see the kids, and he came to see me while she spent time at the group home. He found me in the church, studying.

"Just thought I'd check and see how you're doing," he said. "Thought you might need some encouragement."

I looked at Dan and suddenly felt completely comfortable sharing my worries with him.

"I am a little worried." I closed my Bible. "It's strange that you'd come to see me right now. I was just thinking about this."

"It's not strange at all. I felt a strong urge from God to come here."

"You did?"

"Of course. Now what's the problem?"

I told Dan all about it. "I know it will all be okay, but I do think about it. What will people think when they see a twenty-year-old kid in the pulpit?"

"You don't worry about that. You're where you're supposed to be, doing what you're supposed to be doing. That's what matters. Remember Timothy?"

I knew the books of Timothy in the Bible, but I was a little rusty on the history. "Tell me."

Dan explained that the apostle Paul had left Timothy, a young, inexperienced pastor, in charge of the important church at Ephesus. Paul wrote two letters, which are now the books of 1 and 2 Timothy in the Bible, to encourage him and instruct him in practical matters related to running a church. Dan opened his Bible and scanned until he found the verse he wanted. "Look at 1 Timothy 4:5. Read it aloud."

I looked at it and smiled, then read aloud, "Let no one look down on your youthfulness, but rather in speech, conduct, love, faith and purity, show yourself an example of those who believe." I looked up at Dan.

"Sounds like he's talking straight to you, doesn't it?"

"Yes."

"You take this to heart. Carry it with you. Act like you know a Christian is supposed to. Do the things and make the decisions you feel led to. You'll be just fine."

62

Because I had been duly appointed by an official body of the Baptist church, I could do anything any other pastor could do. I could plan events and spend money. I could baptize, marry, and bury. I could make big decisions in the life of the church. Whatever came up, I was authorized to handle it for those seven weeks.

I would have thought the prospect of preaching would be terrifying, but it wasn't. I'd taught enough lessons here already that I felt comfortable sharing aspects of the Gospel with this congregation. In fact, I couldn't wait. It was the mechanics of it that had me a little unsettled. To deal with that, I fell back on my closest resource. I called my dad.

Phone calls home had been rare. Not only was the phone bill astronomical, but it was downright difficult. Because the call had to bounce off a satellite relay, there was a delay of several seconds before my voice reached home, and another several seconds before their voices came back to me. It was weird and, usually, just not worth the trouble. Our communication had been almost exclusively via United States mail since I'd been here. My mother had sent me packages, letters, and tapes, and I'd sent a few things back.

Now I sat in my office during my lunch break and calculated the time difference. Dad should be home and supper should be over. I picked up the phone and placed the collect call. After several seconds, I heard my mother accept the charges.

"Mark! Mark?" Her voice sounded distant and crackly.

"Yes, it's me, Mom."

"Is everything all right?"

I wanted to tell Dad first. "Everything's fine. I just have something I need to ask Dad. Is he home?"

"Yes, yes. We just finished eating. You're okay? You're not sick?"

"Yes, Mom, I'm fine. Really. Couldn't be better. We'll talk after I talk to Dad, okay?"

"Okay. Here he is. Richard! It's Mark!"

My dad got on the phone, and after another delay of several seconds I heard his voice.

"Well, this is a surprise. How's it going up there?"

"It's kind of amazing, Dad. I really need to get your advice about something."

"Shoot."

"Will's leaving, and I've been named the pastor here." I said this with a private grin, as this was exactly the kind of thing he used to do to me when I was smaller, until I got old enough that I didn't fall for it anymore.

"You're what?" His voice was incredulous. "You're not coming home?" I heard my mother's distressed squawk and a clatter as something heavy hit the floor.

"He asked me Sunday, and the committee just approved me as his replacement today."

"Well . . . that's terrific, Mark."

I couldn't pull it off anymore. "Sorry, Dad. I couldn't help myself. It's true that they asked me to replace Will, but it's only for seven weeks while he takes a leave of absence. I start April 14. My first sermon is April 20."

I heard Dad giving my mother an update so she'd calm down, and then he evidently went off by himself.

"That's great, then. What did you want to ask me about?"

"I'm pretty comfortable with the idea of Bible teaching. I've been here long enough that I have a pretty good grasp of these people and the kinds of lessons they need to hear. What I don't quite understand is the mechanics of getting a sermon ready and preaching it."

"I don't follow you."

"Do you write it all out and read it from the pulpit? Do you make an outline? Do you just write down a few points? How exactly do you, as a pastor, do it?"

He paused and considered. "I think you could ask a hundred pastors that question and get a hundred different answers. Each pastor comes up with a system that works for him."

"Well, tell me what works for you. How do you do it?"

"Hmmm. Let me think how to explain it. First let's back up a little. You might think you know what they need to hear, but you have to be sure. The first, most important thing is to spend time with the Lord. Ask Him to show you what He wants you to say to the people every week. He will have something He wants you to say. Remember my private room at the church?"

I did remember. He had turned a Sunday school room into his own private retreat. It was separate from his office, where he did his counseling and had a telephone and a secretary. This special room was completely private, behind a locked door, and few people even knew it existed. No one was ever invited inside, although he did show it to me. Once. He did his studying, praying, and meditating there. "I remember."

"You have to have some place like that, where you can spend uninterrupted time with God. Study the Scriptures. Pray for inspiration. Pray for discernment and enlightenment. He will always answer those prayers in some way. When He does, then you start putting together your sermon.

"For my actual sermons, my system is a combination of outline and speech. I make a detailed outline and then practice until I have the first part down pat. I never write down all the words, but I memorize them through practice, if that makes any sense. Then I put the outline on paper a little smaller than the pages of my Bible, and I have those pages in my Bible when I go up to give the sermon. That way if I forget anything, I have it right there in my open Bible. Once I get through the memorized part, I'm off and going."

"That's really smart." A new appreciation dawned for my dad. "I never would have thought of that."

"I came up with that system after years of trial and error, starting in seminary."

"That's why I asked you. I have to give my first sermon as the pastor in a little over a week. I don't have years to develop a system, and I haven't even been to seminary yet."

"Yet?" Of course, he picked up on that word. I hadn't meant to tell him now. I wanted to tell him that face to face.

"It's just something I'm thinking about, that I want to talk to you about when I get home," I said evasively. "I know Mom is standing over you waiting for the phone. Do you have any more advice for me?"

"Just listen for the Lord's voice. He put you in this position for a reason. He'll tell you what to do."

"I will. Thanks, Dad. See you in a few weeks. Oh, Dad?"

"Yes?"

"I need you to order me a new car. Will you do that for me?"

"Sure." Now his surprise was complete. "You've made enough money to order yourself a new car?"

"Sure have, and I need it to be there when I get home. Order me a two-toned Chevette, with camel on the bottom and black on the top. Camel interior. I'll send you six thousand dollars to pay for it. Got it?"

"Got it. I'll take care of it for you. Why a Chevette?"

"It's what I can afford. Thanks a lot, Dad."

I talked to my mother for a few minutes, and I could hear Dad in the background telling her this call was expensive. She said she loved me and hung up.

I held the receiver for a long time, smiling, after the connection was broken. Notes in his Bible. Ingenious.

63

I told Jack offhandedly about what I'd be doing the next seven weeks, and he had a concern I hadn't even thought about.

"Your last day as interim pastor will be June 1?"

"Yes."

"That's our wedding day. Will is going to be gone on our wedding day?"

"I guess so."

"Oh, brother. This is terrible. How am I going to tell Connie? All the invitations are out and everything! People have their plane tickets. How can we postpone the wedding now?"

At first I shared his anxiety, but then I remembered what Will had said. "There's nothing to worry about. You don't have to wait for Will. I can marry you."

"You cannot."

"I can. I've been duly appointed as pastor by a committee of the Baptist church. I can do anything Will can do."

"It will be a real wedding? We'll be really, officially married?"

"Just as real as if Will did it."

He started to grin. "That would actually be kind of cool." Then his brow furrowed again. "But if you marry us, who'll be my best man?"

"Can't help you there, brother. You have to figure out some things for yourself."

64

The days flew by, and April 13 arrived quickly. As Will preached that Sunday, I realized that today would likely be the last time I ever saw him. He and Denise would be back in Nome on Wednesday, June 4. I was leaving on Monday, June 2. Even though the first few months of 1980 had been rough, I knew that I would always remember Will West as a visionary, a tireless evangelist, someone who was dedicated to change. He'd been determined to make a difference here, and he had. In the last year he had discipled me, and he wasn't finished yet here in Nome, either. I'd bet that when he came back, rested and refreshed, he'd have new ideas for ways to reach out to the people of Nome and the surrounding Norton Sound area.

He stayed after the service as long as anyone wanted to talk to him, just like my father always had. I deliberately got in the back of the line so I'd be the last one to shake his hand. When I got to him, I stuck out my hand. "Thanks, man. For everything."

"Don't thank me yet. I'd like it if you'd come home with me for Sunday dinner."

I stared at him. "I'd love to, but are you sure that's okay?"

"It was Denise's idea."

"Then I'd love to."

We locked up the church and walked upstairs to the pastorium, which was now part of the church. Will and Denise no longer lived in the house I'd shared with them last summer. I smelled something wonderful the second we walked in the door.

"Denise?" Will called. "We're home."

"I'm in the kitchen." I hadn't heard her voice since that awful day in January, and I hadn't thought it would make my eyes sting. No matter what bad things had passed between us, she had taken good care of me until that day. If she wanted to make up, I was willing.

We hung up our coats and went on into the kitchen. The layout was different, but the furniture and the overall feel of the room were the same. It was welcoming and homey. Denise turned from the stove, where she was stirring something.

"Hi." She folded me in a hug. As soon as I stepped back from the hug, she whacked me on the chest, hard. Twice. Just like she did the day I came down from the mountain. "That's for Janice, and now it's over." She hugged me again. "Welcome back to the family. I'm glad you could come for dinner."

"I wouldn't miss it." I rubbed my chest and caught Will's eye. He shrugged and smiled.

The meal of roast moose, instant potatoes, gravy, canned beans and biscuits was like countless others we'd had together, with easy chatting and bantering. At the end Denise grew serious. "Thank you for stepping in while we're gone. It's a relief to know the church will be in good hands."

"It's what the Lord wanted. I'll do my best. You two just get back here safe and sound and rested. I guess this will be the last time I'll see you. Thanks for everything. I wouldn't have made it without the two of you."

"It's been a privilege," said Will. "You're going to make a heck of a pastor."

With that I thanked them again and walked out the door. I felt like a part of the family again. I guessed this had been Denise's way of apologizing, and that was fine with me.

65

I took my dad's advice to heart. He'd had a room dedicated to meditation and study. This new building had plenty of rooms I could use that way. I had already decided to move into one of the apartments at the church for the rest of my time in Nome. It just made more sense to be on site, as I still had to work my hospital job but I needed to be at the church every minute that I could. And, I admitted to myself, it sure didn't hurt that I would now have running water, heat, a toilet, and an actual kitchen with a freezer full of food. Denise had said to feel free to eat whatever I found. I took stock, and my jaw dropped. There were frozen soups, stews, casseroles, salmon, cuts of moose, and much more. I wouldn't have to worry about food for the remainder of my time here. I felt like I'd gone from the pit to the palace, and I silently blessed her.

I didn't have any time to waste, as I had to give my first sermon in just six days. I decided to use one of the apartments to live in and the other as a study. The pastor's office would be where I would conduct official church business. The Wests had left their Bronco here for me to use, and I spent a couple of hours clearing out my half of the apartment I'd shared with Jack and moving in at the church.

After I'd gotten everything situated in my living quarters, I went next door to my new study. My "library" seemed feeble, at best. It was limited to my Bible, my concordance, and the books on Revelation my father had sent me. I didn't think most of the people here were ready for Revelation just yet. They were still on a milk diet of Scripture. Revelation was meat. I still didn't understand a lot of it myself.

I went into Will's office and surveyed his resources, which were considerable. After some thought, I chose several books to borrow and carried them into my study. I arranged them to my satisfaction and stood, deliberating. Dad had said to seek the Lord and ask Him for discernment and enlightenment. Find out what He wanted me to say to these people, then go from there.

I closed and locked my study door and got on my knees. "Lord, I know You've given me this opportunity for a reason. I know there are things You want me to do and say while I'm in this position. Please show me, Lord. Guide me. Help me to do Your will by these people. Show me the things they need to hear. Help me to find the words that will open their hearts. I'm listening, Lord. In Christ's most holy name and all for Your glory I pray, amen."

I stayed on my knees for a long time, soaking in the silence and listening for that still, small voice. When I finally got up, I had a basic path forward. What I needed was something that would appeal to everyone. There would, hopefully, be people at Sunday's service that weren't believers. There would be new believers, and there would be mature Christians like the Vaughns, the Sanders, and the Leos. I had to come up with something that would be meaningful for everyone. I pored through the Scriptures.

I found the answer in the parables of Jesus. I started with Matthew, and bells went off in my head when I reached chapter twenty-two, the parable of the marriage feast.

Heaven, Jesus taught, may be compared to a king who gave a wedding feast for his son. First, he sent out his slaves to those who had been invited, but they were unwilling to come. Then, he sent other slaves, again to those who had been invited, with more information on the delectable foods and other attractions at the wedding. Still, they paid no attention. Some went on their way, doing their personal business, while others actually seized the slaves and killed them. The king got really angry and sent his armies to destroy the murderers and set their city on fire.

Then, he told his remaining slaves that the feast was ready, but those who had been invited were not worthy. He instructed them to go out to the main highway and invite everyone they saw. In this way, the wedding hall was filled with a variety of people from all walks of life.

There was more to the parable, but this part made the point I wanted to make. *Heaven*, I thought. *That's a topic that is pertinent for everyone.* For the rest of the week I prayed, meditated and planned, and spent hours in my study working on the nuances of my message. The week flew by. I got up each morning, ate breakfast, had a short devotion, and put in my hours at the hospital. Then I went home, ate supper, and spent the evening studying, writing, and practicing. By Saturday night I was satisfied. Hank, my big friend from the jail, would be pleased to find out that he was, in a roundabout way, the inspiration for my first sermon.

66

Sunday morning I was nervous, just like before Don Sanders and I had our talk and he showed me the verse in Timothy. That verse was now etched in my memory, and I repeated it over and over to myself as I prepared for the church service. *Youth doesn't matter*, I reminded myself. What matters is that I am obedient. Obey God, as Dr. Stanley says, and leave the consequences to Him.

At about eight-thirty, I headed downstairs to make sure all was ready. Sunday school would begin at nine-thirty, and the worship service at eleven. The church looked neat and welcoming, just as it should. I still looked around this building and marveled. Just a year ago, this piece of land was a dismal piece of real estate holding six run-down shacks. Now, it was a vibrant, thriving house of the Lord.

People began arriving for Sunday school, and I roamed the classes to see what was being taught. All the group home kids were in their age-appropriate classes. Prissy was now six years old and had graduated to a class for elementary school students being taught by Jack Barker and Connie Vaughn. I saw her through the cracked doorway but didn't want to interrupt, so I went on to the next class. Everywhere I went, I saw people listening intently, fellowshipping with one another, growing in their faith. Was this what being a pastor was like? If so, I liked it a lot.

Eleven o'clock approached, and I made my way to the worship center. People who hadn't come to Sunday school were already seated, waiting for the service to start. I went around and visited with them, shaking their hands and thanking them for coming. As the Sunday school attendees started filing in, I sat on the front row near the podium and spent the last few minutes before the service in silent prayer. I asked for guidance and wisdom, and words to communicate the points I felt God wanted me to.

My mind and heart began to settle, and the nervousness began to melt away. Just before the sermon, the pianist began the introductory strains of "Standing on the Promises," and the congregation stood to sing. By the time the last notes faded away, I was calm and ready. I stepped up to the podium.

"Please turn in your Bibles to Matthew 22:1-14." Pages rustled as people reached for their pew Bibles or opened ones they'd brought with them. I read the parable aloud, then looked up and asked, "What do you think of when you think of heaven?"

I didn't expect an answer and didn't get one. People looked at me expectantly. "I recently asked that question to a group of inmates here in the Nome jail. I expected them to say things like pearly gates, streets of gold, mansions, and the like. But one big, rough-looking guy with scars and tattoos said, 'No one knows.'

"I collected my thoughts and rephrased the question. I said, 'Well, that is true, but what do you think?'

"I was about to settle back and watch them scratch their heads as they pondered this profound question, when the same man said, 'It don't matter what we think. It's where God is.'

"With that, ladies and gentlemen, this simple Christian man captured the essence of Jesus' teaching. When we think of heaven, it's not the place or what we get there that's important. The important part is that we will be with the Person, God Himself. If you are with the One you love, surroundings lose their importance.

"That's what Jesus was saying in this parable. That's what the people in the parable didn't understand. The king invited them to a feast. He didn't demand that they come. He even gave them a second chance after they rejected him, which must have hurt his feelings. The people were too busy living their own lives, tending to their own business, and they totally missed the most important thing, which was to be with the king and honor him.

"Have you ever gotten something all ready, and then your guests didn't show up? That's what has happened to God, all through the ages. He has loved us, and given and done everything for us, and most of us can't be bothered to accept His invitation or even give Him a few minutes of our time.

"The king in the parable tried more than once, just as God has done all through time. The people's response? They made excuses. They had misplaced priorities, just like too many of us do today. We are too busy with our television shows, our jobs, our reading, our hunting and fishing. God does often call at inconvenient times, and it means we have to give up some luxuries or conveniences. Many people just aren't willing to interrupt their busy lives for Him.

"Finally, some of the people went so far as to kill the slaves who brought the invitation. Now, imagine James here invites me to dinner. He sends Connie with the invitation. I'm in a bad mood and don't feel like accepting the invitation, so I just kill her, right? No, that's not a fair illustration, because no one can turn down Lily's cooking, but you see the point."

I went on to touch on the profound mystery of the kingdom of God. "Man cannot be repeatedly confronted with the Word of God and take a passive attitude toward it. There comes a point where God's patience wears thin and the invitation is withdrawn and given to others, just as it was with these wedding guests. The king in the parable said the people he originally invited were unworthy, and he sent his slaves back out to the highway to invite everyone they encountered. In this way, the house was filled with people from all walks of life, but they were people who wanted to be there. They wanted to fellowship with the king.

"That's how we have the opportunity for salvation. The ones who were originally invited were the Jews, God's chosen people, who were supposed to be the light to all other nations. They were treated with extra special care by God, but they have a long history of not being appreciative for all God did for them for hundreds of years. They forgot, ignored, or rejected His invitations and killed His prophets, and even finally killed His own Son, Jesus, who came to heal and to save. That's when the invitation was extended to all peoples and nations. See, we are in God's master plan. We have a direct invitation from the King.

"We have a choice now, but we may not always. The people on the highway responded to the king's invitation because they wanted to be with him and accept what he was offering them. They accepted the invitation with joy and gratitude. Their need was obvious.

"Today we can hide our real need with possessions and jobs, but we have the same needs as the drunks at the Board of Trade. Too often, we don't see the need because we are too busy with our own plans or we just don't care.

"Everyone please bow your heads and close your eyes and really think. Do a needs inventory of yourself right now. Ask yourself, 'Do I need God?' We all do. The important thing is whether you see that need. Are you willing to let down the walls of your security fortress, which are keeping you from making a commitment to Christ? Or, if you are already a Christian, could you have a closer walk with Him?

"Jesus said, 'Behold, I stand at the door and knock. If any man hears My voice and opens the door I will come in to him.'

"God requires one thing—repentance. That means giving up your old way of life in exchange for God's. Would you give your life to God? He gave His Son for you.

"I'll end this service now, but I'll be here for as long as necessary. Maybe you want to accept Christ as your Savior. Maybe you want to be baptized. Maybe you want to join this church. Or maybe there's just something you need to talk or pray about. I'll be here.

"Please stand with me, and let's sing the final hymn."

In the hour that followed, my respect for my father ratcheted up another few notches. Many people stayed, mostly to welcome me and tell me they enjoyed the sermon. Three Christians wanted to talk about baptism. Two families wanted to join the church, now that it had an actual structure. A couple of people had problems they wanted to talk about. Each situation was unique and required my focus and concentration. It wasn't just hand-shaking and pats on the back, which was how I'd viewed my father's after-church activities during my growing up years. No, it was far more than that. This mattered to people. It made a difference.

When it was over, and I was once again alone in my upstairs apartment, I sat next to the window, thought about the morning and smiled. It had been a good first Sunday, and suddenly I felt more confident than ever about the next six weeks.

67

That confidence was short-lived, as the very next day I was confronted with some of the hard realities of running a church.

I woke on Monday to a distinct chill in the air. Snuggling under the covers, I waited for the heat to kick on. Nothing happened. I waited as long as I could, then finally had to get up and dress for work, shivering the whole time.

I thought and worried about it all morning, and finally called James Vaughn and asked if he could go to the church and check on the heat. He called back a short while later and gave me some bad news.

"The problem's obvious."

"What is it?"

"You're out of fuel oil."

Good grief. Oil and gas came in once a year on the barge, and the entire town had to make do with that amount. This was only April. The barge wouldn't be here until July. This wasn't good.

"Do you have any suggestions, James?" I asked in desperation.

"Let me think on it."

The situation got worse when I got home after work. A thin line of water snaked across the worship center, and I traced it to a leak in the baptismal tank. And, on top of that, the refrigerator began making ominous noises and then gave up the ghost in a final death gasp.

This was a new building. It wasn't supposed to do this. Was it? I called James back and told him the new developments, and he came over. He took a look at the baptismal and refrigerator and shook his head.

"Being a new building doesn't mean it's perfect," he said. "New buildings almost always have kinks that need to be worked out. You just found three."

"We need to get this stuff fixed before Sunday. Eventually the pipes will freeze up if we have no heat, and there are people who want to be baptized. I don't think we have the money to get this stuff fixed or buy new."

At my wits' end, I decided not to worry about it tonight. I'd make some calls tomorrow and see what kind of resources we had and what could be done. I plugged in a small electric heater and locked myself in my study to start seeking illumination and guidance about the upcoming Sunday's sermon.

Almost immediately I stumbled onto the story of Jehoshaphat in 2 Chronicles. In those days Israel was a split kingdom. Judah, which was originally one of the twelve tribes of Israel, was at that time a separate entity. Jehoshaphat was the king of Judah. Three other nations were getting ready to make war against him, and those three nations would greatly outnumber Jehoshaphat's army. Jehoshaphat knew he had no chance to beat them on his own, so he sought the Lord's help.

He proclaimed a fast throughout the entire nation. All of Judah gathered together in one place, and Jehoshaphat stood in the assembly among them. There, he prayed a heartfelt prayer that saved his people. He threw himself and his nation on the Lord's mercy and prayed for deliverance. Basically, he tossed the problem on the Lord's doorstep, telling Him His people were about to be destroyed, and asking Him what He was going to do about it.

He pointed out that the three nations that were gathering against Judah were ones that, many years before, Israel had chosen not to invade. "See how they are rewarding us by coming to drive us out from Your possession, which You have given us as an inheritance. O our God, will you not judge them? For we are powerless before this great multitude who are coming against us; nor do we know what to do, but our eyes are on You."

Jehoshaphat got an immediate answer to his prayer through the Lord's prophet, Jahaziel. In a nutshell, the Lord said, "You rest easy. This is not your battle. I got this." Then He gave some instructions.

The next morning Jehoshaphat followed God's directions and sent out his army behind a singing choir. And they watched in amazement as their enemies destroyed each other. When they went to gather the booty from the corpses, it took them three days to carry it off because there was so much. Word spread that the Lord Himself had fought Judah's battle, and Jehoshaphat had peace for the rest of his reign.

I sat back and thought. My little problems seemed pretty insignificant after reading this. Then another thought struck. God cares. Of course He does. If He would literally fight the battle for Judah because Jehoshaphat asked for help, what might He do here if we but ask? These were different kinds of problems, but they were just as real and just as serious to us. I got back on my knees.

"Lord," I prayed, "we have a situation here. You got us this far. You made some incredible things happen to get this church standing and get us where we are today. This is Your church and Your people. Please don't let us stumble now. Help us find answers and get these things fixed. In Christ's name, amen."

God uses people to get things done and, in this case, He used Lily Vaughn. She spread the word so far and so well that the community bonded together just as it did when we were building this church. Again, my hat went off to Will West, who'd created such tremendous good will in Nome. Dozens of families donated some of their precious oil so we'd have enough to get us through until the barge came in July. George Allen came through again, sending a crew the next day to find and patch the leak in the baptismal tank. And the hardware store just happened to have one brand new refrigerator in stock that they donated to the church to replace the second-hand one we'd had since construction.

I watched all this happen, smiling and shaking my head. As Will said the day Matthew Hawkins came through, we serve a mighty God and should never forget it. He can do what He likes, when He likes. Sometimes He just wants to be asked.

The topic of Sunday's sermon was easy. I just told both stories, first of Jehoshaphat and then of my prayer and what had subsequently happened at the church. People sat spellbound, their mouths open.

"Those of you who gave us oil, I want to thank you. God used you to help meet a need, and doesn't it feel great? George Allen, thank you again. You've come through for this church over and over again. And Mark Huff, from the hardware store, are you here?" He waved from the middle of the crowd. "May God bless you. You are a generous man. Thank you.

"It was especially important to get our baptismal tank fixed because today is a very important day in this church. Several people have expressed their desire to make their faith public through baptism."

The three who'd come forward last week, plus five kids from the Lighthouse—Darren, Paul, Thomas, Atka and Kim, came up one by one and gave their testimonies. And one by one, I took them into the tank and said, "Because you have professed Christ as your Savior, I baptize you, my brother—or sister—in the name of the Father, and the Son, and the Holy Spirit." Then I held their noses, gently leaned them back until they were immersed in the water, and lifted them back up.

I knew baptizing the kids was going to be emotional. When they stood before the church and gave their testimonies, my eyes began to sting. Darren said, "Jesus loves me just as I am, and I love Him too. He saved me. I want to do whatever He wants me to do, for my whole life."

I could hear sniffles beginning somewhere in the congregation.

Paul said, "I don't know why things happen like they do. I don't know why my parents had to die or why I lost my eye. But God knows and He's got it all figured out. One day I may know, too. I'll just have to trust Him, and I really do."

Thomas and Kim went next. The sniffles got louder and became sobs. Then came Atka.

"I wish my dad had done this, I wish I was going to see him in heaven. It's like Mark said last week, why wouldn't you take a really good gift when it's offered to you? I'm not going to make the same mistake my dad did. I think he'd be happy to know that."

The weeping coming from somewhere in the middle of the congregation grew louder. I gently dunked Atka under the water, tears flowing from my own eyes. As I issued the weekly invitational, I scanned the crowd to see who had been so overcome by the testimonials. As I scanned, George Allen made his way down his row and down the aisle to me. Tears streamed down his face.

"God spoke to me." He tapped his heart. "Right here. Those kids know something I don't. I want it, Pastor. I want to feel that too. I want to be saved. Will you tell me how?"

68

Five more weeks, then four. The first of May came and went.

I had taken Darren's comments in March to heart when he opened up and told me how much he was going to miss me. I thought hard about it, and realized that it wouldn't be fair if I went from being a big part of the kids' lives, to all of a sudden not being there at all. It was like a physical pain, but I slowly began to ease away from the kids. Where once I was the center of their lives, the one person they looked forward to being with, now I watched as others took over that role.

In Sunday school, I watched with an aching heart through the cracked door as Prissy attached herself to Connie Vaughn like she once had to me.

Paul began to assert himself and become a leader, alongside Darren. And one Sunday in early May, Darren's prayers were answered. He stayed behind after church and told me with shining eyes he had something to tell me. Could he stay until everyone left and talk to me?

"Sure, of course. I'll just be another minute, and then we can get something to eat and talk."

Fifteen minutes later we were sitting in the kitchen eating one of Denise's casseroles. Darren was obviously bursting with some news.

"Remember when we prayed that God would send someone into my life that I could talk to, to be my friend?"

"Sure, I remember."

"He did. He did!"

"Really? Who?"

"The Sanders!"

I was confused. This was not news. The Sanders had been in his life since he was a small boy. "What do you mean?"

"They're adopting me!"

"No way."

"Yes, they are!"

"That's terrific, Darren!"

"They came to the home yesterday and got me off by myself and told me. I almost busted waiting until today to tell you. I wanted to walk here right then and tell you." His eyes were shining now with a sheen of happy tears. "God answered me, Mark!"

"Yes, He did. He knew you needed someone, and He sent some-one. And aren't you extra glad it's someone you already love and trust?"

"I'm so happy, Mark. Thank you."

"For what? I didn't do anything. You should thank the Lord."

"I did. I've been thanking Him, over and over."

"Let's thank Him together."

We bowed our heads to give thanks, this brave, sturdy boy and me. I started the prayer and Darren interrupted and finished with one of the most heartfelt prayers I had ever heard in my life.

The next day I was restless. All throughout my hours at the hospital, I felt as if I were supposed to be doing something, but what? It was times like this when I knew God was trying to tell me something. I blanked my brain and concentrated on hearing Him. Faces of all the people I cared about flashed through my mind. Precious little Prissy. I was still worried about her, and what would become of her when I left. Paul was becoming more of a confident leader with the other kids and was taking on more responsibility at the home, but he still wanted a family, and I hoped and prayed he would get one. My mother and father, my sisters, Doug, and Sandy. I thought fondly of each of them and couldn't wait to see them. Janice. I still had regrets there but had made peace with the fact that I would likely never have the opportunity to make things right in person. Darren. There the swinging pendulum stopped, and I knew my restlessness had something to do with Darren.

I followed my instinct, got in the Bronco, and drove to the group home. They were all happy and puzzled to see me on a Monday. I greeted them all, then pulled Darren aside. "You up for a little walk?"

"Sure."

I still wasn't sure where we were going, but I let my feet carry me and soon realized we were headed up to Anvil Rock, on the same path I took when I stormed up that mountain so many months ago. Then I knew what I was expected to do. I'd shared that experience with Will and Denise, but had never talked about it with anyone else. This was an opportunity to do that, to disciple this extraordinary young man.

We walked quietly up the mountain, enjoying the cool breeze and the silent camaraderie. Nome grew smaller below us. Sounds carried on the breeze. We heard the chirring of sea birds and the hum of mosquitoes, which were beginning to come back after the winter cold. Thankfully, they were still too small to torture us.

We got to the top and rested, taking in the vista below us. I was reminded of another time when I'd sat on a mountaintop and taken in a view, only that time I was with Charles Chandler on Gunsight Mountain near Anchorage and he was counseling me. Now everything was different, and I was on the other side. Suddenly I felt that this was what I was born to do—educate, mentor, and disciple other Christians. It was an exciting thought.

"Darren," I said, "I have a story to tell you."

I went back to the beginning and told him how I'd come to be here in the first place, with that retreat at St. Simons Island two years ago. I described how I'd arrived at my conviction that coming back here was what God wanted of me, including what had happened to Sandy and me on the park bench in Maryville. Then I slowed down and described in detail the events when I landed in Nome and discovered that the job I'd traveled seven thousand miles and given up everything for had gone away.

"Looking back. I believe it was another example of the devil or one of his minions trying to get rid of me. I can look back and see several times when that happened. I couldn't see it at the time. God always protected me."

I went on and told him about my experience on the mountain. We got up and walked over to the mighty rock, and I showed him the cleft where I'd taken shelter from the storm. We crawled up into it together, just as I had that night. It was hard and cold.

"It's freezing in here," he said.

"I know. Imagine spending hours in here with a storm outside."

"How on earth did you survive?"

"I really believe that God put His hand over that opening and protected me. When I crawled in I was drenched with sweat and half frozen. I passed out or went to sleep, I'm still not sure which, but when I woke up I was dry and warm. It was the most incredible experience of my life."

Darren was listening, wide-eyed. "God did that for you?"

"Yes, He did. He saved my life."

"Why?"

That was a good question, and one I'd asked myself repeatedly.

"All I can think is that He just wasn't finished with me yet. There were more things He had planned for me. I'm trying to be really careful to hear His voice and stay in His will."

"How do you know?"

"It's hard at first," I told him honestly. "You just have to keep praying, and keep listening to the Holy Spirit inside you, and keep reading your Bible. The more you read, the more you get to know God, and the more you are aware of His voice. It can come from all kinds of places. Sometimes you'll feel directed to a specific Scripture that gives you an important answer. Sometimes the direction will come from someone you trust. Sometimes you'll hear a little voice or impulse in your heart. Other times you'll get an obvious sign. But that doesn't happen often. The point is, if you're honestly and sincerely searching for His will, He'll make sure you find it."

I paused. "It was an impulse that led me to bring you up here today. I felt this morning that there was something I was supposed to do. This is what it was."

"God told you to bring me up here?"

"Yes, in a way He did. He led me to you, then I felt Him drawing us up here."

"Wow." He thought that over. "Maybe He has plans for me, too."

"There's no question about that. I'm sure He does."

"I wonder what they are."

"That's something you'll discover as time goes on."

We sat for a while longer in comfortable silence. Then Darren spoke again.

"Mark?"

"Yes?"

"What if He wants me to do something I don't want to do?"

I could hear echoes in my memory of Robert Wallace asking almost the exact same thing, months ago in my apartment. I gave Darren the same answer. "I can almost guarantee that at some point, He will want you to do something you're not comfortable with. For me, coming here was a big leap of faith, but it was the best decision I've ever made. I think I'll still be saying that even when I'm old and gray and have great-grandkids. I've done things and grown in ways that I never would have otherwise. Following where God leads you may be scary and uncomfortable, but you'll never have regrets."

Suddenly I knew. I shifted and looked into his eyes. "Remember last summer I told you that you have the gift of leadership?"

"Yes, I remember."

"God wants you to use it."

"How?"

"To start with, the Lighthouse kids need you."

"How?"

"They haven't gotten their Bible stories since I've been pastor. You could do that."

He looked horrified. "You want me to teach?"

"Not teach. Just pick out a Bible story each week and tell it to them in words they can understand."

He mulled that over. "I guess I could do that."

"I know you can. Then see where God leads you after that."

"This is pretty cool," he said. "I can't believe God actually wants to use me."

"Darren, you have no idea."

69

I'd heard about the spring thaw, but couldn't believe the things I'd heard could possibly be true. I soon found out for myself.

The Bering Sea gave the first sign that the thaw was coming. I was walking along Front Street one Sunday afternoon, on my way to the jail, when slight movement caught my eye. The water no longer looked like solid ice. It looked like slush, and if I listened closely I could hear ice cracking. I told the guys at the jail, and they nodded wisely.

"Tomorrow," Jasper said, "it will all be open."

Tomorrow? I couldn't believe that much ice could thaw that fast, but that was exactly what happened. The next day, the sea was once again water, not ice, with waves pounding the sand and rocks. And that was just the beginning. In the days that followed, in the hills and mountains near Nome, the melt began. In Nome itself, the snow and ice that had been piled up to rooftops, burying cars completely, began to melt and flow toward the sea. The amount of water was incredible. For a few days, streets became rivers as water rushed seaward.

During the cold winter months, people had used their honey pots until they became full. Then they ventured a few steps outside their doorways and buried the contents in the snow, a couple of feet down. Those materials, frozen for months, thawed along with the snow and ran into the streets.

The stench was amazing. A person could be walking along in what he thought was mud and notice a bit of toilet paper sticking to his shoe. That was the indication that the mud wasn't mud at all. And the flies! Small black flies, the likes of which I'd never seen before, were everywhere.

We saw a tremendous spike in illnesses at the hospital. From my office near the emergency room, I saw firsthand the impact of sanitation on human health. I'd always known, but here was proof. Thankfully, I now had a shower and could clean up.

Spring thaw also meant the bodies that had been accumulating in the metal box at the edge of town could now be removed and buried. This had to happen fast to avoid even more sickness and smell. Atka had begged me weeks before to do a graveside service for his father when the time came. It would be my first funeral, but Nome seemed to be a place of firsts for me.

The scene was unlike any I'd ever seen before. The cemetery covered one hilltop and was simply a forest of white crosses. There were no headstones. Tall grass grew on and between the graves. The metal box had contained dozens of bodies, and the rush was on to get them all into the ground. Most were natives, but some were whites. Of the whites, only a few were Christians. The natives and most of the whites were simply buried without fanfare. The Christians who belonged to a church here had a simple graveside service, like the one we were doing for Robert. Multiple graves were being dug and services being held, all at the same time.

More people had come to pay their respects to Robert than I had anticipated. Besides the people at our church who loved Atka, many in town knew and respected Robert because of his art. Perhaps twenty people were around the grave that day, many more than at any other service.

I had closely consulted with Atka and Missy as to what they wanted. They wanted me to talk about my friend, pray, and sing one song. I wanted to say something uplifting, but it was hard to be positive about a man whom I was 99 percent sure had never accepted Christ, and I still felt an overwhelming despair at my failure to help him.

A service like this was not for the dead, I reasoned. It was supposed to comfort the living. I had to give them hope and purpose for the future, and not dwell on whether Robert had or had not been a Christian.

"We're here today to celebrate the life of Robert Wallace. He had a gift unlike any I've ever seen before. I personally know of many people he touched with that gift, myself included.

"I first met Robert while doing a sermon at the jail. After he got out, we spent hours and hours talking about Jesus and salvation. I got to know him pretty well, and I can tell you he was a good man. It's my fondest hope that he accepted Jesus before he died. It's never too late. We know that through the example of the thief who died beside Jesus on the cross. I hope we will see Robert in heaven someday. I miss him.

"When I first saw Robert's art, my first thought was that this man had the talent to be an important artist. He didn't want fame and fortune, though. He just wanted to earn enough money from his art to support himself and his family." I pulled out the first skin I'd bought and held it up. "Isn't this incredible? This is one of my favorites, and I'll treasure it always.

"Robert was a troubled man, troubled by the same thing that affects many people. It's something Will West has fought against, and I take up the fight in his absence. Alcohol. It transformed a good, talented man into one who was reduced to living on the street. He loved his family, he loved them very much, but once alcohol gets its hooks into a person, it's hard to shake those hooks out.

"This does not change the fact that Robert Wallace was a good person who loved his family and fathered three amazing children. Robert is the reason some people here came to Christ, and that's a fine legacy to leave. I am personally very proud of his son, Atka, who took this very bad situation and used it for good in his own life. I know Robert would be pleased to see people learn from his mistakes, and treasure his art. He would also want his family to remember that he loved them very much, and find the strength to carry on without him. Let us pray."

Conscious of the cold and incoming rain, I said a brief prayer and led the people in singing one verse of "Amazing Grace"—still the only song I knew in Inupiaq. When the service was over, Atka and Missy came up to me, tears in their eyes. Missy had one child by the hand and was holding another in her arms.

"That was as good as anybody could do for a man like Robert,"

Missy said. "Thank you."

"I meant every word. Missy, you're a strong woman and a good mother, but you may need help with these three little ones. I want you to promise me you'll let the church know what we can do."

"Sure, Mark. I will." She took my hand and looked into my eyes. "It sure was a great day for this family when you and Atka met at the riverbank. You changed my son's life. I see something different in him. I'd like to talk to you about that sometime."

"Anytime, Missy. I'll be here for three more weeks."

70

My time in Nome was quickly dwindling. After nearly a year here, I was down to my last three weeks. I had no idea what exactly I was going to do when I got back. My dad had ordered me a car, and I'd sent him the six thousand dollars to pay for it. It should be waiting for me when I returned. I planned to reenroll at UT for the fall semester, but didn't know where I would live or how I would support myself. I had my savings from this past year, but that money was earmarked for tuition at UT and seminary, and I didn't want to touch it. I prayed hard about my situation and tried not to think too much about it otherwise. I knew it would all work out.

One afternoon I was sitting in the church office when the phone rang. I picked it up.

"Nome Baptist Family Center, this is Mark."

There was a delay of several seconds, and I almost hung up. Then a voice that sounded like it came from far away said, "Mark?"

"Yes, this is Mark." I resigned myself to another satellite call where I would have to wait several seconds for our voices to go back and forth.

"Mark, this is Bob Hall at the BSU in Knoxville."

I sat straight up and grinned. "Bob! How in the world are you?"

"Just great, Mark, just great. How's it going up there?"

"Really good. I'm learning more than I ever expected to. Did you hear that I'm the interim pastor here?"

"No, I didn't know that. That's incredible. How'd that happen?"

"Will West and his wife were burned out. They took a leave of absence and went home to Wyoming. They're coming back right after I leave here."

"You're really getting yourself an education, aren't you?"

"And how. I did a funeral two days ago, and I get to do a wedding right before I come back." I could picture him sitting in his office, shaking his head. Suddenly I missed him and couldn't wait to see him.

"Say, Mark, there was a reason for my call."

"I thought there must be. What is it?"

"Two reasons, really. Do you plan to come back to UT this fall?"

"That's my plan, yes."

"I'd like you to consider living at the BSU. We really need your character and leadership here. You'd have a free place to stay for the next two years."

I stared at the phone, mouth open. "Bob, that's incredible. I'd love that. Yes, I accept."

"The other reason for my call is that Pleasant Grove Baptist is looking for a youth minister, and they called me to see if I knew of anyone who might be a good fit. I immediately thought of you, and I gave them your name. They're expecting you to contact them when you get home."

"It doesn't matter that I haven't been to seminary yet?"

"Absolutely not. What you've been doing there in Nome is more than training enough for them. What do you think?"

"I think it's an answer to prayer, and yes, I'd absolutely like to talk to them."

"Good enough. Give me a call when you get back and we'll firm things up."

"Great. Bob, thanks for thinking of me. It means a lot."

"No problem. I'll see you in a few weeks."

We hung up, and I immediately bowed my head. "Thank you, Lord, for answering my prayers and providing a possible job and a place to live back home. I wasn't worried about it. I knew You'd provide. Thank You. Please help me through the rest of my time here. Help me to do Your will by these people. In Christ's name, amen."

71

Two weeks to go. It seemed as if everyone, now that my time was short, wanted me to "do just one thing" for them before I left. I barely had time to work my job and keep up with my responsibilities at the church. Get up, go to work, come home, eat supper, see to church business, study and prepare for my next sermon, and drop into bed—exhausted.

One afternoon at the end of the third week of May, I heard a knock at my office door at the hospital.

"Come in." I thought it was Susan, as it had been several times a day, every day, for a couple of weeks now. She was jumping up and down on my last nerve, but she was my boss for one more week. I pasted a smile on my face and looked up.

It wasn't Susan opening the door, but Brian Mull, the hospital administrator. I'd never met him before but I knew who he was. He came in, closed the door behind him, and sat in my visitor's chair.

"Hello, Mr. Smith. I'm Brian Mull. I apologize that we haven't met before now. I certainly know of the good job you've been doing for us."

"Well, thank you, Mr. Mull. I appreciate that. Please call me Mark."

"Mark. I'll come straight to the point. I have to ask for your absolute discretion in this matter. We're looking for a new director of finance, and your excellent performance has put you right at the top of the list."

Director of finance? But that was Susan's job. My confusion must have shown on my face.

"There are a few issues with the current director," he said, and didn't elaborate further. "Would you be interested in the job? It would be double your current salary."

Double my current salary. Forty thousand dollars. I sat stunned, then a clear picture came into my head of Satan and Jesus in the wilderness. Jesus went away for forty days and forty nights, and during that time Satan tempted Him. One of the temptations was tangible things of this earth. I knew then that my prayers had already been answered, and home was where I was supposed to go.

"Mr. Mull, I appreciate the consideration, but I'm already committed to go back and finish my education in Tennessee. Maybe the issues will work out and you can keep your current director. I hope so."

"We'll see. I hope so, too. When's your last day here?"

"Friday, May 30. One week from today."

"I wish you all the best, and thank you for the excellent job you've done for us."

"You're welcome. Thank you again for the opportunity."

When he left and closed the door, I stared after him for a few minutes. Timing was everything, I thought. If he'd asked before I got the call from Bob Hall, I might have thought I was supposed to stay here. God knows what He's doing, all right.

The tumult wasn't over, either. The next day I was in my office at the church, putting the final touches on my next-to-last sermon, when the phone rang.

"Nome Baptist Family Center, this is Mark."

"Mark, it's Will West." The delay wasn't quite so bad since Will was only in Wyoming, not on the East Coast.

"Hey, Will! How's it going?"

"We're feeling much better and about ready to come back. How are things?"

"Great." I spent a few minutes catching him up.

"That sounds terrific. You're doing a good job. I knew you would. That's actually why I'm calling."

"Oh?" *What now?*

"I'd like you to consider staying on and being my assistant pastor. You'd be on salary, on my permanent staff at the church. You can stay for free in one of the apartments. I know you want to go to seminary, but that could wait for a while. What do you think?"

This really was tempting. It was a chance to stay in a town I'd grown attached to and continue the work I'd started, with people I'd come to love. It was much more tempting than the hospital job, but I still had a strong conviction that home was where I belonged, where a path had already been laid out for me. God had things for me to do in Tennessee, although I didn't know yet what they were. My work here was nearly finished.

"Will, I appreciate the opportunity, and it's really tempting. I love this place and these people, but I'm comfortable that it's time to go home." I told him about the call from Bob Hall and how things had taken shape in Knoxville. A thought struck. "You know, Will, I'll be living at the BSU for the next two years. It's possible I could arrange for some help for you next summer. Think you could keep another missionary or two busy?"

"Absolutely. You send us one or two. We'll take good care of them."

I also told him about the visit from Brian Mull at the hospital.

"Just so you know," Will said, "the issues with Susan, I'm pretty sure, are related to alcohol. She's having some problems."

"That's a shame. Are you trying to help her?"

"I'm trying. That's how I know about it. I'll go see her when I get back. Maybe I can help her keep her job."

"I hope so." I paused. "Will, do I need to tell you how much you've meant to me over this past year? I hope you know."

"I do. And I'm proud of you, Mark. You've changed from a promising boy to an outstanding young man. You go on from here and do good things."

"I'll do my best. And thanks."

72

Just two days later, the Monday of my last week in Nome, yet another prayer was answered. On Monday evening, as I sat in the church office looking over finances, someone knocked at my door.

"Come in." I added up the last figures in a ledger as I spoke, then looked up as Jack Barker and Connie Vaughn opened the door. "Well, if it isn't the soon-to-be newlyweds. How are y'all today?"

"We're really good, Mark." Connie glanced at Jack.

"Any problem?"

"Absolutely not. Everything's wonderful. That's kind of what we want to talk to you about," Jack said.

"Okay, shoot."

Connie was silent for a moment, holding Jack's hand, obviously gathering her thoughts. I waited. "I've been feeling so blessed lately, Mark," she said softly.

"That's good that you see your blessings. A man who loves you, about to get married, life's looking pretty good I'd say."

"It really is. It's so good, I'm feeling like we need to share it." She looked up at me. "We want a child."

"Okay. You've got things in the right order. You're getting married on Sunday, so you can get started on that whenever you want."

"No, I mean now. And not just any child." She looked at Jack, who nodded encouragingly. She took a deep breath. "We want Prissy. We've gotten really attached to her. We just don't know how to go about getting her, or even if we can."

"Well, you know her background, right?" They nodded. "Her parents are alive, but when they abandoned her she became a ward of the state. It's certainly possible to adopt her, but that's not something I've even looked at. Leo Roberts would know, or Will when he gets back."

"What do you think about it?"

I had been worried about the kids at the group home, especially Prissy. She was so small and delicate, and she and I had developed a strong bond. I'd been gently pulling away for weeks, but she still looked at me wistfully whenever she saw me. She loved only a few people, and I was one of them. I had worried about what my departure might do to her.

I thought this was wonderful, but had to make sure it was right. "I think it would be wonderful to give Prissy a good, stable home, and I think you'd make excellent loving parents for her. Have you prayed about it? Most families start with two, not three. Are you sure you want to start out like this, with a child who's not yours?"

"Yes. We look in her eyes and feel like she's ours already. My parents have already agreed to help in any way we need them. We wanted to see what you thought."

"I think it's great. Talk to Leo and see where you go from here." I paused as a thought struck. "Do you think I could be there when you tell her? She's kind of been my special child since I've been here. I'd love to see her face when she hears."

"Absolutely," said Jack, eyes twinkling. "How about if we come up before church Wednesday night? I'll clear it with Leo. We'll even bring supper."

"Lily's cooking? Now that sounds like a plan."

The next day Jack called me at work with an update.

"Leo says we have to go through the state, but he can't imagine any problem. He also says it would help if you write a letter of recommendation for us. He said since you're the pastor and a state employee, your word will carry some weight."

"I'll have it for you when you come over tomorrow. I can't wait to see her face."

On Wednesday afternoon, I was so excited I could barely stand it. I paced. The clock crawled. I went to work early and left early, so I could be at the church at five o'clock. At five on the dot, Jack and

Connie walked in with Prissy. Connie carried a pot with something that smelled amazing. They had picked Prissy up from the group home and brought her with them, telling her we were going to have supper together before church because it was my last Wednesday night service. I handed Jack a sealed envelope with my letter of recommendation, and we went to the kitchen for our meal.

When we were settled at the kitchen table, savory roast and mashed potatoes on our plates, Jack spoke up.

"Your mother makes the best roast I've ever tasted, Connie. Is this the kind of thing I can expect to eat every night from now on?"

"I'm learning. One day maybe I'll be as good as my mom."

"I'll be your guinea pig."

Prissy said nothing. She just looked back and forth at all of us and daintily ate her meal.

"You tell her, Mark," said Connie. "It's fitting."

I wasn't expecting this and couldn't think of anything to say at first. I gathered my thoughts and moved my chair so I was looking directly at Prissy.

"You like this food, Prissy?" She nodded, chewing and looking at me with those big, heart-breaking doe eyes.

"How'd you like to eat food like this every night, and learn how to make it when you get bigger?"

She nodded, her eyes never leaving my face.

"That really could happen, sweetie. Jack and Connie are getting married Sunday, and they want to be your parents. They want you to be their daughter."

"They do?" She stopped eating and looked at them with big eyes. "You do?"

They nodded, tears in their eyes.

"Why?"

Of all the questions she could have asked, that one was the one I least expected and it was the most heartbreaking. She'd been through such disappointment in her six years, first being abandoned by her parents, then being deemed not good enough by prospective foster parents who'd taken her home with them. They'd always brought her back to the group home, and she'd long since stopped hoping. When she asked why, I knew that what this sweet, beautiful child was really asking was why anyone would love her. It nearly broke me. I couldn't speak.

"Because we love you, Prissy," said Connie. "We love you and we feel like you're our daughter already. Do you want to come live with us and be a family? It would make us so happy."

She looked worried, and I knew what she was thinking. "It's not like all the other times, Prissy. Jack and Connie aren't foster parents. They're real parents. They want to adopt you, and that means they won't ever take you back to the group home unless it's to visit. This is for keeps."

She looked at me, and then looked at her new parents, and the wall began to come down. I could actually see in her eyes when she began to believe and trust. She said, "I'd like that," and crawled onto Connie's lap and snuggled in.

By then we were all weeping, and I was rejoicing inside that one of my biggest worries had been taken care of. Prissy was going to be just fine.

73

Susan wasn't stupid. On Thursday, the day before my last day at work, she came into my office and shut the door.

"I know," she began abruptly.

I looked up from my calculations. It was at the end of the month, which was always a frenetically busy time in the bookkeeping world. And tomorrow was my last day. I was trying madly to get everything wrapped up here. I struggled for patience.

"You know what?"

"I know that Mr. Mull offered you my job."

This was unfortunate. I'd hoped Will could help her keep her job, and she'd never have to find out what had happened between Brian Mull and me.

"I'm sorry. How did you find out?"

"Malina saw him coming in here, and I asked him point blank. He was honest with me. You should have told me."

"Why? I turned down the job, and the last thing he said was that he hoped whatever issues there are would be worked out and you'd be able to stay. He didn't say what the issues are, and I don't want to know."

"He didn't say?"

"No."

She mulled that over. "Then I guess I'm not so mad at him after all."

"You're really good at your job, Susan. The hospital needs you. I hope you can work it out and stay if you want to."

"What about you? That was a heck of an opportunity to turn down."

"My immediate future isn't here. The Lord has things for me to do at home."

"You really believe all that God stuff?"

"Without any doubt whatsoever." Then I reissued an invitation I'd been issuing for weeks. "I'd really like it if you'd come to church Sunday. It's my last Sunday as pastor, and then I leave for home on Monday."

"I'll think about it." It was what she said every time, and I had no hope things would be any different. I hadn't been able to make any sort of dent in her, and she was a loose end that I would just have to continue to pray about. Maybe it would be one of those situations where I planted the seed, and someone else down the road would see it sprout. I hoped she wouldn't be another Robert Wallace.

74

My last day at the hospital came and went uneventfully, and I was able to focus my complete attention on Sunday. It was going to be a big day, with my last sermon and Jack and Connie's wedding. They had issued invitations, but they had no problem with anyone attending who wanted to. They planned to come to church, offer a buffet meal after the service, and have the ceremony at two o'clock.

I was getting agitated, because I'd had no inspiration for my final sermon. So many things begged to be said. Thoughts kept darting into my mind, and I had no idea which ones were from me and which were from God. Clearing my thoughts so I could listen for His voice was almost impossible, with everything that was going on.

Then I told myself, this is ridiculous. Doing what He wants, especially in this situation, is the absolute most important thing there is. I simply need to block out everything else. He'll give me guidance. He always does.

I determinedly went into my study on Saturday morning and buried myself in Scripture, and the answer quickly became obvious. It was as if God was just waiting for me to give Him my undivided attention. Jack and Connie. This was a day about love, and what love is more powerful than that of God for us? The two could easily dovetail into a powerful message.

It didn't come like all the others had, in an outline that I could massage and flesh out. It flowed out of my brain in one gush, as one complete, coherent message. It came so fast that I had trouble writing it all down. When I finished writing, my hand aching, I looked at the result in astonishment. Where did that come from? I knew exactly where, and I knew that this would be one I'd have to read verbatim. For the rest of the day and into the night I practiced, hoping to commit some of it to memory so I could give it the inflection and heart it deserved.

I went to bed that night completely satisfied and at peace, with anticipation for the day ahead.

75

As usual, I went downstairs early the next day to make sure all was ready. Connie and Lily were already there, preparing food and looking harried.

"Hello, young bride." I kissed Connie on the cheek. "How are you today?"

"I'm happy and terrified." She looked like the seventeen-year-old girl she was.

"Me too," said Lily. "I'm not ready. I can't imagine how I'm going to be ready in just six hours. There's the food, the decorations . . . oh my goodness, the decorations. How am I going to do that while church is going on? Why we did this on a Sunday afternoon is beyond me." She was babbling now.

"Lily." Slowly those wild eyes focused on me. "What's the most important thing today?"

"The wedding."

"And the most important part of the wedding is that Jack and Connie will be married. Not the food, not the decorations, none of that. All of that will just make for stories down the road. As long as they are married, and they will be, everything else is just noise and icing on the cake."

She took a deep breath. "You're right, of course. How did a boy as young as you get to be so smart?"

I shrugged, not knowing how to answer that one. "You'll get all the help you need to get ready. I'll see to it. Now relax."

People began arriving for Sunday school, and Connie had to go teach her class. In no time at all, it was eleven o'clock. I took my place on the front row, and the service began. Amazingly, I wasn't nervous at all. The sermon was etched in my head, and I knew I could do it justice. When it was time, I stood up and took my place at the podium. I had notes, but I didn't need them.

"How many times do you hear the word 'love' in a day? People use it to talk about anything—from the purest love of God the Father to the way they feel about Spam and grits.

"Did you know that love can do just about anything? It can even make people disappear. Whenever Jack Barker and I are together and he hears of or sees or even thinks he sees Connie, I disappear. It's like I'm not even there. His mind shifts into a different world.

"My aunt and uncle in Oklahoma had a special bond of love—they truly fit the saying 'They loved each other more than their own life.' Because of them, I think I understand how that is possible. Two weeks after my uncle died, my aunt passed on quietly. My family thinks that their love was so strong that without that life-giving love between the two of them, neither could survive.

"To me that shows the importance of love in our daily life. Do you realize how much we depend on the love of others? When you were that small, ugly, fat baby that only screamed and messed up diapers and threw up, it took the love of a mother. You were defenseless, helpless.

"It's not just babies that need love. Grown-ups—doctors, teachers, drug addicts, alcoholics, criminals, even pastors—we all need love. I think that drugs, alcohol, premarital sex, et cetera are only symptoms of a starvation disease . . . lack of love.

"You've heard that song, 'What the world needs now is love, sweet love. That's the only thing that there's just too little of.' I think that little song captures the essence of what Jesus had to say about love in Matthew 22:37-40."

I heard Bibles coming out and pages being turned. I looked up and, for the first time, saw Susan sitting in the second row. She stared at me. I looked back at her and gave her a small nod and a smile.

"You know when I was first really struck by that verse? When I was a first grader back home. It was the motto of a church club I was in.

"These were God's two greatest commands. One, love God with

all you have. Two, love your neighbor as yourself. This means everyone . . . enemies, families, fellow countrymen, ministers, saints, and strangers. If you're not included there, you're an animal, and God even wants us to be kind to animals.

"The Bible describes three types of love. First is *agape* love, which is a deep, unconditional love that comes from God. It is sacrificial and unselfish. It gives and does not expect anything in return. Second is *phileo* love, which is a brotherly, friendly love. Like the way I feel about Jack. There is some give and take as we show each other that we are more special than just anybody. Third is *eros*, which is physical and romantic love. It is passionate, emotional, and explains a strong attraction.

"If I've learned one thing through my experiences here in Nome, I think this would have to be it. 1 Corinthians 16:14 says, 'Let all that you do be done in love.' Let me read that again, 'Let all that you do be done in love.' Whether it's with your students, your patients, your boss, your coworkers, your parents, your children, or the gas station attendant, some type of love is a suitable response for every situation.

"God created us to experience all kinds of love, but He wants us to know that His love for us is *agape* love. It's hardest for us to understand love like that. God knew that. He knew that at just the right time He would show us His love by sending His own Son. Think about God creating the universe, the sun, moon and stars, earth, and eventually all of us. For thousands of years, He sat in heaven watching the people on earth. They were worshipping golden idols, the sun, the moon, and the stars . . . everything He made, but not Him. God even sent messengers—prophets—to explain to them and warn them of what they were doing, but they ignored and even killed the prophets.

"God must have been sad. He must have been angry, too. He could have just said 'Forget it' and smeared everybody right then and blown them all to hell. But He didn't. I can imagine what He said with tears in His eyes. Tears of hurt this time, and pity. 'They really don't understand. They don't know Me and My love for them. It is time to send my Son to show them in their own flesh and blood, on their own soil.

"So God sent Jesus, His only Son, and even allowed Him to die as the ultimate expression of *agape* love. To bear the punishment and consequences of sin, even though Jesus Himself did not sin. Isn't that neat? 'For God so loved the world that He gave His only begotten Son, that whosoever believes in Him should not perish but have everlasting life.'

"Isn't God beautiful? From the way I see it, there is only one way to describe God, our heavenly Father. God . . . is love."

I ended the service by reminding everyone that a wedding was coming up in a couple of hours, and asking for help setting up. As I'd anticipated, Lily had more help than she wanted or needed.

As usual, I stayed as long as anyone wanted to talk to me. Susan stayed in her seat until everyone had left the worship center. Many people left; some migrated to the kitchen for the wedding buffet. I went to where she was seated and sat down beside her. "I'm glad you came."

"That was amazing. I've never heard anything like it. How did you get those words? How did you come up with that?"

"It came from the Bible and God inside me. I asked Him to show me what to say, then I started writing it down. He led me in every word. I could barely write fast enough to get it all down. It was really neat."

"I've never heard such. But I will tell you, I felt something inside. You really gave me something to think about." With that, she got up and left the worship center.

I stared after her, mouth open. I ran to the window and made sure she was gone, then jumped into the air and pumped my fists. "Yes!" I shouted. In the months I'd known Susan, I'd come to the conclusion that she was an impossible nut to crack. I'd invited her to church over and over. I'd tried to model Christianity the best I knew how. I'd tried everything I knew, to no avail. This was the most promising thing I'd ever heard come out of her mouth.

Maybe the seed was planted. Maybe it would sprout. I hoped and prayed so.

76

As people went through the line at the buffet lunch, I prepared for the final act I would perform as interim pastor at the Nome Baptist Family Center. It was probably the one act that meant the most to me, as Jack and Connie were very special, and I'd watched their relationship from the first moment they'd set eyes on each other. I wanted to make this a special day for them.

Since I couldn't be the best man, and there never had been a maid of honor, they'd opted to go without honor attendants. Prissy would be their flower girl and junior bridesmaid, and would carry Jack's ring. Paul would be junior groomsman and would carry Connie's ring. Lily would play the piano, as she did for every church service. And proud daddy, James, of course, would escort the bride and give her away.

Jack had invited the people he worked with at the airport. The Vaughns had invited pretty much the entire town of Nome, many of whom had been at the church service. It was a small, simple wedding, but in attendance would be almost all the white population and a good smattering of natives as well.

Several weeks ago, before I'd moved into the church apartment, Jack had opened a package from home and gasped. Inside had been his mother's engagement and wedding rings. His mom had passed away years before, and these rings had gone to his older sister. When she'd heard he was engaged, she'd given the rings to him for his bride. The engagement ring was a stunning one-carat, emerald-cut center diamond surrounded by smaller diamonds. Brother and sister had worked secretly to get the rings sized appropriately, and they would be a big surprise for Connie today. To explain why he hadn't gotten her a ring yet, Jack had mentioned that they would honeymoon in a place where he could buy her a diamond. She had been happy with that.

Connie had her secrets as well. She'd worked with a native ivory carver and today would slip an exquisite hand-carved wedding ring of priceless, dark ivory on Jack's finger. It was exactly the kind of jewelry he would wear and treasure.

I was privy to all these secrets, and I could not wait to see them revealed today.

One secret I was not in on, however, was the wedding dress. Connie and her mother had made a trip to Anchorage to shop just after her engagement and had come back with a large white bag that disappeared somewhere in their house as soon as they arrived home. Literally no one had seen the dress. I was a guy and dresses did not interest me much, but I had to admit I was curious.

I spent the last hour before the ceremony with Jack, and he was beside himself. He alternated between nerves and happiness. He paced. He sat and stood. He looked out the window. He glanced at his watch. Then he did it all again. I gave him the same speech I'd given Lily hours before. It seemed to work with her. Not so much with him. He paced some more.

"Jack," I finally said in amused exasperation, "don't you have a knife to sharpen or something?"

He looked at me with vague panic in his eyes. "Mark, tell me I'm doing the right thing."

"You absolutely are." I didn't hesitate. "You and Connie are going to be just fine. You are so made for each other. You keep Christ at the center of your marriage, and you can't go wrong. You two need to agree that when you get mad at each other you will make up before the day is over."

Then we heard the first strains of the piano. Lily was playing music while the guests seated themselves. I knew that meant we had about ten minutes before we had to walk out there. I took Jack's hand and said, "Let's pray." We bowed our heads.

"Father, please be with Jack and Connie today. It's the biggest day of their lives. Help them to always remember that You are the center and the reason for everything. Your *agape* love is the glue that will keep them together. Help Jack to be a patient and kind leader in their new home. Bless them as they start their family with Prissy. We know You are with us and will help everything go well. And use me, Father, as I try to help make this day special for them. In Christ's name, amen."

We opened our eyes, released hands, and smiled at each other. "It's going to be all right, isn't it?" Jack asked.

"You bet it is. It's time to go."

Jack and I walked out and took our places at the front of the worship center. Lily began playing the wedding march, and Paul and Prissy walked down the aisle and took their places on either side of me.

Connie appeared on the arm of her father. Slowly they walked down the middle of the worship center, in time to the music. She wore a long, simple, classic white dress with short puffed sleeves and no train. Her veil was modest, only to the middle of her back. A sheer short veil covered her face, but her shining eyes were clearly visible.

I glanced sideways at Jack and saw him staring raptly at his bride, his love for her in his eyes.

I cleared my throat. Getting choked up was not an option right now.

Connie arrived at her groom's side, and the music stopped. James placed her hand in Jack's, lifted her veil and kissed her cheek, and sat down.

"Dearly beloved," I began, and the ancient words echoed in the big room. They'd wanted a classic ceremony, with traditional vows. They stared into each other's eyes and promised to have and to hold for better for worse, for richer or for poorer, in sickness and in health, to love and to cherish, till death do them part.

The couple had wanted me to say a few words in addition to the traditional ceremony. I'd thought long and hard about it, and in the end had decided to simply speak from the heart.

"I was there the day Jack first set eyes on Connie. He'd come here from California as part of a crew that was donating their time to help finish this building. He planned to stay only one week. He had a life and work back in California.

"Then the Vaughns pulled up in their truck. Connie stepped out with her parents, and Jack's whole world changed. I've never believed in love at first sight, but that's exactly what I witnessed that day. He took one look at her, and she at him, and they were instantly in love. After that, leaving Nome for long was not an option. Jack went back to California just long enough to tie up some loose ends so he could be with Connie from now on. Nome is now Jack's home, because of her.

"It hasn't always been easy and, as his roommate, I can tell you this for a fact. He is human, after all. But their love for each other always triumphed, and here we are today. I am privileged to be standing here, with the honor of joining these two in holy marriage.

"Paul, please give the bride's rings to Jack." As Jack slipped the two rings on Connie's finger the amazement washed over her face. She wasn't expecting an actual ring, not until their honeymoon. She stared at her shaking hand and then into his eyes, tears falling down her cheeks. "With this ring, I thee wed." He smiled broadly and tenderly at her.

"Prissy, please give the groom's ring to Connie." Connie smiled because she had her own surprise. She slipped the ring on his finger and watched his face as his eyes grew huge. It was a one-of-a-kind ring, carved in ancient, dark, rare ivory. I knew the engraving inside read, "My Man Forever."

"With this ring, I thee wed."

"I now pronounce you man and wife." I stood beaming as Lily played the recessional. Paul looked so proud to be an important part in this ceremony, and Prissy jumped into Jack's waiting arms. The three of them walked away together. I could not think of a better way than this to end my time in Nome.

77

I had plenty of time to think during my trip home. The Chandlers expected me to stop in Anchorage on my way out and debrief them on my mission work. So I chose to do it in a roundabout way and see parts of Alaska I'd not seen yet.

I flew to Fairbanks, stayed overnight, and saw some of the sights there. The Museum of the North fascinated me. Actual reindeer grazed in open fields. Then I took the Alaska Railroad from Fairbanks to Anchorage. The domed cars provided a wonderful view of the Alaska Range as we rattled through it. It was a completely different vantage point of the mountains from when I'd first arrived on the milk run. The train went through Talkeetna, and we would have had a view of Mt. McKinley except for the ever-present cloud cover. Eight hours after leaving Fairbanks, I arrived in Anchorage. The Chandlers met me.

There was so much to tell them, but I was only there for one night. They most wanted to hear about my time as interim pastor, and I gave them a complete run-down of those seven weeks.

"I have to thank you. You did a terrific job of equipping me, in every way. Every single thing you made sure I knew turned out to be really, really important. I'm an outdoor-type person and I thought I was ready, but I don't think you can be prepared for the extremes in Alaska without considerable help from someone who has lived here. Even being an Eagle Scout was not adequate preparation. The gear you got for me literally saved my life. The things you taught me saved my sight and helped me help my roommate when he got snow blindness. And your spiritual guidance was right on target. So thank you."

"You're welcome," Patsy said, looking warmly at me. "That's what we're here for."

"I'd like you to take back the gear you got me, and use it for some other unprepared missionary. That would make me really happy. Would you?"

"Of course, we will," Charles said. "You're more than welcome to keep it, you know."

"I know, but it would make me feel good to think someone else who needs it is using it."

"Then we'll make sure that happens."

"One more thing." I unrolled one of Robert's best rabbit skins. "I want you to have this." I related most of the story of Robert, his family, his struggle with alcohol, and ultimate death as the Chandlers both gently stroked the soft fur and admired the skillful drawing on the tanned side, turning it over several times as they listened intently.

"Thank you, Mark. What are you going to be doing when you get back?" Patsy asked.

"I'm going to be living at the Baptist Student Union at UT for the next two years, and the director recommended me for a youth minister job, so I hope I'll get that. I'm thinking I'll go to seminary after that, but I'll take it one step at a time and see where God leads me."

They both stared at me. "Yours is an amazing story, Mark," Patsy said. "I've never heard of a missionary that's had quite the extent and variety of experiences that you have in just one year. If you use them well, you'll have a good foundation for wherever God leads you."

"I'm going to do my best. I know He has plans. I'm just going to stay close to Him and figure it out as I go."

"That's all you can do," Charles said. "We'll be praying for you every day, and you let us know if there's ever anything we can do."

The next day I hugged them, waved goodbye, and boarded the plane for home.

78

What a difference, I thought. Everything is different. The trip is different. I am different. When I came here a year ago, I thought I had everything figured out, but I really had no clue. Patsy was right, my experiences had changed me.

I definitely did not want to be a dentist, but I planned to finish UT and earn my degree in biology. I already had two years in, and changing majors now would extend my time there. I wanted to get on with my life.

I hadn't chosen a seminary yet, but I knew I wanted one that would encourage free thought and expression, not one that would indoctrinate all its students with one and only one way of thinking. I wanted to be forced to ask and answer tough questions. Somewhere down the road, someone might be struggling with a bitter life's lesson, and I wanted to be equipped to help. I had confidence that God and science work hand in hand. Creation? Evolution? Bring it on. History, philosophy, world religions? It wouldn't challenge my faith in the least. Not now.

The one thing I did know was that I wanted to serve God from now on. I didn't know exactly how, but I was leaning toward youth or education ministry. It would be fun to see how that all worked out; it was in His hands. I had never felt so secure in my life.

I remembered an old hymn that I sang as a child, and it had special meaning now after my experience in the cleft of Anvil Rock.

A wonderful Savior is Jesus my Lord,
A wonderful Savior to me;

He hideth my soul in the cleft of the rock,
Where rivers of pleasure I see.

He hideth my soul in the cleft of the rock,
That shadows a dry, thirsty land;
He hideth my life in the depths of His love,
And covers me there with His hand.
A wonderful Savior is Jesus my Lord,
He taketh my burden away,
He holdeth me up and I shall not be moved,
He giveth me strength as my day.

With numberless blessings each moment He crowns,
And filled with His fullness divine,
I sing in my rapture, oh, glory to God!
For such a Redeemer as mine.
When clothed with His brightness transported I rise
To meet Him in clouds of the sky,
His perfect salvation, His wonderful love,
I'll shout with the millions on high.

The plane flew steadily east, back across the continent. It had been an incredible year, one in which the Lord had done some amazing things in my life and through me. He had provided opportunities in one of the most remote places in the world, and I hoped I'd done my best with them. Then I thought about the people and the opportunities that were waiting at home, and I could not wait for what lay ahead.

I looked out the window at the majesty and grandeur of Alaska and smiled. Maybe my path would lead me back here someday. I hoped so.

EPILOGUE

I remember the first time I heard the story. It was Halloween of 2011. I was sitting in a restaurant with Mark Smith, who's now my husband. We had met on Match.com a few days before, and this was our first face-to-face meeting.

There was something magnetic about him, even then. He had said on his online profile that he was a Christian and an Eagle Scout, which was what led me to message him in the first place. Sitting with him, I was happy I did. His energy, his commitment, his sincerity—all pulled me in.

He was telling me about the turning point in his life. His year in Nome, Alaska, at the age of nineteen was pivotal in shaping him into the incredible man he is today. It began with a life-threatening blow when he got off the plane, but God used some unforgettable experiences to shape and mold him. His time in Alaska gives life to the Scripture verses that refer to the Lord as the Potter and us as the clay, and being protected in the cleft of the rock.

My husband and I traveled to Nome in July 2013. I had the chance to see the church he helped construct, the arctic doorways he built to earn money to survive, the sea where he fished through a hole in the ice so he'd have something to eat, the jail where he preached his first sermon at the age of twenty, the Lighthouse where he touched the lives of so many children, and other places I'd heard about.

I actually stood in the church he helped build and talked with the current pastor. The building is standing strong and firm and is the home of weekly church services and vibrant mission work. Areas of the church that were once open, vaulted ceilings have now been refurbished to take advantage of the space to house mission teams. A new area had just been built to hold food for a food pantry, especially needed during the Iditarod when the town's population quadruples. We walked around the church and the grounds, and Mark showed me the beam that it required a miracle to hoist into place, the baptismal that the church was built around, another thick beam that is still protruding past the foundation in the back of the church because they didn't have the tools to cut it to size, and the large room where he preached during the seven weeks he served as interim pastor.

Mark's story reminded me of the classic, inspirational novel, *Christy*, by Catherine Marshall. It's the tale of a young person coming of age in her relationship with God, through experiences that caused her to come to grips with some tough questions. *Christy* has always inspired me. I knew Mark's story could do the same for a new generation.

I've always been able to put words together. Since I was a young teenager, I knew that I had this gift for a reason. I hadn't used it for the Lord to date; my professional career had been spent in journalism and corporate communications. Now I knew the time had come. I had to tell Mark's story. But could I do it justice? Of course I could, if the Lord helped me. And I knew He would, if this was His will.

For months, Mark and I spent hours reminiscing, as I tried to get into his head and imagine what it feels like to go outdoors and mush dogs when it's forty below zero. Or to stand before a group of prisoners, as a youngster of twenty, and preach the Gospel. Or to minister to young, tortured children when you're not much older than them yourself. So many things that happened to him that I can only imagine.

It's my privilege to tell the story with him, and it's our hope that it will bless and inspire someone else.

Frances Smith

The construction site, before the church was built

Pastor Will West preparing the church's foundation

The church frame, nearly completed

Mark (middle), Darren (left) and Atka working on the church

Paul, near
the church
construction site

The Lighthouse

Prissy during Lighthouse activities

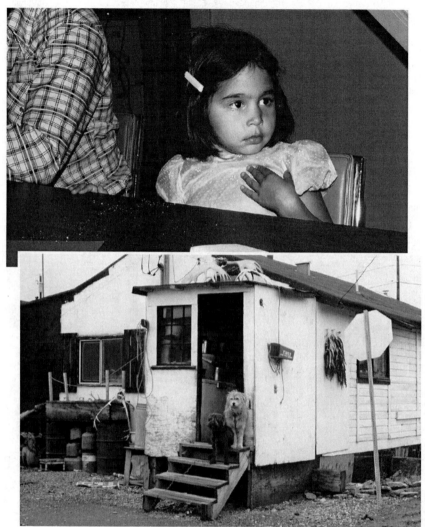

A typical Nome home in 1979

A gold dredge near Nome

A heated
outhouse

An Alaskan mosquito

An old train, bogged down and abandoned in the soggy tundra

Flowers on the tundra

Nome's only ambulance

The crew from California, in August 1979

Charles and Patsy Chandler, near Anchorage
in September 1979

Anvil Rock close up

Sunrise over the mountains east of Nome

Patricia Boston working with some of the Lighthouse kids

Jack Barker in the doorway of the apartment
he and Mark shared

Mark with cabin fever, in his and Jack's frigid apartment

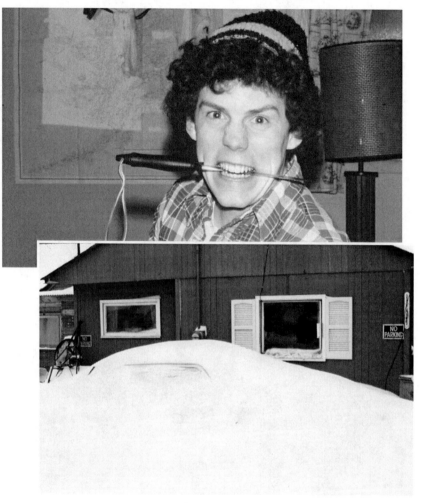

A car almost covered in snow

Children building snow forts between houses

A typical dog team

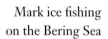

Mark ice fishing
on the Bering Sea

Doug throwing
boiling water out
the front door of
Mark's apartment
during his visit to
Nome. The water
froze before it hit
the ground.

Sunset over the Bering Sea, with ice chunks in the foreground

Mark's willow branch Christmas tree, decorated with an unraveled sock

The ice beginning to break up on the Bering Sea during the spring thaw

The Strong Dog Pull at the 1980 Iditarod

The Nome airport in 1979

Mark at the Nome airport in July 2013

The completed church in March 1980

The church in July 2013

Mark and the church's pastor, Bruce Landry, in July 2013

Mark with Anvil Mountain in the background, July 2013

The Bering Sea in 2013

The Nome cemetery in 2013

The Nome River in 2013

One of the arctic entryways Mark built, still standing in 2013

ABOUT THE AUTHOR

Until 2013, Frances Smith spent her professional career in journalism, corporate communications, and public relations.

In 2011, God used match.com, an online dating service, to bring her to Mark Smith. Almost instantly they knew they were meant to be together. They married in 2012, and God called Frances to write full-time for Him in 2013. Her first book, *Cleft of the Rock*, was published in 2014. *Thorn in the Flesh* was finished in 2015, and the third book in the trilogy, *Lamp to My Feet*, should be complete by mid-2017.

Frances has also been active in church leadership, serving as wedding director, Presbyterian Women moderator, and Presbyterian deacon. Today she is a baptized member of Pleasant Grove Baptist Church, where she is part of the Sunday School teaching team.

She holds a Bachelor of Arts in English and a Master of Arts in English education. She and Mark live in East Tennessee and, between them, have four sons and a daughter. They enjoy fishing, hiking, and nature.

Visit Frances at www.cleftoftherock.org, or email her at fran@cleftoftherock.org.